Internet Adventures

Version 2.0

Step-by-Step Guide to Finding and Using Educational Resources

Cynthia B. Leshin

Allyn and Bacon

Boston   London   Toronto   Sydney   Tokyo   Singapore

DISCLAIMER

While a great deal of care has been taken to provide accurate and current information, the Internet is a dynamic and rapidly changing environment. Information may be in one place today and either gone or in a new location tomorrow. New sites come up daily; others disappear. Some sites provide forwarding address information; others do not. The publisher and author assume no responsibility for errors or omissions. Neither is any liability assumed for damages resulting from the use of this information.

As you travel the information superhighway and find that a resource you are looking for can no longer be found at a given Internet address, there are several steps you can take:

1. Check for a new Internet address or link, often provided on the site of the old address.

2. Use one of the search engines described in Chapter 5, with the title of the Internet resource as keywords.

3. Explore Internet databases such as Excite, Yahoo, Infoseek, or Galaxy which have large directories of Internet business resources.

Refer to the Appendix for detailed information on how to find outdated URLs.

The author welcomes readers' feedback, correction of inaccuracies, and suggestions for improvements in subsequent editions. Cynthia Leshin can be contacted by email at: **cleshin@xplora.com**

ABOUT THE AUTHOR

Cynthia Leshin is an educational technologies specialist with her doctorate in educational technology from Arizona State University. Dr. Leshin has her own consulting company—XPLORA. She consults with businesses and schools interested in learning about and implementing technology rich environments for student success, improved learning, and customer support. Currently she is working as a consultant for Private Networks designing and developing university courses, continuing education, and training courses that are delivered using advanced communication technologies—digital satellite and the Internet.

She has authored twelve books for Simon and Schuster including *Internet Adventurer — Step-by-Step Guide to Finding and Using Educational Resources; Netscape Adventures — Step-by-Step Guide to Netscape Navigator and the World Wide Web; Student Resource Guide to the Internet—Student Success Online; Management on the World Wide Web*, and seven discipline-specific Internet books with Internet-based learning activities. She has also written a book, *Instructional Design: Strategies and Tactics*. Her expertise in educational psychology and theories of learning provides her with a unique background for translating complicated technical information into an easy-to-use, easy-to-understand, and practical learning resource.

Dr. Leshin has taught computer literacy and Internet classes at Arizona State University West and Estrella Mountain Community College. She has taught college accredited Internet classes using distance learning technology for Educational Management Group, a Simon & Schuster company. The Internet serves as a tool for teaching and communicating with her students. She is freqently an invited speaker at national and local conferences and for staff development programs.

In Dr. Leshin's "other life" she rides mountain bikes and races for Cannondale's HeadShok team. She also enjoys organic gardening, hiking, skiing, scuba diving, and exploring southwestern trails with her three dread-locked Puli dogs and her husband, Steve.

ACKNOWLEDGMENTS

The author would like to thank several people for making this guide possible:

I am most grateful to my editor Nancy Forsyth for her continued support, encouragement, and patience during the writing of this book. She has provided me with most appreciated opportunties to grow as an author and professional.

To Gail Hartman, a special friend and colleague, who has provided the Internet-based curriculum in Chapter 6. This curriculum was taken from the *Internet Adventures Newsletter* published in 1995-1996 by XPLORA and sponsored by Apple Computer. XPLORA received so much positive feedback on the newsletter and the curriculum that we decided to include it in this book to share with more educators. Gail's expertise and knowledge of the K-12 classroom environment have greatly contributed to this book's content. Gail has acted as a subject matter expert and reviewed much of the content relevant to the classroom, making most appreciated suggestions and in some instances helping to construct information that a teacher would find useful when trying to learn how to integrate the Internet into the curriculum.

To Marianne Mollerup for her creative work and support with desktop publishing. Her book design and art work have greatly contributed to my vision of making this an inviting, fun, and easy-to-understand guide for educators.

To all those at Allyn & Bacon who have transformed these words into this guide, especially those who read the manuscript and made valuable and most appreciated suggestions.

To my husband, Steve, for his continuing support and for helping to make this Internet adventure possible.

PREFACE
The Adventure Begins...

In this book you will embark on a very exciting trip along the information superhighway. You will learn about the newest and fastest growing communication medium that some have called the fourth media positioned to take a place with print, radio, and television as a mass market means of communication. You will take Guided Tours where you follow step-by-step procedures for learning how to navigate and find useful and valuable information in cyberspace. You will also find the three thematic curriculum units very helpful as models of how the Internet can be integrated into the classroom.

As you travel and explore Internet sites you will quickly appreciate the power of the Internet to bring timely and valuable resources to the classroom for your students as well as for yourself as a professional. Some of the ways in which Internet resources can be used for teaching and learning include:

- access to the latest information on a subject or classroom theme;

- participation in global online learning adventures;

- access to online curriculum, lesson plans, and invitations to join in global collaborative projects;

- opportunities for collaboration on projects and learning adventures with other educators and classroom from around the world;

- capabilities for collecting information from a global and diverse worldwide community;

- opportunities to meet and learn from subject matter experts on virtually any topic;

- access to resources such as dictionaries, encyclopedias, and library catalogs worldwide;

- access to literature such as the classics and novels;

- access to libraries world wide;

- access to news publications and electronic journals; and

- access to databases of diverse information at universities, educational institutions, and government agencies.

Educated individuals understand that we are rapidly moving into a new world, a digital world where the way we live, work, and play is about to be changed forever. Those who want to be successful in this world are learning about the digital tools and resources that are transforming our lives. Those who do not join this webolution will be left behind. As educators of our nation's young it is imperative that we learn about and understand the driving technology behind this movement.

The Internet is not a trend. It is like an ever-cresting wave being driven by the force and momentum of international currents, spraying its global magic from the monitor and inviting us to jump in—the world awaits. Travel, information-on-demand, and communication make the Internet a technology that is here to stay.

No one, not even the corporate giant such as Microsoft, envisioned how the Internet would change our world. No once could have prophesied that the Internet of the 1970s and 1980s based at our educational institutions would become the fastest growing communication medium of all times. Today, we are experiencing perhaps the greatest revolution in communication.

But we are still pioneers in exploring the uses of this powerful new tool. *Internet Adventures* provides the foundation you need to begin to understand how this tool can be used for teaching, learning, and professional development, and for preparing our students for the life in a digital world.

This book uses a travel metaphor to help make your learning journey more fun, more interesting, and easier to understand. In this travel guide you will visit the following places:

Chapter 1 begins with the Tourist Information Center. Before beginning any journey it is often helpful to visit a travel center and obtain some basic information on the destination that you are about to travel to. In this chapter you will learn about the Internet and the World Wide Web.

In Chapter 2 you will learn about how to use a browser—Netscape Navigator or Microsoft Internet Explorer—to travel in cyberspace. You will take Guided Tours where you follow step-by-step procedures for using a browser. Knowing browser basics is especially important today when new versions of browser software are being released several times a year. After you complete this chapter you will be able to use any browser version for your travels.

After becoming familiar with Internet travel and navigation, you are ready for the ultimate Web experience—multimedia-oriented Web environments. At the end of Chapter 2 you will learn about Web environments filled with live objects—animation, streaming audio and video, virtual reality, and more.

In Chapter 3 you will travel to virtual communities and learn how to communicate on the Internet using electronic mail, listserv mailing lists, Usenet newsgroups, chats, MOOs and MUDs, and Internet phones. People today are on the Internet because they value and enjoy the interactivity and relationships they build within the virtual community of cyberspace. Virtual communities provide opportunities for you and your students to meet, work with, learn from, and exchange information with Netizens all over the world.

In Chapter 4 you will learn about Gopher, FTP (File Transfer Protocol), Telnet—the earliest Internet tools for accessing information. Although the World Wide Web is the center of Net activity, there are many different and useful non-Web resources available.

Chapter 5 provides the foundation for finding and evaluating useful, valuable, and perhaps most importantly reliable resources on the Internet. You will learn about search directories and search engines as tools for finding Internet resources. You will also learn how to become *infocritical* of information you find on the Internet. The Internet is analogous to a wilderness untamed frontier. With an estimate of 20 to 50 million pages of data created from a variety of sources—individuals, businesses, corporations, non-profit organizations, schools, special interest groups, or illicit if not illegal sources—it is inherent that not all the information is accurate, unbiased, reputable, scientifically valid, and up-to-date. Unlike many of your professional publications, there is not editorial board for Internet information. It is therefore essential that you learn how to evaluate information found on the Internet and teach these skills to your students.

You will also find information in this chapter on how to record and reference Internet information very useful. Additionally, there are many excellent references to valuable Internet collections that you will enjoy exploring.

In Chapter 6 you will go on three learning expeditions exploring three thematic units offering online and off-line interdisciplinary activities that encourage an active approach to learning and help minimize the lines of division among content area. These units offer many opportunities for students to analyze information, distinguish between fact and opinion, and identify cause and effect as they learn about the Oceans, Ancient Civilizations, and the Rain Forest. At the end of this chapter you will find an excellent article on performance-based assessment by Jay McTighe and Steven Ferrara.

Chapter 7 has a plethora of educational and useful resources for you to explore.

Every foreign country has its own vocabulary and language. In the Foreign Language Center you will find a glossary of words and terms to help you better understand geek speak.

Internet Adventures takes you on a learning journey to help you understand and explore the exciting possibilities of the Internet as a new tool for teaching, learning, and professional development.

HAPPY INTERNET ADVENTURES.

TRIP ITINERARY

CHAPTER 3
Visiting Virtual Communities   55

CHAPTER 4
The Internet Landscape   101

CHAPTER 5
Internet Research   137

CHAPTER 6
Internet-Based Learning Expeditions   181

CHAPTER 7
Expedition Experience   263

1

Tourist Information Center

CHAPTER CONTENTS

What is the Internet?

TOURIST INFORMATION CENTER

The first stop before beginning a journey is frequently the Tourist Information Center. The Center is a place where general information can be obtained about destinations. This information is helpful before beginning a trip in that it provides basic and essential facts on places of interest. This information sets the stage for the journey and begins to open the doors through which we will pass on our adventures.

This book begins the learning journey at the Travel Information Center where you will learn about the Internet. In this chapter you will learn

- what the Internet is.
- the history of the Internet.
- what it means to "be on the Internet."
- the difference between the Internet and the World Wide Web.
- Internet addressing protocol—the URL.
- the three standards used by the World Wide Web.
- how to connect to the Internet.

WHAT IS THE INTERNET?

in'ter·net n
1. world's largest information network **2.** global web of computer networks **3.** inter-network of many networks all running the TCP/IP protocol **4.** powerful communication tool **5.** giant highway system connecting computers and the regional and local networks that connect these computers **syn information superhighway, infobahn, data highway, electronic highway, Net, cyberspace**

A term frequently used to refer to the Internet is "information superhighway." This superhighway is a vast network of computers connecting people and resources around the world. The Internet is accessible to anyone with a computer and a modem.

History of the Internet

The Internet began in the 1960s at the height of the cold war when the United States Department of Defense was trying to figure out how U.S. authorities could communicate with each other in the aftermath of a nuclear attack. The foremost military think tank at the time, the Rand Corporation, worked on the first communication network that evolved into today's Internet.

1962: The Rand Corporation begins work on the packet-switching network to facilitate the transfer of data over a network.

1969: ARPANET is created connecting four U.S. campuses: Stanford Research Institute, the University of Utah, UCLA, and UC Santa Barbara.

ARPANET became an immediate success allowing military institutions and universities to share its research. In the 1970s, government and university networks continued to develop as many organizations and companies began to build private computer networks.

1971: ARPANET expands to include 23 university and government research centers.

1974: Telnet, the first commercial version of the ARPANET, is introduced.

1979: The first Usenet newsgroup is introduced by two graduate students at Duke University.

In the 1980s the ARPANET continues to grow at what soon will become a phenomenal pace. These early computer networks that made up the ARPANET evolve into the "internet" as TCP/IP (the protocol used today on the Internet to communicate and share information) is created. The explosion of the personal computer market in the 1980s and powerful network servers make it possible for the first time for companies to connect to the Internet.

1982: The word "internet" is used for the first time.

1984: The novel, *Neuromancer*, by William Gibson is published introducing the term "cyber space."

1986: The National Science Foundation creates NSFNET when it establishes five super-computing centers at universities to provide powerful computing power.

1988: Internet Relay Chat (IRC) is developed by Jarkko Oikarinen.

1990: The ARPANET ceases to exist and is replaced by the Internet, whose backbone is the National Science Foundation's NSFNET.

1991: The National Science Foundation lifts its restrictions on the use of NSFNET for educational institutions only. Electronic commerce is born.

Mark McCahill leads a team from the University of Minnesota and releases Gopher.

Tim Berners-Lee, working at CERN in Switzerland, introduces the World Wide Web.

1993: The first Web browser, Mosaic, is created by Marc Andreesen and a group of student programmers at the National Center for Supercomputing Applications (NCSA) at the University of Illinois at Urbana-Champaign.

1994: Netscape Communications Corporation introduces Netscape Navigator.

The age of the Internet arrives as a 30-year-old Cold War concept explodes into the fastest-growing interactive communication medium that the world has ever known.

1995: The browser war between Microsoft and Netscape Communications Corporation begins as Microsoft introduces Internet Explorer in the summer of 1995.

Security—encryption, Internet viruses, secure online business transactions, and company security—becomes an important focus for Internet hardware and software.

1996: Microsoft continues the race for Net surfer's hard disk space as the war with Netscape escalates. The release of Explorer 3.0 matches Netscape 3.0 browser features and performance.

Most of the other Internet browsers collapse under the weight of the two most powerful browsers from Netscape and Microsoft.

The browser has developed into an extremely complicated and sophisticated software technology. Plug-ins and helper applications bring rich and creative multimedia enviroments to the Net surfer's desktop.

New buzzwords and computer jargon are created by the digerati.

Issues related to free speech on the Internet are addressed. The Internet scores as three judges called Government attempt to regulate content on the Internet, a "profoundly repugnant" affront to the First Amendment (June 1996).

PointCast—free software delivering personalized news to the desktop over the Internet—overtakes the browser war to win the title of the year's most compelling innovation.

1997: Intel introduces the next generation of fast and powerful computers with its MMX-technology PC.

An interest in collaborative computing and groupware sparks the third generation of browsers. Netscape brings groupware to the Internet with the introduction of its Netscape Communicator suite of group-friendly applications for sharing data and collaborating over the Net.

Microsoft integrates the Internet into the computer desktop as Web standards become a part of Windows and its software applications.

Visit the following Web sites for more information on the history of the Internet and computers. Additional sites can be found in Chapter 7.

COMPUTER HISTORY WEB SITE
http://granite.sentex.net/~ccmuseum/hist_sites.html

HOBBES INTERNET TIMELINE
http://info.isoc.org/guest/zakon/Internet/History/HIT.html

PUBLIC BROADCASTING SYSTEM— HISTORY OF THE INTERNET
http://www.pbs.org/internet/history

What Does it Mean to "Be on the Internet"?

"Being on the Internet" means having full access to all Internet services. Any commercial service or institution that has full Internet access provides the following:

- Electronic mail (email)
- Telnet
- File Transfer Protocol (FTP)
- World Wide Web

Electronic Mail
Electronic mail is the most basic, the easiest to use, and for many people, the most useful Internet service. Email services allow you to

- communicate with friends or new acquaintances
- interact with professional colleagues
- participate in electronic discussion groups—listserv mailing lists
- interact with others on bulletin boards such as Usenet newsgroups
- request information from an individual, company, or institution
- receive technical support for hardware and software
- send résumés to a company
- participate in electronic workshops or conferences

The type of electronic mail program you use will usually depend on how you are connected to the Internet. If you are connected to the Internet through a college, school, business, or government agency that is using a local area network (LAN) then you may be using an email program that runs on the network server such as Lotus's CCMail, Microsoft Exchange, or BeyondMail.

If you are connecting to the Internet with an organization with no LAN or from home, then you have more choices of which email software program to use. Home users most often use Eudora and Eudora Pro, shown in Figure 1.1. Browsers such as Netscape Navigator and Microsoft Internet Explorer have email programs built-in eliminating the need for additional email software. Still, many Net users prefer the features and expanded capabilities of programs such as the highly-rated and very popular Eudora Pro.

FIGURE 1.1
Electronic mail window for Eudora Pro

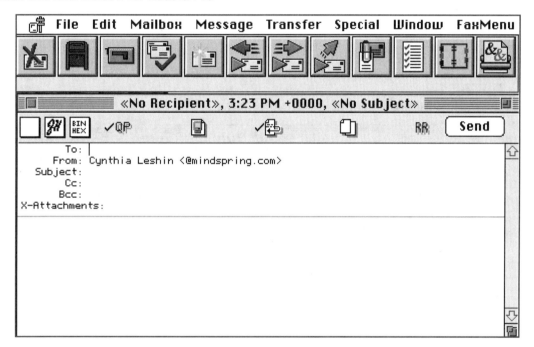

Notice the pop-up menus (File, Edit, Mailbox, Message, Transfer, Special, Window, and FaxMenu—only available if fax software is installed) for performing email operations. The toolbar below the pop-up menus provide easy access to the frequently used email operations: deleting a message, checking your **In Box** messages, accessing messages to be sent in the **Out Box**, checking for new messages, creating messages, replying to or forwarding messages, checking the spelling of a new message, accessing your address book, or printing a message.

In Chapter 3 you will learn more about email programs and how to use them.

Telnet

Telnet is one of the oldest Internet tools that allows users to log onto another computer and run resident programs. Although Telnet is not as visually interesting as the World Wide Web, it is essential to Internet travel. Telnet is a text-based environment requiring commands to navigate. Some Telnet access sites automatically link you to Web pages. Many Telnet sites, such as libraries, allow anyone to login without having a special account. Others require users to have a valid account before accessing many of the resident programs.

There are things you cannot do on the Web that Telnet can do. For example, when you Telnet to a remote computer, frequently a mainframe supercomputer, you are working on another machine and are using that machine's speed and power. College students and business travelers dial a local Internet service provider and then Telnet to their college or business accounts to get their email. Telnet saves them the cost of a long distance phone call.

Telnet also provides direct access to Internet services not always available from your Internet provider. Many of these services are exciting and interesting (see Fig. 1.2). Some open doors to alternative learning environments.

Some of the Internet services available using Telnet include

- databases (such as earthquake, weather, special collections)
- libraries (public, academic, medical, legal, and more)
- Free-Nets (noncommercial, community-based networks)
- interactive chats
- MOOs, MUDs
- bulletin boards

FIGURE 1.2
The Smithsonian Telnet site at telnet://siris.si.edu

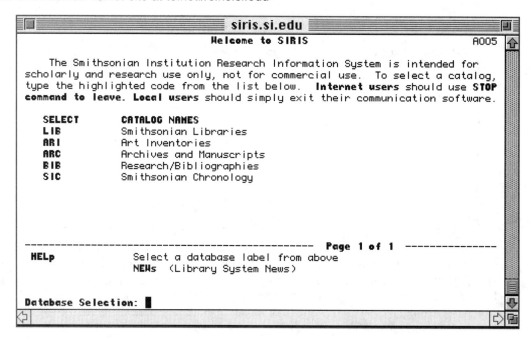

You will learn more about Telnet in Chapter 4.

File Transfer Protocol (FTP)

FTP is a special method used to transfer files between two Internet sites. Files or data can be sent to another site—uploading a file—or can be retrieved from a remote site—downloading a file. Many servers that make files available to Internet users are known as anonymous FTP sites. Any Internet user can log onto these sites and retrieve files. Before Web browsers, users would connect to an FTP site and login using anonymous as their username, and their email address as their password. When using a Web browser such as Netscape or Explorer, this login procedure is taken care of by the browser software.

FTP resources contain computer software, databases, updates to most retail software, electronic texts, technical reports, journals, magazines, news summaries, books, images, and sound. One of the most widely used FTP services is to travel to FTP servers to download the most current versions of software such as Netscape, Explorer, Eudora, utility programs, or applications for experiencing multimedia environments on the Web. Using a browser makes file retrieval easy. FTP surfers just enter the URL for the FTP site or the Web site that has a link to the FTP server and follow the links (see Fig. 1.3).

FIGURE 1.3
Goddard Space Center FTP site: ftp://dftnic.gsfc.nasa.gov

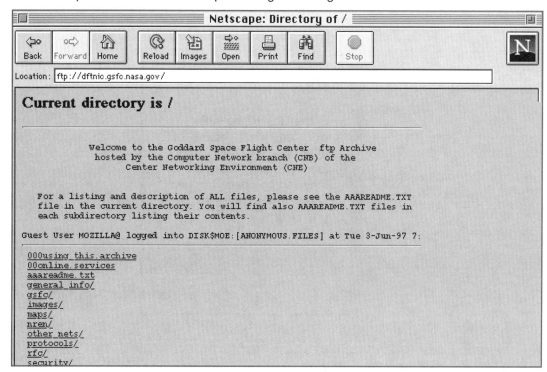

Files that are sent using FTP are usually compressed to facilitate faster transfer over the Internet.

Most PC compression and decompression is done with a package called, PKZIP. Macintosh compressed file extensions include

.hqx	(BinHex or a textual representation of binary files)
.sit	(files compressed using Stuffit)
.cpt	(files compressed using Compact Pro)

One of the most commonly used decompression programs for Macintosh is Stuffit Expander. There are many Internet sites where you can find a copy of Stuffit Expander and download it to your computer by double-clicking on the Web link. After you obtain a copy of Stuffit Expander, place a copy on your desktop. When you receive files that need to be decompressed, drop them onto the Stuffit icon.

Visit the following Web sites for free compression programs.

TUCOWS (Windows only)
http://www.tucows.com

JUMBO
http://www.jumbo.com

SHAREWARE
http://www.shareware.com

NOTE

Some files will be self-extracting which means that after they have been down-loaded to your desktop,
they can be opened by just double-clicking on their pro-gram icon.

You will learn more about FTP and file compression in Chapter 4.

World Wide Web

The World Wide Web (WWW or Web) is a collection of standards and protocols used to access information available on the Internet. This information is in the form of documents linked together in what is called a hypermedia system. Hypermedia is combined-use multimedia (text, images, video, and sound) in a Web presentation page.

Using the World Wide Web requires a browser to view Web documents and navigate through the intricate link structure. Today, the two premiere Web browsers are Netscape Navigator (shown in Fig. 1.4) and Microsoft Internet Explorer (shown in Fig. 1.5). Both of these browsers combine a point-and-click interface design with an "open" architecture that is capable of integrating other Internet tools such as electronic mail, FTP, Gopher, and Usenet newsgroups. This architecture makes it relatively easy to incorporate images, video, and sound into text documents.

FIGURE 1.4

Netscape Navigator browser showing Netscape's Yahoo online tutorial

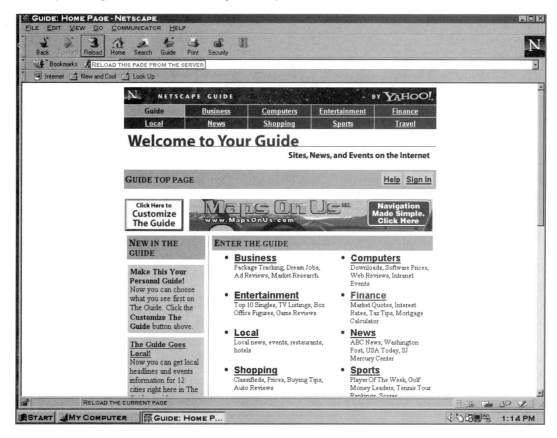

FIGURE 1.5

Microsoft Internet Explorer showing Microsoft's K-12 Education page

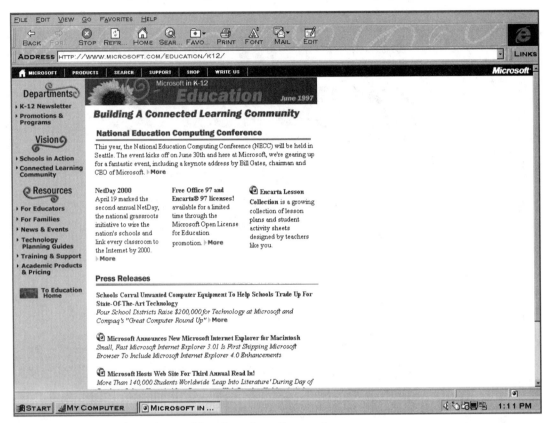

You will learn more about the World Wide Web in Chapter 2.

Tool Kit of Internet Resources

Although "being on the Internet" means that a user has access to email, Telnet, FTP, and the World Wide Web, there are many tools that Internet users have available to them to access these and other Internet resources. To better understand these tools and their uses, it is helpful to think of the Internet as a medium for

- information access,
- information sharing, and
- communication.

Information Access and Sharing Tools

Electronic tools that are actually software applications help Internet users access and share information include:

> electronic mail (email)
> listserv mailing lists
> Usenet newsgroups
> Telnet
> File Transfer Protocol (FTP)
> Free-Nets
> Gopher
> World Wide Web

Communication Tools

Communication tools that make it possible to interact with other Net users include:

> electronic mail—delayed response media
> listserv mailing lists—delayed response media
> Usenet newsgroups—delayed response media
> Internet Relay Chat (IRC)—real-time media
> MOOs, MUDs, and MUSE—real-time media
> Internet Phones—real-time media
> Internet videoconferencing—real-time media

Browsers such as Netscape and Explorer are most often used to access these Internet resources. Netscape's third generation browser introduced in January, 1997—Netscape Communicator (version 4.x series)—is a collaborative tool for expanded interaction, group discussions, and the sharing of multimedia data over the Internet. Microsoft has focused its development efforts on totally integrating the Internet into the desktop as its browser becomes a part of Windows and Microsoft software applications.

The Web and the Internet

The Web and the Internet are *not* synonymous. The World Wide Web is a collection of standards and protocols used to access information available on the Internet. The Internet is the network used to transport information.

The Web uses three standards:

- URLs (Uniform Resource Locators)
- HTTP (Hypertext Transfer Protocol)
- HTML (Hypertext Markup Language)

These standards provide a mechanism for WWW servers and clients to locate and display information available through other protocols such as Gopher, FTP, and Telnet.

URLs (Uniform Resource Locators)

URLs are a standard format for identifying locations on the Internet. They also allow an addressing system for other Internet protocols such as access to Gopher menus, FTP file retrieval, and Usenet newsgroups.

URLs specify three types of information needed to retrieve a document:

- the protocol to be used;
- the server address to which to connect; and
- the path to the information.

The format for a URL is: **protocol//server-name/path**

FIGURE 1.6
Sample URLs

World Wide Web URL:	http://home.netscape.com/home/welcome.html
Document from a secure server:	https://netscape.com
Gopher URL:	gopher://umslvma.umsl.edu/Library
FTP URL:	ftp://nic.umass.edu
Telnet URL:	telnet://geophys.washington.edu
Usenet URL:	news:rec.humor.funny

NOTE

The URL for newsgroups omits the two slashes. The two slashes designate the beginning of a server name. Since you are using your Internet provider's local news server, you do not need to designate a news server by adding the slashes.

HTTP (Hypertext Transfer Protocol)

HTTP is a protocol used to transfer information within the World Wide Web. Web site URLs begin with the http protocol: **http://** and this Web URL will connect you to Netscape's Home Page: **http://home.netscape.com.**

HTML (Hypertext Markup Language)

HTML is the programming language used to create a Web page. It formats the text of the document, describes its structure, and specifies links to other documents. HTML also includes programming to access and display different media such as images, video, and sound.

CONNECTING TO THE INTERNET

Now that you have a basic understanding of the Internet, you are ready to begin your cyberspace adventure. Before you can travel and explore the information superhighway you will need the following:

- an Internet account

- a username and password (required to log onto your Internet account)

- instructions from your institution on how to log on and log off

There are three ways to obtain these requirements.

- **Network**. Network connections are most often found in colleges, schools, businesses, or government agencies and use dedicated lines to provide fast access to all Internet resources. Special hardware such as routers may be required at the local site. If you are at one of these institutions you will only need to apply for an Internet account. Many of these institutions provide opportunities for accessing your account from a home computer.

- **Internet Service Provider (ISP)**. Internet access providers offer SLIP (Serial Line Interface Protocol) or PPP (Point-to-Point Protocol) connections (SLIP/PPP). This service is referred to as Dial-Up-Networking and makes it possible for your PC to dial into their server and communicate with other computers on the Internet. Once you have established a PPP, SLIP, or direct Internet connection, you can use any software that speaks the Internet language called TCP/IP. There are several TCP/IP software applications including Eudora, Netscape Navigator, and Explorer.

  Internet Service Providers should give you the required TCP/IP software to get you connected to the Internet. Additionally, many will provide Internet applications such as Eudora, Netscape Navigator, or Microsoft Internet Explorer. Prices are usually based on hours of usage, bandwidth, and locality.

- **Commercial Online Service Providers**. Examples of online services include America Online (AOL), CompuServe, Prodigy, Delphi, and Microsoft Network (MSN). Online services are virtual communities that offer services to their subscribers including electronic mail, discussion forums on topics of interest, real time chats, business and advertising opportunities, software libraries, stock quotes, online newspapers, and Internet resources (Gopher, FTP, newsgroups).

Finding an Internet Provider

There are several Web sites to help you find an Internet access provider:

http://thelist.com
http://www.clari.net/iap/iapcode.htm
http://www.primus.com/providers

To find the names of providers in your area, click on the link to your area code. You will find descriptive information of providers within your area code and a description of their services. All providers that service your area will be found by the area code listing.

TIPS FOR FINDING A PROVIDER

TIP

If your area code is not listed
There are providers who have nationwide access. Some of the Web sites have information on these service providers.

TIP

If there is no local dial-in number
Look for service providers that are the closest to you or who have an 800 number dial-in access. Many providers are also listed on these Web sites.

TIP

Choosing a provider
Contact providers by phone, fax, or electronic mail. If you want to use Netscape or Explorer you will need to get a SLIP or a PPP account.

Ask about the following:

- Type of Internet accounts available.

- Price and hours of access. How much will it cost per month for a SLIP or PPP account? How many hours of Internet access are included? An average price is $20 per month for 150 hours of graphical access.

- Technical support. Does the provider offer technical support? What are the hours (days, nights, weekends, holidays)? Is support free?

- Software. Do they provide the TCP/IP software? Is the software custom configured? Do they provide free copies of an email program such as Eudora and a Web browser such as Explorer? Good Internet providers will supply custom-configured TCP/IP software and the essential Internet navigation and communication software.

Touring with Browsers

CHAPTER CONTENTS

TOURING WITH BROWSERS

This chapter provides a guided tour of the tools and resources you will use to surf the Net. In this tour, you will

- learn how to navigate the Internet using a browser.
- travel on a guided Net tour.
- surf to cool Web sites.
- save your favorite Internet sites (URLs).
- learn how to export and import your favorite URLs.
- learn how to use and navigate Web page frames.
- learn about the Web's multimedia-oriented environment.
- learn how to use and install helper applications and plug-ins.
- visit cool multimedia Web sites.

INTERNET NAVIGATION USING BROWSERS

A *browser* is a software program for viewing a Web document. In 1995 the browser war began between Netscape Communications Corporation (NCC) and Microsoft. At this time approximately 30 browsers had been developed for exploring the World Wide Web and the Internet. In 1996 the browser war between Microsoft and Netscape escalated with the release of Microsoft Internet Explorer, featuring browser capabilities to match those of Netscape Navigator. When 1996 drew to a close there were only two premiere browsers—Netscape Navigator and Microsoft Internet Explorer—others collapsed under the weight of these two popular and powerful Net tools. In 1997 Netscape and Microsoft headed in different directions as the fourth generation browser was introduced. Netscape Communications Corporation (NCC) focused on providing network services for business and Microsoft integrated the Internet into the desktop.

NCC introduced the Netscape Communicator Suite featuring
- **Navigator 4.0**—for Internet browsing
- **Messenger**—an email application for local area networks
- **Collabra**—a tool for public and private discussions
- **Composer**—a more advanced HTML editing tool
- **Conference**—a collaboration tool for sharing multimedia files
- **CoolTalk**—Internet telephone for telephone conferencing

Microsoft's Explorer 4.0 integrates Internet Explorer into the Windows operating system. This integration between the desktop and browser allows users to edit and work with documents from within the browser as they surf the Net. Both software application and browser are viewed simultaneously on the computer screen.

The one common thread between these two browsers is the increased ease for the playing and viewing of multimedia files on Web pages. For example Netscape 4.0 has an automated plug-in installer. Microsoft's ActiveX supports many audio and video formats. Both browsers also feature more personal customization options such as the ability to create toolbar buttons and to hide or make visible icons and buttons.

IMPORTANT

The browser war to determine who will control Net surfers' desktop and hard disk space makes one thing certain—new browser versions will be introduced every few months. What is important to remember is that their navigational functions will remain basically unchanged. Tools for communication and interaction such as email and Usenet news features may change slightly and take on a new appearance. New features may be added. HOWEVER, if you have a basic understanding of the browser it will be easy to transfer this knowledge and learn the new functions and enhancements. This section is designed to give you the basic information to use a browser—no matter which version. The basics for Netscape Navigator and Microsoft Internet Explorer will be presented.

Browser Basics

When a browser is opened you will see a Web page or *window* that may contain text, images, movies, and sound. Each multimedia resource on a page has associated locational information to link you to the resource. This locational information is called the URL. For example, the URL or address used to connect to the Home Page for the White House is **http://www1.whitehouse.gov/ WH/ Welcome.html** (see Fig. 2.1).

FIGURE 2.1

Home Page for the White House using Netscape Navigator
http://www1.whitehouse.gov/WH/Welcome.html

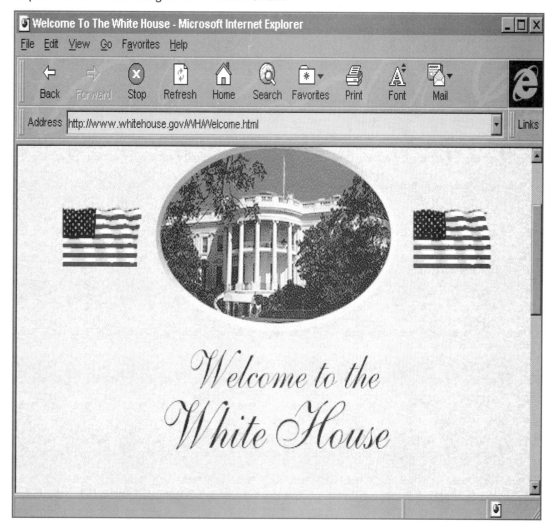

Netscape and Explorer include the following features to assist you with your Internet travels:

- *Window Title Bar* shows the name of the current document.
  In Figure 2.1 note the title bar with the name Welcome to the White House.

- *Page display* shows the content of the Web window. A page includes text and links to images, video, and sound files. Links include highlighted words (colored and/or underlined) or icons. Click on a highlighted word or icon to bring another page of related information into view. In Figure 2.1 the White House page has links to the President and Vice President and commonly requested federal services.

- *Address location* field shows the URL address of the current document. In Figure 2.1 you will see the address or URL for the Home Page for the White House. **http://www1.whitehouse.gov/WH/Welcome.html**

- *Status Bar* indicates the status of the document or file you are trying to transfer. The status bar displays three types of information from left to right: the Web address of the document; the progress indicator displays downloading progress; and the progress bar displays the completed percentage of your document layout as your page downloads.

- *Toolbar buttons* activate browser features and navigational aids.

- *Pop-up menus* also activate browser features and navigational aids. Many of these features perform the same functions as the toolbar buttons.

Navigating the Net Using Toolbar Buttons

A browser's *toolbar* has buttons (Fig. 2.2 and Fig. 2.3) that perform commands that you will use most frequently when surfing the Internet. You are probably already familiar with toolbar buttons from other software application programs, such as a word processing application.

FIGURE 2.2

Netscape Navigator (version 4.x) toolbar buttons

FIGURE 2.3

Microsoft Internet Explorer (version 3.x) toolbar buttons

Notice that both browsers, Netscape and Explorer, have navigational buttons for

- taking you to a previous Web page—**Back** button.

- moving forward the next page in your history list—**Forward** button.

- taking you back to the first opening page— **Home** button.

- finding information and newsgroups—**Search** button.

- saving your favorite URLs—Bookmarks button (Netscape); **Favorites** button (Explorer).

- printing the currently displayed page—**Print** button.

- stopping the transfer of a Web document or file—**Stop** button.

Other tools include a button for

- reloading the same page that you were viewing—**Reload** button(Netscape) and **Refresh** button (Explorer). This tool is useful if you have used the **Stop** button and would like to view the entire document or page.

- using larger or smaller fonts on the Web page you are viewing—**Font** button (Explorer only).

- accessing the browser's email program—**Mail** button (Explorer only).

Netscape and Explorer both provide options for users to create buttons on the toolbar for frequently used navigational aids or tools.

Netscape and Explorer share features for assisting the Internet traveler. Each of these browsers also has what their developers believe are other important and frequently used Internet commands that have been made into toolbar buttons. When you have used one browser it is very easy to transfer your knowledge of Internet navigation to other browsers.

Pop-up Menus
Pop-up menus (see Fig. 2.4 and 2.5) appear when you point to something within your browser or page and click on it. For example, click on the **Help** menu and the following pop-up menu appears.

FIGURE 2.4
Help pop-up menu for Explorer

This menu gives options for finding help on Internet Explorer as well as other Microsoft services designed for the Internet.

Clicking on some objects, such as an image on a page (Fig. 2.5) presents a pop-up menu that lists things you can do to whatever you clicked, such as saving the image to your hard drive.

FIGURE 2.5
Clicking on Mapquest's map provides this pop-up menu for image options

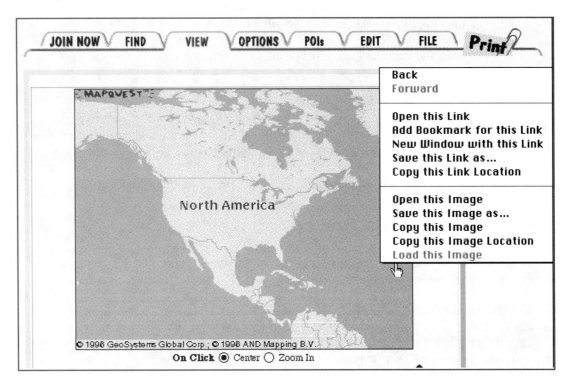

NOTE

If you are using a PC your mouse will have two buttons. Use the right button to click on an image or menu.

Directory Buttons

Other toolbar buttons within browsers provide features helping you to find information and resources on the Internet. For example, Netscape's Places buttons (version 4.x) as shown in Figure 2.6 provides links to new Web sites (What's New?), interesting Web sites (What's Cool?), business and after hour Web sites (Destinations), tools for helping you to find people on the Net (People), and information on how to upgrade your browser or find plug-ins and viewers (Software).

FIGURE 2.6
Netscape's buttons providing additional features for Net surfers

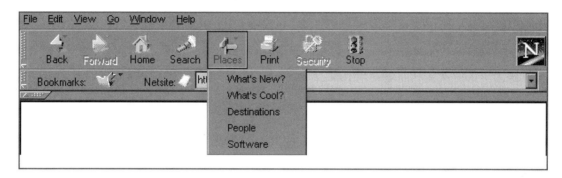

GUIDED TOURS—NETSCAPE & EXPLORER

Guided Tour 1
Surfing the Net

In this guided tour you will use Netscape Navigator or Explorer to

- connect to World Wide Web sites and Home Pages;
- use pull-down menus and navigational toolbar buttons to navigate World Wide Web sites; and
- save bookmarks of your favorite pages.

STEP 1

Log onto your Internet account. When you have connected, open the Netscape or Explorer browser by double-clicking on the application icon.

Netscape Navigator Icon   Microsoft Explorer Icon

You will be taken to a Home Page. Notice the Location/Address URLs in Figure 2.1. This Home Page may belong to Netscape Communications Corporation (http://home.netscape.com) or Microsoft (http://www.microsoft.com), or it may have been designed by your college or university. Look at the top of the Home Page in the Title Bar to see whose Home Page you are visiting.

Notice the highlighted text on Web pages containing built-in URL information for linking to that information. You can also type in new URL text to link a page.

STEP 2

Begin exploring. Use your browser toolbar buttons and pull-down menus. Depending on which version of Netscape you are using, either click on the **What's New** button or the **Places** button to find **What's New** and **What's Cool**. You will see a list of highlighted underlined links to Web sites. Click on a link and EXPLORE. HAVE FUN! If you are using Explorer, investigate the Home Page that you are viewing or click the pop-up menu **Go** and select **Best of the Web**.

STEP 3

Save your favorite pages. When you find a page that you may want to visit at a later time, click on the pull-down menu, **Bookmarks** or the **Bookmarks** button (in Netscape 4.x). Next, click on the menu item **Add Bookmark**; in Explorer select the **Favorites** menu.

Click on the **Bookmarks** (Favorites) pull-down menu or button again. Notice the name of the page you marked listed below the **View Bookmarks** menu item. To view this page again, select the **Bookmarks** pull-down menu and click on the name of the page you saved. Later you will learn how to organize your bookmarks.

Explore Home Pages and cool Web sites.

STEP 4

After you have linked to several pages, click on the **Go** pull-down menu. Notice the listing of the places you have most recently visited. If you want to revisit any of the pages you have already viewed, click on the name of the Web site.

Netscape creates a history list of every Web sites you have visited in a "history" file. The file keeps track of the text and images of every site visited. To reconnect to a site you have visited, type **about:globalhistory** in the URL location (netsite) dialog box and the history list file appears. The history list in Netscape (versions 2.x and 3.x) is available for your current working session only. Netscape 4.x can easily summon the history list that recalls Web sites visited days or weeks ago.

Explorer also creates a History list or folder that keeps track of your Internet visits for a user-definable number of days. To view your history list, select the **View** menu then the **Navigation** tab or, for a shorter list, select the **Go** menu. Use these history lists to re-visit sites.

Guided Tour 2
Surfing to Cool Web Sites

In this guided tour you will enter in URL addresses to link to World Wide Web (WWW) sites, but before you begin, remember these URL Tips.

URL TIPS

TIP

Do not capitalize the protocol string. For example, the HTTP protocol should be **http://** not **HTTP://**. Some browsers such as Netscape correct these errors; others do not.

TIP

URLs are case sensitive, be sure to copy the address capitalization exactly.

TIP

Don't place any spaces within an address.

TIP

If you have trouble connecting to a Web site, check your URL to be sure you have typed the address correctly. Check to be sure you placed the slash marks in the right direction—forward slash (/) , not backward slash (\).

TIP

Netscape accepts abbreviated Net addresses, without the http://www. prefix. If you type a single word as your URL, Netscape adds the prefix **http://www.** and the suffix **.com**. For example, to connect to Netscape's Home Page, type **Netscape**.

There are three options in Netscape for entering a URL:

- the **Netsite** text field (see Fig. 2.1).
- the **File** menu—Open Location; or
- the **Open** toolbar button (only in Netscape 2.x or 3.x series).

If you are using Explorer, you have two options:

- From the menu bar choose the **File** pop-up menu, then click on **Open**.

- Highlight the URL in the Address text field (see Fig. 1.5) and type your URL over the highlighted address.

Select one of the above options. It will take you to the window where you can enter your choice of URL text.

The Web sites below link to some of the best and coolest places on the Net. Practice using your browser and saving your favorite Web sites by entering the following URLs.

AWESOME LIST
http://www.clark.net/pub/journalism/awesome.html

CNET'S BEST OF THE WEB
http://www.cnet.com/Content/Reviews/Bestofweb

EXCITE REVIEWS
http://www.excite.com/Reviews

LYCOS TOP 5% SITES
http://point.lycos.com

NETGUIDE LIVE'S BEST OF THE WEB
http://www.netguide.com

PLACES TO SEE WINNERS PAGE
http://www.astep.com/award

THE RAIL
http://www.therail.com/cgi-bin/grand

WORLD WIDE WEB TOUR
http://www.derossi.com/tour/tour.tg

YAHOO INTERNET LIFE
http://www.zdnet.com/yil

Guided Tour 3
Saving Your Favorite Web Sites

In this guided tour you will use Netscape Navigator or Explorer to organize, modify, save, and move bookmark files.

Netscape Navigator Bookmarks

Before you can organize and work with bookmark files, you must access Netscape's **Bookmark** window (Fig. 2.7). Go to the **Window** pull-down menu and select **Bookmarks** or use the **Bookmark** toolbar button.

Organizing your bookmarks

Before you begin saving bookmarks, it is helpful to consider how to organize saved bookmarks. Begin by thinking of categories that your bookmarks might be filed under such as Software, Business, Education, Entertainment, Research, and so forth. For each category make a folder. These are the steps for making your bookmark folders.

a.   Go to the **Window** menu and select **Bookmarks**.

FIGURE 2.7
Netscape's **Window** pop-up
menu for working with **Bookmarks**

Window	FaxMenu
Netscape Mail	
Netscape News	
Address Book	
Bookmarks	⌘B
History	

FIGURE 2.8
Netscape's **Bookmarks** window

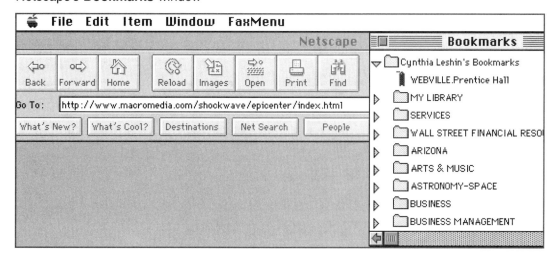

Notice the Web sites saved in the Bookmarks folders in Figure 2.8. This Bookmarks window gives you three new menus for working with your bookmarks: File, Edit, and Item (Fig. 2.8).

    b.   Create a new folder for a bookmark category by selecting the Item menu (Fig.2.9).

FIGURE 2.9
Opened **Item** menu from within
the Bookmarks window

Item	Window	FaxMenu
Edit Bookmark...		⌘I
Go to Bookmark		
Sort Bookmarks		
Insert Bookmark...		
Insert Folder...		
Insert Separator		
Make Alias		
Set to New Bookmarks Folder		
Set to Bookmark Menu Folder		

c. Select Insert Folder (see Fig. 2.9).

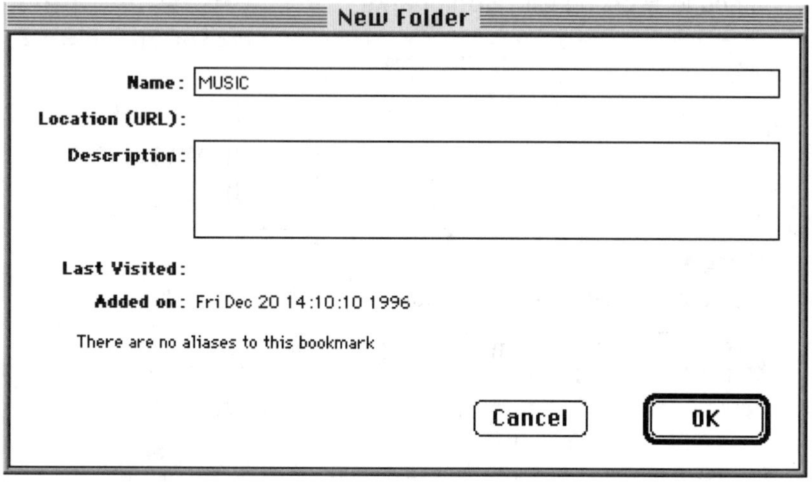

FIGURE 2.10
Insert Folder
window

```
═══════════════════ New Folder ═══════════════════

        Name : │MUSIC                                    │

Location (URL) :

   Description : ┌──────────────────────────────────────┐
                │                                      │
                │                                      │
                │                                      │
                └──────────────────────────────────────┘

  Last Visited :

      Added on : Fri Dec 20 14:10:10 1996

        There are no aliases to this bookmark


                              ┌──────────┐  ┌──────────┐
                              │  Cancel  │  │    OK    │
                              └──────────┘  └──────────┘
```

d. Type in the name of your folder in the Name dialog box. As shown in Figure 2.10, a folder called Music has been created.

e. Enter in a description of the bookmark folder (optional).

f. Click OK.

Add bookmarks to a folder.
Netscape provides an option for identifying the folder into which you would like to put your bookmarks in.

a. Select the folder you would like to add your new bookmarks to by clicking on the name of the folder once. The folder should now be highlighted.

b. Go to the Item menu and select **Set to New Bookmarks** Folder shown near the bottom of Figure 2.9.

c. Go back to the Bookmarks window and notice how this newly identified folder has been marked with a colored bookmark identifier. All bookmarks that you add will be placed in this folder until you identify a new folder.

Modify the name of your bookmark.
Bookmark properties contain the name of the Web site and the URL. You may want to change the name of the bookmark to indicate more clearly the information available at this site. For example, the bookmark name STCil/HST Public Information has very little meaning. Changing its name to Hubble Space Telescope Public Information is more helpful when later selecting from many bookmarks.

a. To change the name of a bookmark, select the bookmark by clicking on it once.

b. Go to the **Item** menu from within the Bookmarks window.

c. Select **Properties**. (For the Macintosh, select Edit.)

FIGURE 2.11
Properties window from Bookmark **Item** options

```
═══════════════ Hubble Public Pictures ═══════════════

        Name : │Hubble Space Telescope Public Information        │
Location (URL) : │http ://www.stsci.edu/pubinfo/Pictures.html      │
  Description : ┌───────────────────────────────────────────────┐
              │                                               │
              │                                               │
              │                                               │
              └───────────────────────────────────────────────┘

 Last Visited : Tue Jul 23 07 :06 :52 1996
    Added on : Sat Feb 10 14 :34 :34 1996

  There are no aliases to this bookmark

                              ( Cancel )      ╭───  OK  ───╮
```

d. Enter in the new name for your bookmark by either deleting the text shown in Figure 2.11, or begin typing the new name when the highlighted text is visible.

e. Notice the URL for the bookmark; you can also enter a new description for the URL.

Make copies of your bookmarks.
Occasionally you will want to save a bookmark in several folders. There are two ways to do this:

a. Select the bookmark that you would like to copy. Go to the **Edit** menu from within the Bookmark window and select **Copy**. Select the folder where you would like to place the copy of the bookmark. Go to the **Edit** menu and select **Paste**.

b. Make a copy of your bookmark for another category folder by selecting **Make Alias** from the **Item** menu. When the alias of your bookmark has been created, move the alias bookmark to the new folder (see "Note").

NOTE

Bookmarks can be moved from one location to another by dragging an existing bookmark to a new folder.

Delete a bookmark.
To remove a bookmark:

    a.   Select the bookmark to be deleted by clicking on it once, then pressing the delete key; or

    b.   Go to the **Edit** menu from within the Bookmarks window and choose either **Cut** or **Delete.**

Export and save bookmarks.
Netscape provides options for making copies of your bookmarks either to save as a backup on your hard drive, to share with others, or to use on another computer. Follow these steps for exporting or saving your bookmarks to a floppy disk.

    a.   Open the **Bookmarks** window.

    b   From within the Bookmarks window, go to the **File** menu. Select **Save As**.

    c.   Designate where you would like to save the bookmark file—on your hard drive or to a floppy disk—in the **Save** in box (Fig. 2.12).

FIGURE 2.12
Netscape Bookmarks
window for saving
bookmark files

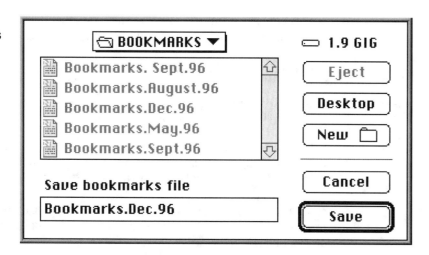

    d.   Enter a name for your bookmark file in the **File** name dialog box.

    e.   Click **Save**.

Import Bookmarks.
Bookmarks can be imported into Netscape from a previous Netscape session saved on a floppy disk.

    a.   Insert the floppy disk with the bookmark file into your computer.

    b.   Open the **Bookmarks** window.

    c.   From within the Bookmarks window, go to the **File** menu and select **Import** (Fig 2.13).

FIGURE 2.13
Netscape **File** menu from
within Bookmarks

d. Designate a location for the bookmark file. The Look in window displays a floppy disk
or you can click on the scroll arrow to bring the hard drive into view.

FIGURE 2.14
Import window allows a
bookmark from a floppy disk
to be imported into your
Netscape application

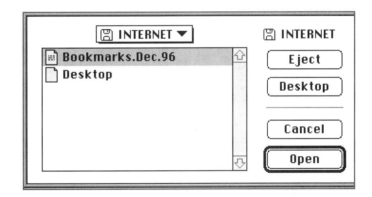

e. Click on **Open**, shown in Figure 2.14. The bookmarks will now be imported into your
Netscape bookmark list.

Internet Explorer Bookmarks

Organize your bookmarks.
Before you begin saving bookmarks, it is helpful to consider how to organize saved bookmarks.
Begin by thinking of categories that your bookmarks might be filed under such as Software,
Business, Education, Entertainment, Research, and so forth. For each category make a folder. These
are the steps for making your bookmark folders.

a. Go to the **Favorites** menu and select **Organize Favorites** (Fig. 2.15).

FIGURE 2.15
Explorer's menu for adding,
organizing, and viewing favorite URLs

FIGURE 2.16
Explorer dialog box for organizing favorite URLs

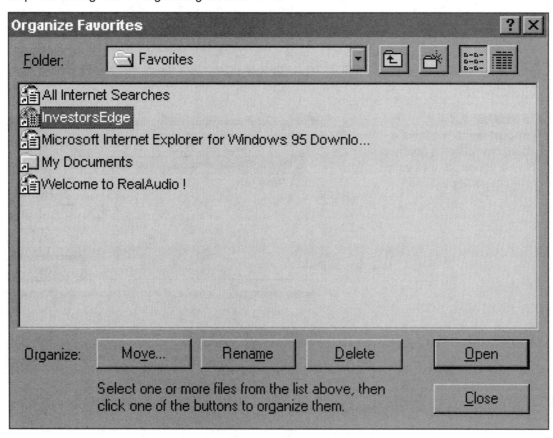

  b. Click on the **Folder** icon.

A new folder will be created (see Figure 2.17). Type a name for the folder in the highlighted folder
box.

FIGURE 2.17
Explorer creates a New
Folder for your URLs

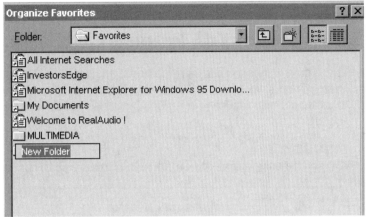

c. To save a URL, click on the **Favorites** menu and select **Add to Favorites**.

d. Use this same Organize Favorites option for organizing, renaming, or deleting your
    favorite URLs (see Fig. 2.17).

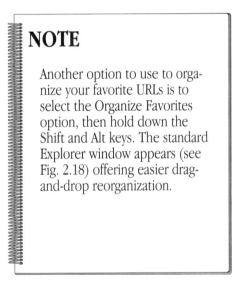

NOTE

Another option to use to organize your favorite URLs is to
select the Organize Favorites
option, then hold down the
Shift and Alt keys. The standard
Explorer window appears (see
Fig. 2.18) offering easier drag-
and-drop reorganization.

FIGURE 2.18
Another option for organizing
favorite URLs in Explorer

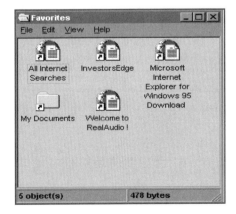

Guided Tour 4
Navigating With Frames

In this guided tour you will visit Web sites with frames and learn how to navigate and work with frames. Frames were introduced as a new feature of Netscape Navigator 2.x. Frames make it possible to create multiple windows on a browser page. Figure 2.19 is an example of a Web page divided into several windows called *frames*.

FIGURE 2.19
A Web site using frames to organize information about books

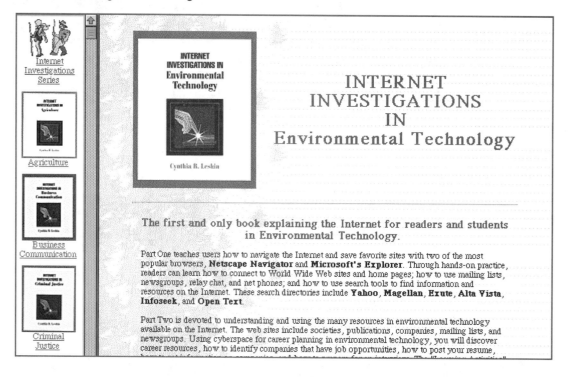

Frames are used to organize and display information. The icons in the left margin are the categories of information that can be linked. Click on an icon and information on that book will be displayed in the right foremost frame.

If you are using Netscape you will need to use your mouse to navigate within frames and to save bookmarks. To move forward and back within frames, position your cursor within the frame and hold down the mouse button (Macintosh users); Windows users hold down the right mouse button. A pop-up menu appears. Choose **Back** or **Forward**. If you are using Explorer, only one frame is active at a time. Click on the **Back** or **Forward** button to navigate with the currently active frame. You can also use the history list found under the **Go** menu.

FIGURE 2.20
The pop-up menu from within Netscape displaying frame navigation

```
Back
Forward

Open this Link
Add Bookmark for this Link
New Window with this Link
Save this Link as...
Copy this Link Location

Open this Image
Save this Image as...
Copy this Image
Copy this Image Location
Load this Image
```

To bookmark a frame in Netscape place your cursor over the link to the frame and hold down the mouse button. The pop-up as seen in Figure 2.20 appears. Select **Add Bookmark for this Link**. In Explorer the active frame will be marked as a Favorite.

To print a frame, click the desired frame and select **Print Frame** from the **File** menu.

Now that you know about frames, let's visit several Web sites where you can interact with Web pages that have multiple panes.

CNN INTERACTIVE
http://www.cnn.com

DISCOVERY CHANNEL
http://www.discovery.com

NETSCAPE'S LINK TO COMPANIES USING FRAMES
http://home.netscape.com/comprod/products/navigator/
version_2.0/frames/frame_users.html

WIRED
http://www.wired.com

Explore the links in the frame table of contents. If you are using Netscape, use your mouse to move forward and back within frames by positioning your cursor within the frame and holding down the mouse button (Macintosh users); Windows users hold down the right mouse button. A pop-up menu appears. Choose **Back in Frame** or **Forward in Frame**.

If you are using Explorer, click on the **Back** or **Forward** button to navigate with the currently active frame or the history list under the **Go** menu.

Save bookmarks of your favorite Web documents by placing your cursor over the link to the frame and holding down the mouse button. A different pop-up menu appears. Select **Add Bookmark for this Link.**

Print a frame that you would like to save by clicking the desired frame and selecting **Print Frame** from the **File** menu.

Point at a border between a frame. If your pointer changes to two parallel lines with two arrows you can drag the frame border or reposition it.

Guided Tour 5
Customizing Your Browser

Navigator and Explorer allow you to personalize your Net surfing preferences. If using Netscape, select the **Options** menu, then **General Preferences** (Netscape 4.x select **Edit** menu, **Preferences**, **General Preferences**). Notice that you can enter your favorite starting Home Page (Fig 2.21).

FIGURE 2.21
Netscape's **General Preferences** for customizing Net travel

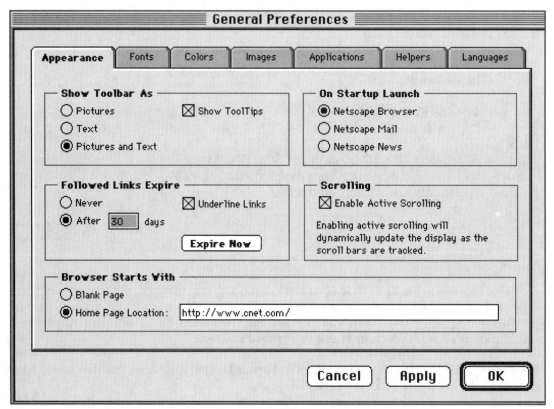

For Explorer, select the **View** menu, then the **Options** tab. Explorer also allows you to customize your toolbar by making your favorite Web sites into toolbar buttons. By default, the Links toolbar contains buttons that link you to Microsoft—services, product updates, Web tutorial, and favorite links (Fig. 2.22).

FIGURE 2.22
Explorer toolbar buttons showing the default Quick Links to Microsoft services

To change the **Links** toolbar sites:

STEP 1

Select the **View** menu, then **Options** (see Fig. 2.23A), then click on the **Navigation** tab.

FIGURE 2.23A
Explorer Navigation tab dialog box for working with toolbar buttons

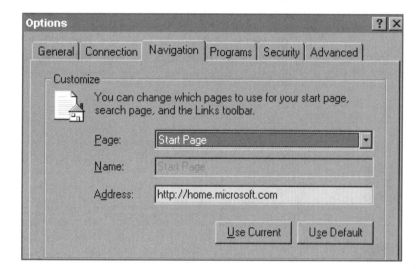

FIGURE 2.23B
Options for selecting and changing the Quick Link button

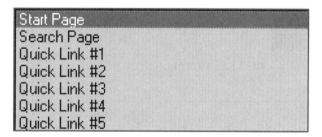

STEP 2

Select the **Page** box. The default is Start Page. You can then select a Quick Link button that you want to change; they are numbered from 1-5 (see Fig. 2.23B).

FIGURE 2.24
Dialog box for changing toolbar buttons

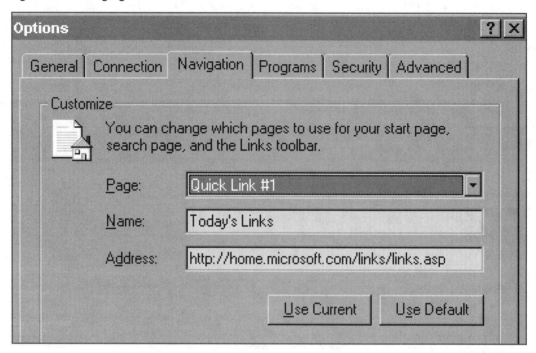

STEP 3

In the **Page** box, type the name for the button (see Fig. 2.24).

STEP 4

In the **Address** box, type the URL for the site that you want to become a button.

STEP 5

Click the **Use Current** button.

Multimedia-Oriented Web Environments

Now that you have used a browser to navigate the Internet, you are ready to explore the ultimate Web experience—multimedia-oriented environments. The term *multimedia* is used when referring to more than one medium—such as the use of text supplemented with animation, video, or sound. When multimedia is integrated into a Web presentation or document, it is referred to as *hypermedia*. Hypermedia is being used extensively to bring life to Web pages with cool graphics, animation, live objects, 3D video, interactivity, streaming audio and video (audio or video files that flow continuously over the Internet to your computer immediately playing the video or sound file as it arrives to your desktop.)

Before You Begin...

Before you can experience multimedia Web environments you will need some basic information about *plug-ins* and *helper* or *viewer* applications. When a graphic image, video, or sound file is created it requires a program for viewing or playing. Although the first browsers did support the viewing of most images, they did not support the playing of video and sound. Net users had to obtain copies of external viewer applications to experience Web audio and video. These external viewer software programs are written by companies other than Netscape or Microsoft and are necessary to experience cool multimedia effects.

Helper applications are stand-alone programs that work with browsers to play or display multimedia files. These same helpers can also operate on their own outside the browser environment. Almost any program can be considered a Helper Application. For example, compression programs such as Stuffit Expander or PKZIP are often configured as helper applications to work with a browser. When a compressed file is downloaded from the Internet the compression program automatically starts to decompress or open it upon successful completion of the download.

In 1995 Java—a programming language that enabled miniprograms to be downloaded and run on a Web page—was introduced by Sun Microsystems. These miniprograms called *applets* made it possible for the first time for Web designers to add life and animation to Web pages creating what is often referred to as *live objects*. Browsers such as Netscape or Explorer ran the miniprogram while the Web page was being displayed. To experience Java visit the following Web sites.

> GAMELAN
> http://www.gamelan.com

> JAVA CENTER
> http://www.java.co.uk

Shortly after Java was introduced, plug-in applications were developed and became the hottest new Web technology for adding special effects to Web pages. Plug-ins are software programs designed to play a multimedia file from within the browser window or page, running as a system resource for as long as they are needed.

Microsoft's response to Java was the ActiveX development platform. This technology, available in Explorer 3.0 or later, has also opened new doors for moving and animating Web objects, creating live audio, scrolling banners, and interactivity.

Today plug-ins and viewer applications are widely used and required to experience cool graphics, animations, video, and sound on Web pages. Most plug-ins and viewers are free and can obtained at Web sites with shareware such as

TUCOWS (FOR WINDOWS)
http://www.tucows.com

JUMBO
http://www.jumbo.com

SHAREWARE
http://www.shareware.com

or connect to Netscape's Plug-in page at http://home.netscape.com/comprod/products/ navigator/version_2.0/plugins/index.html.

Newer versions of Netscape and Explorer have a few plug-ins and viewers already built-in.

How Do Plug-ins and Viewers Work With My Browser?

After you type in a URL requesting a Web page from a server, the components of that page—text, image, video, or sound—begin downloading to your computer. The server where the requested Web document resides sends a message to your browser with the MIME (Multipurpose Internet Mail Extension) type of the requested file. If the file is a MIME text type then the browser displays the file. If the file contains an image with an extension such as .JPEG, .GIF, JPG, JPE, or XMB it is a MIME image type and the browser displays the image on the Web page using a built-in image viewer. Sound or video MIME types may or may not be able to be played depending on whether your browser has the required plug-in or viewer built in. For example, Netscape 3.0 and later can play sound files ending in .AU, .AIF, and .SND.

If the MIME type is none of these, the browser looks for a plug-in or helper to see if it has been configured with your browser to run the file. If no plug-in or helper is found, you will be shown a dialog box such as Figure 2.25 from Netscape Navigator.

NOTE

Before a plug-in or helper can play or display a multimedia file it must be installed or configured for your browser. Microsoft Internet Explorer supports many audio and video formats without requiring plug-in installation and configuration.

FIGURE 2.25
Dialog box from Netscape indicating that the plug-in cannot be found

 This page contains information of type "video/vdo" that can only be viewed with the appropriate plug-in. What do you want to do?

[**Plug-in Info**] [**Cancel**]

This message allows two options:

- Link to information on the plug-in you need to view the multimedia file by clicking on Plug-in Info, or

- Cancel the downloading of the file by clicking on the Cancel button.

> **NOTE**
>
> Explorer uses the same plug-ins as Netscape. If you have been using Netscape and switch to Explorer, you will not need to do anything special. Use Explorer to connect to a site and when Explorer detects the need for a plug-in it will locate it on your hard drive, run the program, and display the multimedia file. Explorer's ActiveX platform performs many of the same functions as Netscape's plug-ins.

Cool Plug-ins and Helpers for the Net

There are many plug-ins and helpers used by Web developers to permit cool graphics, animation, scrolling banners, and streaming audio and video to be added to Net pages. The best site to visit for the latest and hottest plug-ins is Netscape's site at http://home.netscape.com/comprod/products/navigator/version_2.0/plugins/index.html.

Listed below are a few of the more popular and frequently used plug-ins.

ACROBAT READER BY ADOBE SYSTEMS

http://www.adobe.com

Acrobat Reader documents created in word processing, desktop publishing, spreadsheet, graphics, or database files can be saved as Acrobat PDF files and viewed on any kind of computer even if the software and the fonts used to create the application are not present.

APPLE QUICKTIME PLUG-IN

http://www.quickTime.apple.com/dev/devweb.html

This plug-in lets you experience QuickTime animation, music, audio, video, and virtual reality panoramas and objects on Web pages.

BUBBLEVIEWER

http://www.omniview.com

Bubbleview by Omniview lets you experience a 360-degree environment.

COSMO PLAYER

http://www.sgi.com

Experience 3D worlds on the Web with Silicon Graphics's Cosmo Player.

LIVE3D

http://home.netscape.com/comprod/products/navigator/live3d/index.html

Live3D lets you experience a rich world of 3D spaces and the ability to interact with text, images, animation, sound, music, and even video on the Web.

MOVIESTAR BY INTELLIGENCE AT LARGE

http://www.ialsoft.com

An alternative plug-in for QuickTime Multimedia, Moviestar enables the viewing of video, sound, background music, animation, and more.

NETSCAPE MEDIA PLAYER

http://home.netscape.com/comprod/mirror/media/download_mplayer.html

Netscape Media Player brings streaming audio and synchronized multimedia to your desktop.

THE POINTCAST NETWORK

http://www.pointcast.com

Personalize your own news broadcasting system using Pointcast Network. Options include world, national, business and political news as well as weather, sports, investments, lifestyle, or other topics of interest.

REALAUDIO

http://www.realaudio.com

RealAudio is a real-time streaming audio plug-in that lets you listen to live music, news, live events and much more.

SHOCKWAVE

http://www.macromedia.com

Shockwave is one the hottest applications for bringing streamed movies and interaction to your desktop. Shockwave plays files created in Macromedia Director.

VIVOACTIVE PLAYER
http://www.vivo.com
A streaming video player, Vivoactive brings video clips to your Web pages.

VR SCOUT
http://www.chaco.com
Immerse yourself in real-time virtual communities with Chaco Communications's VR Scout.

Installing Plug-ins—Netscape Navigator

You have learned that you need a plug-in or helper application before displaying or playing multi-media files on the Internet. Newers versions (4.x series) of Netscape and Explorer make the playing of plug-ins easier with automatic installers (Netscape) or the built-in cability to play many audio and video files (ActiveX in Explorer).

> **NOTE**
>
> Choose a plug-in for a multimedia file, if it is available, over a helper application. It will take longer for a helper to display or play a file since the helper must first launch then open the file. However, check to see if a helper has additional features that the plug-in may not.

> **IMPORTANT...**
> Read any README files that have been installed with the plug-in application. Many times they contain valuable information to help you with any problems you may encounter with the plug-in and having it work as intended with your browser or computer system software. Since plug-ins and viewers are free there is NO TECHNICAL SUPPORT. You will find that the README files may have all the information you need to solve your problems.

The following guidelines are for installing a plug-in with Netscape Navigator. Most plug-ins come with installation programs that will place the plug-in in the appropriate folder and set up your browser to use it. If the plug-in does not have an install program, read the README file.

STEP 1

After you have found a plug-in that you would like to use with your browser, visit a Web site where you can obtain a copy of a free plug-in. The best site is Netscape's **http://home.netscape.com/comprod/products/navigator/version_2.0/plugins/index.html**.

STEP 2

Download the plug-in from a Web site.

STEP 3

Run the program and an install or set-up will begin. Follow the instructions and the plug-in will be installed. If the plug-in does not have an install or set-up program, read the instructions that accompany the file.

STEP 4

After the plug-in is installed, click on the multimedia object and the plug-in takes over launching the file.

STEP 5

Restart your computer after you have installed the plug-in.

NOTES

Many plug-ins and helpers require the latest system software to play or display the multimedia file. If you are having problems with a plug-in or helper, read the README file. There will probably be information on requirements for running the program.

Netscape Navigator 4.x has a plug-in install feature built-in.

Installing Helper (Viewer) Applications

One important helper application is the program to decompress files sent over the Internet. For the Macintosh the most popular compression program is Stuffit Expander; for Windows, PKZIP is most commonly used. In this example we will use Netscape Navigator to install a compression utility.

STEP 1

Visit a shareware Web site and find the helper application you are looking for, in this case, either Stuffit or PKZIP.

STEP 2

After the program is downloaded to your hard drive, follow the instructions to install it or use the set-up feature.

STEP 3

Open Netscape and select **General Preferences** from the **Options** menu. Click on the **Helpers** tab. (With Version 4.x, go to the **Edit** menu, select **Preferences**, **General Preferences**, then **Helpers**.)

FIGURE 2.26
The Helpers tab showing viewers and plug-ins for Navigator

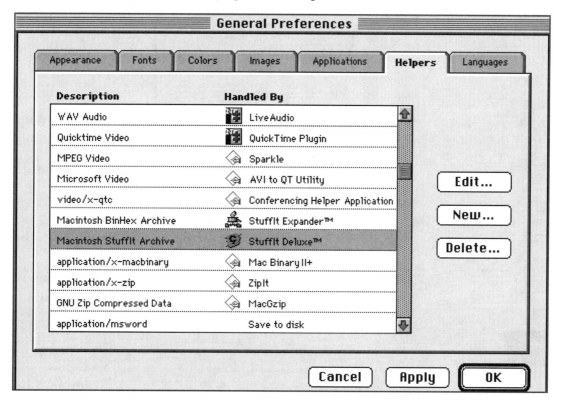

NOTE

Although different versions of Netscape may present different dialog boxes for these operations, the procedure is the same for installing helpers.

This tab displays the descriptions and names of helpers and plug-ins for text, image, sound, and video, as well as other applications that you many want to use with Netscape (e.g., a compression program). The files are listed under Description (see Fig. 2.26) using a naming standard known as MIME (Multipurpose Internet Name Extension).

NOTE

MIME types consist of two parts: the main type and the subtype. For example, the main type for a NASA image would be image and the subtype might be jpeg. The file name extension indicates the subtype for the file. You will find the main type and subtype for many of the different types of files you might encounter on the Net under the Description listing.

STEP 4

From within the Helper listing look for the application you are trying to install, in this case application/x-zip compressed (for the PC) or application/x-stuffit (for the Macintosh). Click on the application, then on the **Edit** button.

FIGURE 2.27
The **Edit** Type dialog box from within **Helpers**

Edit Type

Description : Macintosh StuffIt Archive

MIME Type : application/x-stuffit

Suffixes : sit

Handled By

○ Navigator
○ Plug-in :
◉ Application : StuffIt Deluxe™   [Browse...]
　　　　File type : [SIT! ▼]
○ Save to disk
○ Unknown : Prompt user

[Cancel] [OK]

STEP 5

You must now let Netscape know where to find this helper application on your computer hard drive.

Click on the **Browse** button. Find the application that you want to use as a helper with Netscape, then click on the Open button (see Fig. 2.28). This action indicates to Netscape what file you would like to run from within Netscape whenever a file with the indicated extension is encountered. In this case, if a file from the Internet that needs to be uncompressed—indicated by the file extension **.sit**—is encountered by Netscape, the browser will look for the application, open it, and perform the program action.

FIGURE 2.28
The dialog box for finding
the helper application on
the hard drive

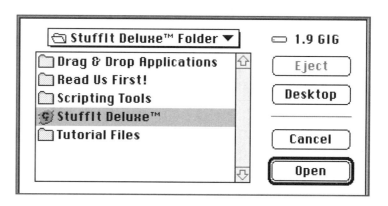

Installing a Plug-in Without an Install Program or a Helper Not Listed in General Preferences

TIP

There will be times when you may want to install a helper that cannot be found under the Helper listing or when a plug-in does not have an install program.

Read the plug-in or helper README file. You will find that these documents usually have the information you need, such as the mime type and subtype.

Some general steps include the following:

STEP 1

Drag the plug-in into your browser's Plug-In Folder. You may need to use your computer operating system's **Find** feature to locate where this folder is kept on your hard drive.

STEP 2

Open Netscape and go to the **General Preferences**; select the **Helper** tab.

STEP 3

Scroll through the list of plug-ins and helpers to see if the program is already there. Netscape may be pre-configured for some plug-ins and helpers even if you do not have them.

STEP 4

If the program is not there, select the New button (in Fig. 2.26). A new dialog box will appear (Fig. 2.29). You will need the data from the README file to enter the information.

The example below illustrates these steps. We will configure Netscape to play the RealAudio helper application for the listening to streaming audio.

FIGURE 2.29
The **New** dialog box for adding a new Helper/Viewer to Netscape

Edit Type

Description: [_____]

MIME Type: [_____]

Suffixes: [_____]

Handled By

○ Navigator
○ Plug-in: [_____ ▼]
○ Application: Unknown   [Browse...]
         File type: [TEXT ▼]
○ Save to disk
◉ Unknown: Prompt user

[Cancel]   [OK]

a.   Complete the information on the helper that is requested. In the Description box enter information about the application—it doesn't matter what you name the program. In this case the helper is RealAudio.

The MIME Type is audio and the subtype is x-pn-realaudio.

The files that RealAudio will open have the file extension of .ra and .ram. Enter these extension types in the Suffixes dialog box, as shown in Figure 2.30.

IMPORTANT
When you enter the extension in the Suffixes box, do not add a period (.) before the extension name.

FIGURE 2.30

Information added to install the RealAudio Player Application

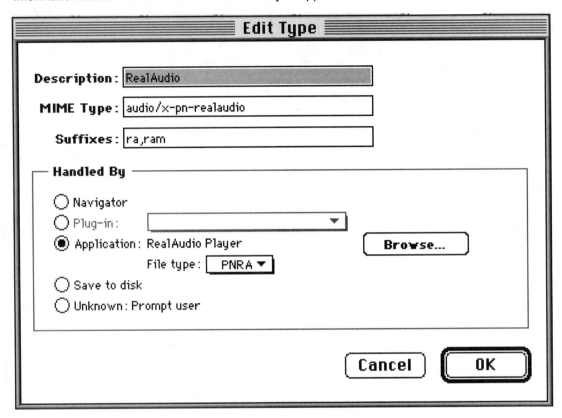

b. Choose from the three options to indicate how the program is to be handled: by Netscape, as a plug-in, or as a helper application.

c. Click on the browse button to show Netscape where the application is located on your hard drive (see Fig 2.31).

FIGURE 2.31

Using **Browse** to show Netscape where the RealAudio Player can be found on the hard drive

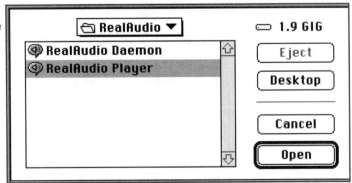

Cool Multimedia Web Sites

Now that you better understand how to play and display multimedia files using plug-ins and viewers, visit the following sites for the ultimate Web experience.

ABC.COM—ABC news heard by RealAudio and viewed by Vivoactive
http://www.abc.com

ALTERNATIVE ENTERTAINMENT NETWORK
http://www.cummingsvideo.com

ARTISTS UNDERGROUND—the place to discover new artists and their music
http://www.aumusic.com

AUDIONET—news, sports, events, and a cool CD jukebox
http://www.audionet.com

AUTO CHANNEL—live broadcasts of races from around the world
http://www.theautochannel.com

CNN INTERACTIVE—the latest world news
http://www.cnn.com

CYBERTOWN—a virtual community in cyberspace
http://www.cybertown.com/cybertown/index.html

CYBERVDO—experience some of the Net's coolest streaming video
http://www.cybervdo.com

DISCOVERY CHANNEL—explore the world with Discovery's interactive channel
http:www.discovery.com

ESPN SPORTSZONE—a multimedia sports experience
http://espnet.sportszone.com

Hot Wired—home of the digiterati where you can experience sensory overload
http://www.hotwired.com

MTV—an electronic MTV experience
http://www.mtv.com

NATIONAL GEOGRAPHIC—explore the world and multimedia
http://www.nationalgeographic.com

NATIONAL PUBLIC RADIO—RealAudio at its best
http://www.npr.org

SHOCKWAVE GALLERY—a gallery of the coolest Shockwave experiences
http://www.macromedia.com/shockwave/epicenter/index.html

Visiting Virtual Communities

CHAPTER CONTENTS

Communicating on the Internet

Electronic Mail

Guided Tours

Listserv Mailing Lists

Usenet Newsgroups

Chats

Free-Nets

MOOS and MUDS

Internet Phones

Expedition Experience

VISITING VIRTUAL COMMUNITIES

If you enjoy surfing on the Net you may enjoy chatting and interacting with people from all over the world. In this chapter you will learn how to communicate with others using

- electronic mail
- listserv mailing lists
- Usenet newsgroups
- Chat Worlds
- free-nets
- MOOs and MUDs
- Internet phones

COMMUNICATING ON THE INTERNET

Although the Internet was created as a research network, it soon became popular for chatting and discussing work-related topics and hobbies. Online services such as America Online, CompuServe, and Prodigy popularized live events and chats. Live events featured guests that online subscribers could talk with. Chats hosted discussions on current events or any topic that subscribers were interested in discussing within the global community of subscribers.

The popularity of live interactive events fostered new technological developments for Internet communication. Today more and more companies are introducing software to make Internet communication easier. For example, Netscape's Communicator Suite provides new options for interaction, collaboration, and the sharing of information within a business or local area network; Web sites such as Yahoo, CNET.COM, the Discovery Channel, Time Warner, and The Palace offer free chat software for live interactive discussions on their site; Internet phones are the hottest new Internet service making real-time transmission of voice possible; desktop video-conferencing is becoming more popular as a communication tool with powerful possibilities for interaction; and multi-user voice technology products are turning the Web into a virtual community where people can socialize, communicate, and collaborate with others one-on-one or in small groups.

People today are on the Internet because they value and enjoy the interactivity and the relationships they build within the virtual community of cyberspace. The way companies, institutions, and individuals communicate has changed. Internet communication involves five major services: electronic mail, electronic discussion groups (listservs and Usenet), Internet Relay Chat (IRC) or chats, Internet phones, and desktop Internet videoconferencing. Email and electronic discussion groups are delayed response media. IRC, Net phones, and desktop videoconferencing are real-time media. Net phones and videoconferencing are usually used for private conversations; IRC is typically used as a public forum, however, many chat clients offer options for private discussions. Electronic mail is most often used for private conversations; electronic discussion groups are used for public conversation.

ELECTRONIC MAIL

What is Email?
Electronic mail, or email, is the most widely used Internet service. Email will make it possible for you to:

- communicate with friends who have email accounts;
- meet and interact with people all over the world;
- participate in electronic conferences and discussions on an unlimited range of topics;
- subscribe to electronic services;
- get answers to technical questions;
- take online workshops or classes;
- mail any electronic text and graphics to anyone with an email address.

Using email is like sending a letter to someone. However, your electronic letter will be created and sent by the computer: you will be sending a file rather than a piece of paper. The file or message you send will go to the electronic mailbox of the person you address. You will also have your own electronic mailbox to receive any mail that comes into your Internet account.

Mail messages are composed of pure ASCII (see Foreign Language Center) or standard text files. This means that:

- your message can be read by users of any type of computer;
- no fancy formatting of the file is possible;
- no graphics may be transmitted;
- no special characters can be accommodated within the message.

In addition to sending a text message, electronic mail supports the following:

- mail messages can be printed out as "hardcopy;"
- files or messages can be attached to a message that you are sending;
- messages can be sent to multiple recipients (carbon copies);
- messages can be filed and stored in folders that you create;
- messages can be replied to and forwarded to another person;
- messages can be read at your convenience.

The Internet Post Office—Email Addresses

The best analogy for understanding how email works is the U.S. Postal Service. When you write a letter and use the Postal Service to deliver it, you probably follow these steps:

1. write the letter;
2. put the letter in an envelope;
3. address the envelope;
4. give your letter to the Postal Service (mail box or post office).

The letter is picked up by a postal truck and is taken to the post office where it is sorted by zip code and then forwarded to another place. When it arrives at its next destination, it is again sorted and then picked up by a mail carrier and delivered to the recipient's mailbox.

A very similar process occurs when you use electronic mail to send a letter. You will follow these three steps:

1. address your email envelope on the computer;
2. write your letter;
3. send your email message.

Two things must happen before you can use electronic mail:

1. You must have an electronic mail account and know your email address;
2. You must know the email address of the person to whom you are sending your message.

An electronic mail account is obtained from one of the following:

- your school, college, or university
- commercial Internet provider
- your state or local network

The Internet Email Address

All individuals who use the Internet must have their own Internet addresses. Each Internet address follows the standard format: **username@host.domain**

My email address is: cleshin@xplora.com

My username is: cleshin
The host for my account is: xplora
The host domain is: com (commercial)

There are many variations of this format. You will frequently see addresses that include sub-domains in order to be more specific. The addressing information may indicate the department or sublocation where the host is to be found, the actual location of the host (state, country), or other information specific to the host's identity.

username@host.subdomain.domain

These are other email addresses illustrating the variation in format.

cleshin@azedlink.state.az.us
(Account with the State of Arizona, AZEDLINK project.)

cleshin@aol.com
(Account at America OnLine.)

ICCBL@ASUVM.INRE.ASU.EDU
(Account at Arizona State University.)

Internet addresses include:

- your account name (also referred to as username, userid, or login name);
- the "at" (@) symbol that follows your account name;
- name of the host for your email account;
- a dot or period (.) that separates each part of the address;
- domain name (type of organization that hosts this Internet account).

Organizational Domains

In the United States most Internet sites have domain names that fall into one of these categories:

.edu	for educational institution
.com	for commercial organization
.mil	for military
.gov	for government

.org	for non-profit organizations
.net	for networking organization
.int	for international organization

In the spring of 1997 the Internet Ad Hoc Committee (IAHC) proposed new domain names to ease the growing demand for domain names such as .com. Proposed domain names include

.arts	for art and cultural entities
.firm	for businesses
.info	for information services
.nom	for individuals
.rec	for recreation and entertainment
.store	for merchants
.web	for Web services

For more information visit IAHC's Web site at **http://www.iahc.org.**

Geographical Domains

Outside of the United States it is more common to use geographic zone names:

at	for Austria
au	for Australia
ca	for Canada
ch	Switzerland
de	Germany (Deutschland)
dk	Denmark
es	Spain
fr	France
gr	Greece
ie	Republic of Ireland
jp	Japan
nz	New Zealand
uk	United Kingdom
us	United States

GUIDED TOURS—EMAIL

Guided Tour 1
Using Email

Electronic mail programs basically work in the same way. Once you have learned one email program it is very easy to transfer this knowledge to other electronic mail programs.

In this Guide Tour you will learn how to use the email program that comes with the Netscape Communicator Suite 4.x series. This email program is built into Netscape and is accessed through the Netscape software. If you are using older versions of Netscape or other email programs you will find this information helpful in using their email programs or version. Netscape's Messenger is a powerful email program offering many different options for sending, receiving, and filing electronic mail.

Before You Begin....

STEP 1

Login to your account

Before you can begin using electronic mail, you must first establish contact with your Internet account. If you are using a commercial online service you will use your telecommunications software to dial your Internet provider. Your Internet provider will give you a local dial-up number. After you have dialed the number using your telecommunications software, you will be prompted to login. The login process consists of two parts:

- entering your username;
- entering your user password.

STEP 2

When you have established contact with your Internet provider, you will be prompted for your username.

login: type your username and press   <RETURN>

STEP 3

Next, you will be asked (prompted) for your password.

password: type in your password and press <RETURN>

FIGURE 2.1
An example of a login to an Internet account

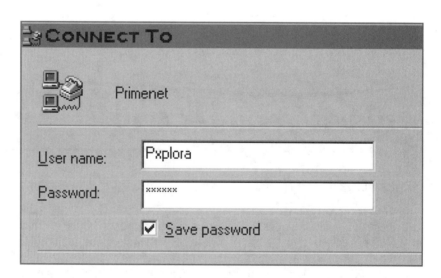

After you have made your connection to the Internet you are ready to begin.

Open your email program. Since we are using Netscape Messenger in this Guide Tour, we will click on the **Mailbox** button (Fig. 3.2).

FIGURE 3.2
Netscape's Navigator showing Mailbox button

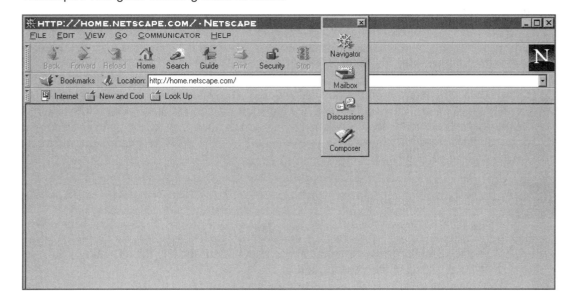

Most email programs today use toolbar buttons and pulldown menus for assisting with email operations.

FIGURE 3.3
Netscape's toolbar buttons and pulldown menus

Email programs usually have toolbar buttons and pull-down menu items for

- sending email messages
- getting email messages
- replying to messages
- forwarding a message
- filing or saving messages
- printing messages
- deleting messages

In addition many have tools for

- saving email addresses in an electronic address book
- sending attachments—files created in other software application programs

Guided Tour 2
Sending Email

After you have opened your email program, look for a toolbar button for creating a new email message. In this case we select the **New Msg** button (see Fig. 3.3).

You will then see the email composition dialog box. Next you address your email message. When you address your email envelope you will need to know the address of the person who is to receive your message. Email addresses are assigned to individuals when they receive an Internet account. When sending an electronic message, it is very important to know the recipient's exact address.

STEP 1

Enter
- the email address of the person to whom you are sending the message,
- the subject of the message, and
- the message.

FIGURE 3.4
Netscape Messenger email Composition box

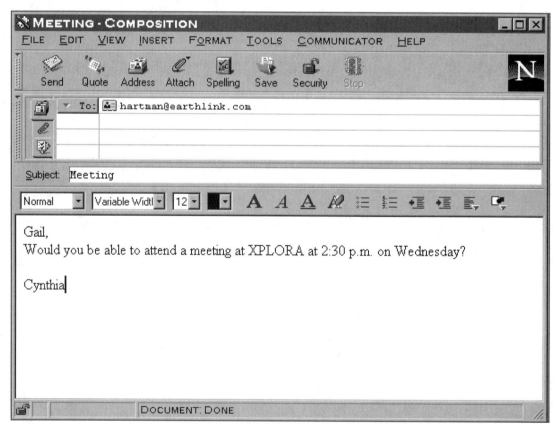

STEP 2

After you have finished addressing and writing you message, click the **Send** button.

Traveling Hint

- When writing Internet addresses, use small (lower case letters).

- If you see some addresses that have both upper and lower case letters, it is safe to change all letters to lower case.

If you decide to change the address to lower case be aware that occasionally the userid is case sensitive and you may have to keep this part of the addrress in capital letters.

EXAMPLES

INFO@delphi.com
JSMITH@aol.com

- Email cannot be depended on as a reliable medium for communication. Messages frequently get delayed and even lost. Some email programs have a Return Receipt option. Use this option to be notified when your recipient has seen your message.

Guided Tour 3
Receiving, Reading, and Replying to Email

Receiving and Reading Email Messages

It takes only a few seconds to receive your message. Many email programs will automatically download your email when you open the mail application. You will first be asked for your password. This prevents others from accessing your email.

FIGURE 3.5
Netscape's login
for receiving email

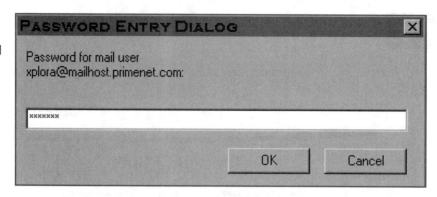

If your email program does not automatically retrieve your messages, look for the button or menu for Getting Messages. You also used the **Get Message** button if you want to check your messages again at a later time, perhaps after working online. In Messenger, click the **Get Msg** button (Fig. 3.3). Messenger displays your messages in the Inbox.

FIGURE 3.7
Email messages in the Inbox

Subject	Sender	Date	Priority
Hey Mac Users: New PaperPort 5.0 S...	Visioneer Customer List	11:54	
Some information, please	**Danette Morse**	**13:21**	

To read your email, click on a message.

FIGURE 3.7
Email message selected and displayed

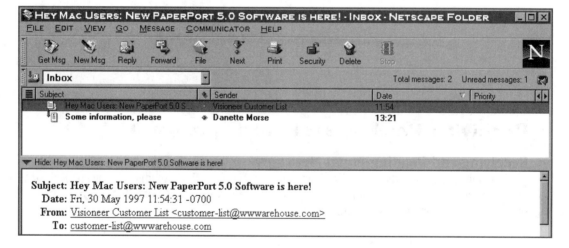

To read the next email message click the **Next** button. The next message may also be displayed when you either file or delete the current message.

Replying to Email Messages

If you want to reply to a message that you have received, you can do so by clicking on an icon that will say **Reply** (see Fig. 3.3). A new message window will appear with the original email sender's address already in the recipient or "To" box and the original subject in the "Subject" box.

Type your reply.

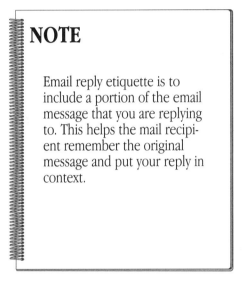

NOTE

Email reply etiquette is to include a portion of the email message that you are replying to. This helps the mail recipient remember the original message and put your reply in context.

FIGURE 3.8
Reply email message

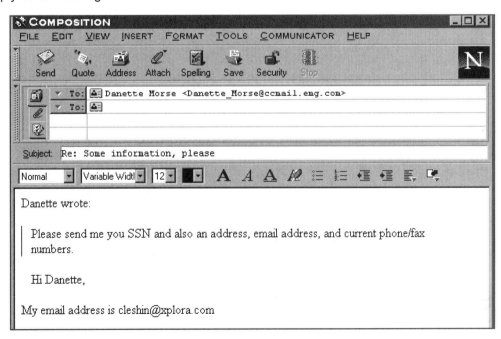

After you have finished your reply, click the **Send** button.

Guided Tour 4
Managing Your Email

All incoming electronic mail is stored in a shared mailbox area by your Internet host. Try to minimize the amount of space your mail takes up by deleting or filing your mail. Your mail may also run faster if your mail box is not full of messages. When you begin to receive electronic mail, practice using these functions.

- save and file a message
- delete messages
- print and file messages
- forward a message

Saving and Filing Email Messages

Messages you want to save can be stored in electronic file folders. Each email system will provide you with filing and saving options. The way you will go about filing will vary among programs. Some programs have a file folder icon that you click on. Others may have an icon that says "File" or "Save." In still others you may have to do something a little different. You may need to refer to the email program documentation as you accumulate more mail and want to create multiple folders.

The basic strategy for saving and filing will consist of the following steps:

STEP 1

Organize your mail

Organize your mail by defining a set of categories. Each category will be made into a personal folder. Think of this as being similar to a filing system that you may use in an office.

STEP 2

Create folders

You may create as many folders as you like. Incoming messages that you want to save will be stored in these folders according to subject or category.

STEP 3

Move message to folder

Messages are usually moved to folders by first clicking on them to select and highlight them. Once the message has been selected you will either click on the file folder icon to which you want to move your message or you may have to select the "Save" or "File" command. When you click on the command icon, you should receive a list of folders. Select the folder into which you want to file your message by double clicking on that folder; your message should be saved there.

Follow these steps to file email messages using Netscape Messenger.

STEP 1

Select and open the message you want to save and file.

STEP 2

Click the **File** button.

STEP 3

Make a folder for saved messages. Click Messenger's **File** pull-down menu and select **New Folder** option.

FIGURE 3.9
Messenger's **File** pull-down menu

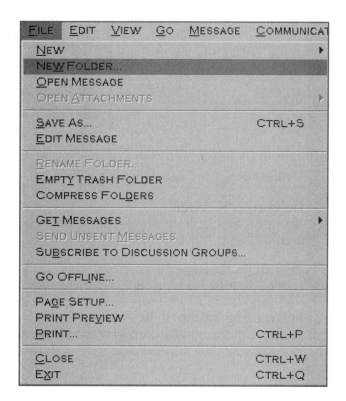

STEP 4

Click the **File** button and select the folder where the message is to be saved.

FIGURE 3.10
Messenger's File button and file folders

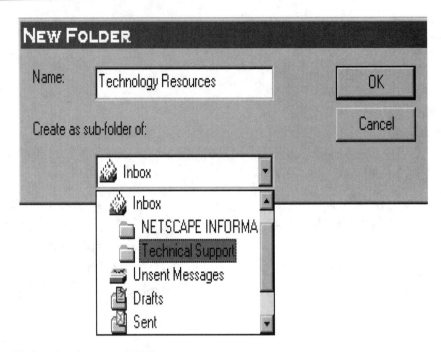

The message is then filed in the designated folder.

Deleting a Message

To delete a message in Messenger, click the **Delete** button on the toolbar when the message is open.

Printing a Message

Click on the **Print** button to print a selected and/or open message.

Forwarding an Email Message

Sometimes you may wish to send all or part of a received message to another person. To forward a message:

STEP 1

Click the **Forward** button.

STEP 2

An email composition window will appear in which to enter the email address of the recipient of your forwarded message. Enter the email address, subject, and any forwarding note in the forwarding message window.

FIGURE 3.11

Messenger forward message box

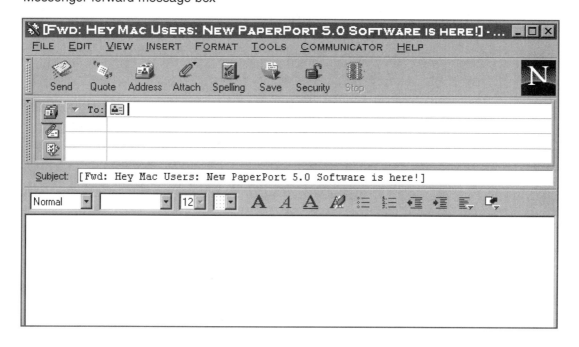

STEP 3

Click the **Send** button.

Guided Tour 5
Creating an Address Book

Email programs provide an address book for saving email addresses. Address books save you from having to type in email addresses for people you regularly send mail to.

To create an address book entry in Messenger follow these steps:

STEP 1

Open the **Communicator** pull-down menu.

FIGURE 3.12
Messenger Address Book option

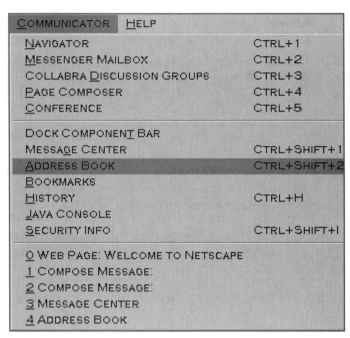

Select the **Address Book** option.

FIGURE 3.13
Messenger Personal Address Book

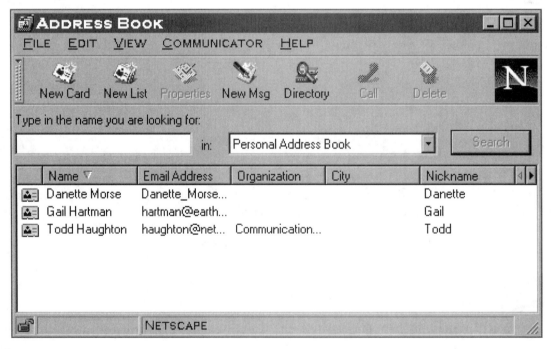

STEP 2

Click the **New Card** button.

FIGURE 3.14
New Address Book
Card for email address
entry

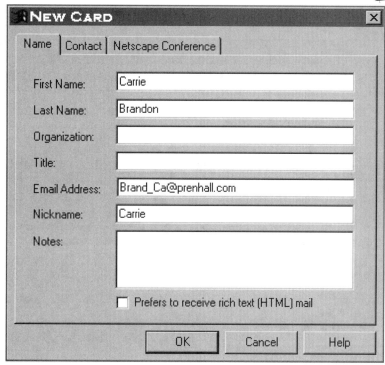

When you have entered the information, click **OK.**

STEP 3

To use your Address Book for sending a email message, click the **New Msg** button. When Messenger opens the Composition box, click the **Address** button. Your address book of email recipients will be displayed.

FIGURE 3.15
Open Address Book

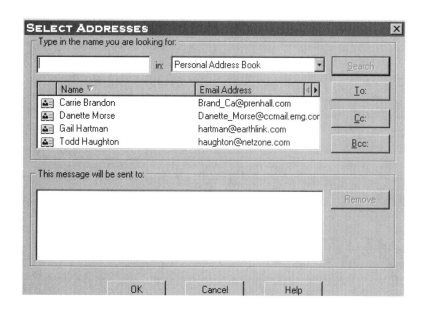

STEP 4

Select the email recipient. Click the **To** button. Then click **OK.**
The email composition box is displayed with the recipients email address entered.

FIGURE 3.16
Email message addressed with entry from Address Book

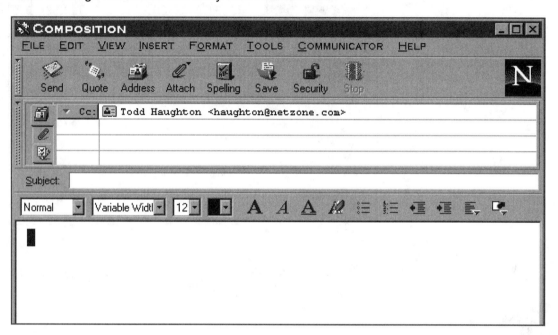

NOTE

You can also open your Address Book, select a recipient and click the **To** button to address an email message.

STEP 5

Adding email addresses from a received message. You can save the email address from a message that you receive by selecting the **Message** pull-down menu and then choosing the **Add to Address Book** option.

FIGURE 3.17
Adding email addresses to the
Address Book

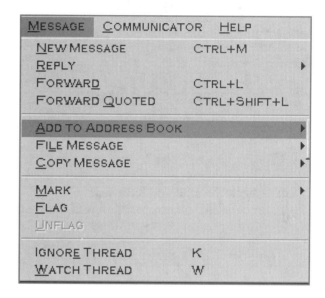

Guide Tour 6
Other Email Tools

Email programs frequently have options available for sending attachments (files created in another application) and for checking spelling. Netscape's Messenger has the following tools.

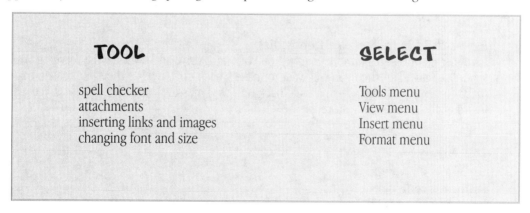

TOOL	SELECT
spell checker	Tools menu
attachments	View menu
inserting links and images	Insert menu
changing font and size	Format menu

Additionally the toolbar button within the Message program provides options for changing the font and font size; for making text bold, italic, or underlined; for creating a bullet or numbered list; indenting text; and for inserting objects.

FIGURE3.18
Messenger toolbar buttons with email tools

Tips for Using Email

Tip

Check the mail you have sent
Occasionally you may want to reread a message that you sent. Mail programs will have a file listing the mail you have sent. This file will be named something like "Mail Sent" or "Out Box."

Tip

Creating mailing lists of groups
You may want to create mailing lists of groups of people who should always receive the same type of messages. For example, if you are on a committee you might want a mailing list of all the members of the committee to receive the minutes of meetings or to announce meeting dates. Mailing lists can be created in your Address Book.

- In the field where you would ordinarily enter the name of a single person, enter the name of your group or mailing list.

- In the field where you would normally enter the address of one person, enter the multiple addresses of your group. Remember, separate each address with a comma and a space.

Tip

Save email file folders to a floppy disk
If your saved messages have been saved on your hard drive and not on a file server at your school or university, then you will want to make a back-up copy. For the same reason that you make copies of your work, you should back up saved messages and files. Check to see where your e-mail file folders are stored.

Tip

Request a return receipt
If you want to be notified when mail you have sent has been read, click on the "Return Receipt" command icon or box. Look carefully for this box. Most mail programs will notify you the instant when your message has been read.

Tip

Replying to mail (all or one)
When replying to a mail message check to see who received copies of the original message. The message header will usually display the names of all the addresses that receive the same message. If you only choose to reply to the sender of the message, you may have several options of how to do this:

- Send a new message and address it only to the sender of the message.

- Check your email program to see if two reply options are available: "Reply to All" or "Reply" (replies only to the sender of the message).

Tip

Creating your personal signature
Signatures are typically used to provide information about the sender of the message. This personal signature may include your name, address, phone, fax, email address. Some people also include a quote. Check to see if your email program provides a signature creation option.

LISTSERV MAILING LISTS

With so much attention on the World Wide Web, many new Internet users miss learning about electronic mailing lists (also referred to as lists, listservs, or discussion groups) as an Internet resource for finding and sharing information. Electronic mailing lists began in the 1960s when scientists and educators used the Internet to share information and research. Early programs, known as *listservs*, ran on mainframe computers and used email to send reports or studies to a large group of users.

Today, listservs perform the same function—the sharing of information. There are hundreds of special interest lists where individuals can join a virtual community to share and discuss topics of mutual interest.

What Is a Listserv Mailing List?

A *listserv* is the automated system that distributes electronic mail. Email is used to participate in electronic mailing lists. Listservs perform two functions:

- distributing text documents stored on them to those who request them, and
- managing interactive mailing lists.

Listservs and text documents
A listserv can be used to distribute information, in the form of text documents, to others. For example, online workshops may make their course materials available through a listserv. The listserv is set up to distribute the materials to participants at designated times. Other examples of documents available through a listserv include: a listing of all available electronic mailing lists, Usenet newsgroups, electronic journals, and books.

Interactive mailing lists

Interactive mailing lists provide a forum where individuals who share interests can exchange ideas and information. Any member of the group may participate in the resulting discussion. This is no longer a one-to-one communication like your email, but rather a one-to-many communication.

Electronic mail written in the form of a report, article, abstract, reaction, or comment is received at a central site and then distributed to the members of the list.

How Does a Mailing List Work?

The mailing list is hosted by a college, university, or institution. The hosting institution uses its computer system to manage the mailing list.

Here are a few of the management functions of a listserv:

- receiving requests for subscriptions to the list;
- placing subscribers' email addresses on the list;
- sending out notification that the name has been added to the list;
- receiving messages from subscribers;
- sending messages to all subscribers;
- keeping a record (archive) of activity of the list; and
- sending out information requested by subscribers to the list.

Mailing lists have administrators that may be either a human or a computer program. One function of the administrator is to handle subscription requests. If the administrator is human, you can join the mailing list by communicating in English via an email message. The administrator in turn has the option of either accepting or rejecting your subscription request. Frequently lists administered by a human are available only to a select group of individuals. For example, an executive board of an organization may restrict its list to its members.

Mailing lists administered by computer programs called listservs usually allow all applicants to subscribe to the list. You must communicate with these computer administrators in listserv commands. For the computer administrator to accept your request, you must use the exact format required. The administrative address and how to subscribe should be included in the information provided about a list.

How to Receive Documents From a Listserv

Email is used to request text documents distributed by a listserv. The Email is used to request text documents distributed by a listserv. The email is addressed to the listserv administrative address. In the body of the message a command is written to request the document. The most common command used to request a document is "send" or "get." The command is then followed by the name of the document that you wish to receive. A command to request a list of interesting mailing lists might look like this:

"get" or "send" < name of document >

o r

get new-list Curriculm Standards

How to Join a Listserv Mailing List

To join an interactive mailing list on a topic of interest, send an email message to the list administrator and ask to join the list. Subscribing to an electronic mailing list is like subscribing to a journal or magazine.

- Mail a message to the journal requesting a subscription.

- Include the address of the journal and the address to which the journal will be mailed.

All electronic mailing lists work in the same way.

- Email your request to the list administrator at the address assigned by the hosting organization.

- Place your request to participate in the body of your email where you usually write your messages.

- Your return address will accompany your request in the header of your message.

- Your subscription will be acknowledged by the hosting organization or the moderator.

- You will then receive all discussions distributed by the listserv.

- You can send in your own comments and reactions.

- You can unsubscribe (cancel your subscription).

The command to subscribe to a mailing lists looks like this:

subscribe <name of list> <your name>

or

subscribe Learning Styles Cynthia Leshin

The unsubscribe command is similar to the subscribe command.

unsubscribe <name of list> <your name>

Active lists may have 50-100 messages from list participants each day. Less active mailing lists may have several messages per week or per month. If you find that you are receiving too much mail or the discussions on the list do not interest you, you can unsubscribe just as easily as you subscribed. If you are going away, you can send a message to the list to hold your mail until further notice.

Important Information Before You Begin

Mailing lists have two different addresses:

1. An administrative address that you will use when you

- subscribe to the list.
- unsubscribe from the list.
- request information or help.

2. A submission address used to send your messages to the list.

The Administrative Mail Address

Most listserv mailing lists use software such as listserv, majordomo, or listproc that automatically processes users' requests to subscribe or unsubscribe. Some examples of administrative addresses used for subscribing and unsubscribing are:

listserv@uga.cc.uga.edu
majordomo@gsn.org
listproc@educom.unc.edu

NOTE

Requests for subscriptions are usually processed by computers, therefore type the commands without any changes. Be sure to enter the exact address that you have received, duplicating spacing and upper and lowercase letters. Do not add any other information in the body of your message. If your email package adds a signature, be sure to take it off before sending your request.

After you join a listserv mailing list, you will usually receive notification of your subscription request and an electronic welcome. This message will provide you with information such as the purpose of the list, the names of the listserv's owners, how to subscribe and unsubscribe, and other commands to use for the list.

Save a copy of this listserv welcome message. Later you may want to refer to it for information on how to unsubscribe or perform other operations related to the list.

The Submission Mail Address

Mail sent to the submission address is read by all of the subscribers to the list. This address will be different and should not be used for communicating with the list administrator.

Here is an example of an address for sending your messages to the mailing list participants:

itforum@uga.cc.uga.edu

For this mailing list, the first word is the name of the list, itforum (instructional technology forum). Any mail sent to this address will be sent to all subscribers to the list. This is the address used to communicate with subscribers to the list.

Finding Listserv Mailing Lists

World Wide Web Site for Finding Mailing Lists

Two of the best resources for helping you to find mailing lists are these World Wide Web sites:

http://www.liszt.com
http://www.tile.net/tile/listserv/index.html

Email a Request for Listservs on a Topic

To request information on listserv mailing lists for a particular topic, send an email message to

LISTSERV@vm1.nodak.edu

In the message body type: LIST GLOBAL / keyword

To find electronic mailing lists you would enter:

LIST GLOBAL / environment

In this case, the request is to find environmental mailing lists.

USENET NEWSGROUPS

What Are Newsgroups?

In the virtual community of the Internet, Usenet newsgroups are analogous to a café where people with similar interests gather from around the world to interact and exchange ideas. Usenet is a very large, distributed bulletin board system (BBS) that consists of several thousand specialized discussion groups. Currently there are over 20,000 newsgroups with 20 to 30 more added weekly.

You can subscribe to a newsgroup, scan through the messages, read messages of interest, organize the messages, and send in your comments or questions—or start a new one.

Usenet groups are organized by subject and divided into major categories.

CATEGORY	TOPIC AREA
alt.	no topic is off limits in this alternative group
comp.	computer-related topics
misc.	miscellaneous topics that don't fit into other categories
news.	happenings on the Internet
rec.	recreational activities/hobbies
sci.	scientific research and associated issues
soc.	social issues and world cultures
talk.	discussions and debates on controversial social issues

In addition to these categories there are local newsgroups with prefixes that indicate their topic or locality.

Some newsgroups are moderated and reserved for very specific articles. Articles submitted to these newsgroups are sent to a central site. If the article is approved, it is posted by the moderator. Many newsgroups have no moderator and there is no easy way to determine whether a group is moderated. The only way to tell if a group is moderated is to submit an article. You will be notified if your article has been mailed to the newsgroup moderator.

What Is the Difference Between Listserv Mailing Lists and Usenet Newsgroups?

One analogy for describing the difference between a listserv mailing list and a Usenet newsgroup is to compare the difference between having a few intimate friends over for dinner and conversation (a listserv) vs. going to a Super Bowl party to which the entire world has been invited (newsgroups). A listserv is a smaller, more intimate place to discuss issues of interest. A Usenet newsgroup is much larger and much more open to "everything and anything goes." This is not to say that both do not provide a place for valuable discussion. However, the size of each makes the experiences very different.

A listserv mailing list is managed by a single site, such as a university. Subscribers to a mailing list are automatically mailed messages that are sent to the mailing list submission address. A listserv would find it difficult to maintain a list for thousands of people.

Usenet consists of many sites that are set up by local Internet providers. When a message is sent to a Usenet site, a copy of the message that has been received is sent to other neighboring, connected Usenet sites. Each of these sites keeps a copy of the message and then forwards the message to other connected systems. Usenet can therefore handle thousands of subscribers.

One advantage of Usenet groups over a mailing list is that you can quickly read postings to the newsgroup. When you connect to a Usenet newsgroup and see a long list of articles, you can select only those that interest you. Unlike a mailing list, Usenet messages do not accumulate in your mailbox, forcing you to read and delete them. Usenet articles are on your local server and can be read at your convenience.

Browsers and Usenet Newsgroups

Netscape and Explorer support Usenet newsgroups. You can subscribe to a newsgroup, read articles posted to a group, and reply to articles. You can determine whether your reply is sent to the individual author of the posted article or to the entire newsgroup. Additional features include the scanning of related references and their associated URL. These URLs are shown as active hypertext links that can be accessed by clicking on the underlined words. News reader buttons and pull-down menus provide the reader with controls for reading and responding to articles.

Newsgroups have a URL location. These URLs are similar, but not identical, to other pages. For example, the URL for a recreational backcountry newsgroup is **news:rec.backcountry**. The server protocol is **news:** and the newsgroup is **rec.backcountry**.

Newsgroups present articles along what is called a *thread*. The thread packages the article with responses to the article (see Fig. 3.19). Each new response is indented one level from the original posting. A response to a response is indented another level. Newsgroups' threads, therefore, appear as an outline.

NOTE

Information on Explorer's news reader begins on page 88, however you may want to read this section on Netscape newsgroups for general information. This section only provides basic information to get you started with Usenet newsgroups.

Reading Usenet News Using Netscape Navigator

Netscape News Window for Usenet News

To display the News window in Netscape, go to the **Window** menu and select **Netscape News.**

FIGURE 3.19
The Netscape News window displaying groups subscribed to (left window) and article threads (right window)

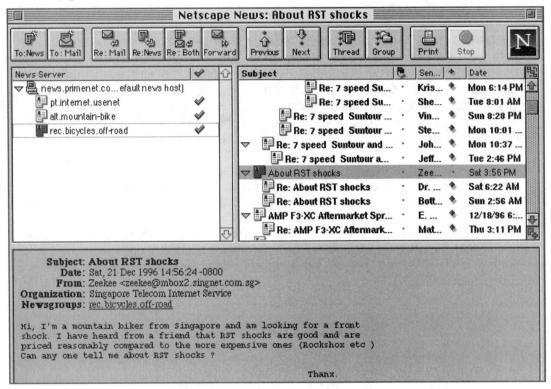

Notice that you have new options in the form of toolbar buttons and pull-down menus for receiving, reading, replying to, and sending messages to newsgroups. Netscape News works in much the same way as Netscape Mail.

This example also illustrates the newsgroup thread where articles are presented in an outline format with their accompanying response.

FIGURE 3.20
Netscape News window buttons

To: News: Displays a Message Composition window for creating a new message posting for a newsgroup.

To: Mail: Displays a Message Composition window for creating a new mail message.

Re: Mail: Click on this button to reply to the current newsgroup message (thread) you are reading. Your reply goes only to sender of original message.

Re: News: Selecting this button replies to the entire newsgroup.

Re: Both: Displays a Message Composition window for posting a reply to the current message thread for the entire newsgroup and to the sender of the news message.

Forward: Displays the Message Composition window for forwarding the current news message as an attachment. Enter the email address in the **Mail To** field.

Previous: Brings the previous unread message in the thread to your screen.

Next: Brings the next unread message in the thread to your screen.

Thread: Marks the message threads you have read.

Group: Marks all messages read.

Print: Prints the message you are reading.

Stop: Stops the current transmission of messages from your news server.

Accessing Usenet News With Netscape Navigator

Netscape Navigator provides four ways to access newsgroups.

- If you know the name of the newsgroup, type the URL in the location field of the Netscape main menu.

- From within the Netscape News window, go to the File menu and select Add Newsgroup. Enter the name of the newsgroup in the dialog box.

- From within the Netscape News window, go to the Options menu and select Show All Newsgroups. From this list, select a newsgroup and check the Subscribe box beside the newsgroup name.

- From a World Wide Web site (e.g., **http://www.cen.uiuc.edu/cgi-bin/find-news**) click on a link to a newsgroup or a newsgroup message.

FIGURE 3.21
Netscape News window
Options menu

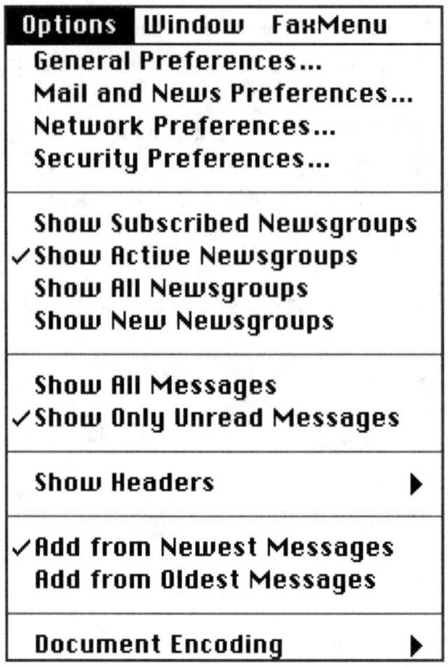

```
Options  Window  FaxMenu
   General Preferences...
   Mail and News Preferences...
   Network Preferences...
   Security Preferences...

   Show Subscribed Newsgroups
 ✓ Show Active Newsgroups
   Show All Newsgroups
   Show New Newsgroups

   Show All Messages
 ✓ Show Only Unread Messages

   Show Headers              ▶

 ✓ Add from Newest Messages
   Add from Oldest Messages

   Document Encoding         ▶
```

Reading Usenet News Using Explorer

If you are using Microsoft Internet Explorer and want to read Usenet newsgroups you will need Microsoft's Internet Mail and News software. This software may already be installed and available if you are at a school, college, or university. Internet Mail and News can also be downloaded at no cost from Microsoft's Home Page **http://www.microsoft.com** or from within Explorer by selecting the link to Microsoft Products. To determine if the news reader has been installed and configured, from the Explorer **Go** menu and select **Read News**. If a news window opens (see Fig. 3.22) then you know that the news reader has been installed. If nothing happens then you will need to download and install Internet Mail and News.

Explorer's News Reader

When you open Explorer's news reader by selecting **Read News** from the **Go** menu you will see this window.

FIGURE 3.22

Explorer news reader window

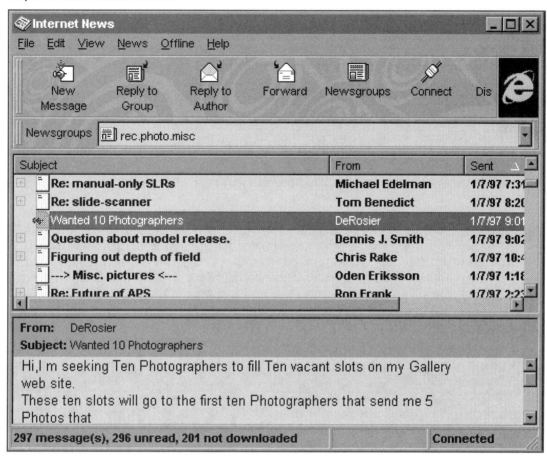

Notice that the news reader has pull-down menus and toolbar buttons for using the reader.

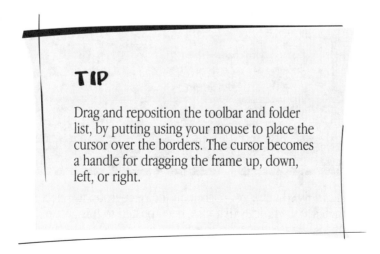

TIP

Drag and reposition the toolbar and folder list, by putting using your mouse to place the cursor over the borders. The cursor becomes a handle for dragging the frame up, down, left, or right.

Before you can view newsgroups the name of your Internet Service Provider's news server must be entered into the news reader. To add a news server follow these steps.

STEP 1

Open the news reader by selecting **Read News** from the **Go** menu.

STEP 2

You will now see the news reader window (Fig. 3.22). Select **Options** from the **News** pull-down menu, then click on the **Servers** tab. Click on the **Add** button to enter in the news server name. If you don't know the news server name, check with your Internet provider.

Once your news server name has been entered you are ready to either view newsgroups that your Internet provider has subscribed to, view newsgroups in a subject area, or subscribe to a newsgroup (see Fig. 3.23). Go to the **News** menu from within the news reader and select the **Newsgroup** options. This window provides you with options for viewing newsgroups. If this is the first time you are using the news reader, the window displaying available newsgroups will most likely be blank. You will need to tell the news reader what newsgroups you would like to view.

FIGURE 3.23

Explorer news window for download newsgroups

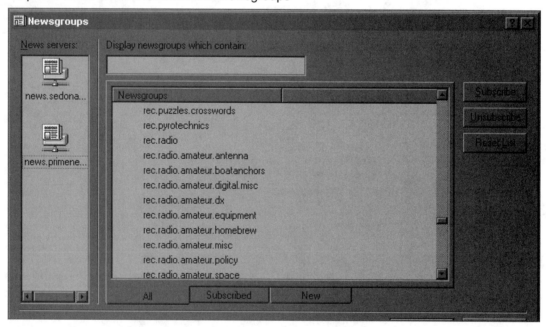

To view the news in a listed newsgroup, click on the newsgroup to select it and then click the OK button. You will then see the articles that have been posted to this group. For example in Figure 3.24 the news group select is **rec.photo.misc**. This example show a few of the news articles posted. To view the newsgroup click once on the news article and the contents will be displayed at the bottom of the news reader (see Fig. 3.24).

FIGURE 3.24
The expanded news reader window for reading and replying to a Usenet news article

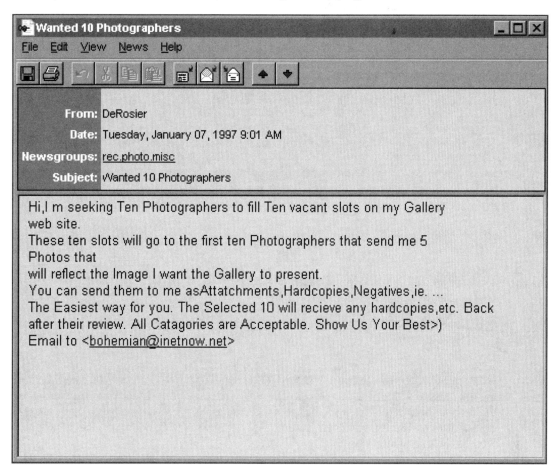

To respond to the author of the article use the toolbar buttons as shown in Figures 3.22 .

NOTE

If your response is only appropriate for the author of the news article, send your response only to the author and not to the entire group. There many be times that the information you want to share will be appreciated by all the readers of this group, in which case, post your response to the entire newsgroup.

TIP

Use search engines such as Infoseek Ultra, Excite, and Lycos to find newsgroups of interest. After entering in keyword(s) select the newsgroup option for the search.

TIPS for New Users of Newsgroups and Listservs

TIP

After you subscribe to a list or newsgroup, don't send anything to it until you have been reading the messages for at least one week. This will give you an opportunity to observe the tone of the list and the type of messages that people are sending. Newcomers to lists often ask questions that were discussed at length several days or weeks before. Begin by reading the Frequently Asked Questions (FAQs).

Tip

Remember that everything you send to the list or newsgroup goes to every subscriber on the list. Many of these discussion groups have thousands of members. Before you reply or post a message, read and review what you have written. Is your message readable and free from errors and typos? When necessary, AMEND BEFORE YOU SEND.

Tip

Look for a posting by someone who seems knowledgeable about a topic. If you want to ask a question, look for their email address in the signature information at the top of the news article. Send your question to them directly rather than to the entire newsgroup or listserv.

Tip

Proper etiquette for a mailing list is to not clog other people's mail boxes with information not relevant to them. If you want to respond to mail on the list or newsgroup, determine whether you want your response to go only to the individual who posted the mail or you want your response to go to all the list's subscribers. The person's name and email address will be listed in their posting signature.

Tip

The general rule for posting a message to a list or newsgroup is to keep it short and to the point. Most subscribers do not appreciate multiple-page postings.

If you are contacting an individual by electronic mail, identify yourself, state why you are contacting them, and indicate where you found their posting. Again, be as succinct and to the point as possible.

CHATS

A popular Internet cartoon shows a dog sitting in front of a computer. The caption reads, "On the Internet, nobody knows you're a dog." This cartoon reveals that the Internet's unique ability for individual anonymity opens many communication doors for individuals who otherwise may feel inhibited with live face-to-face interaction. For many chatting on the Net, and creating alternative identities become a new way of life and for some an addiction. In fact a Usenet newsgroup has been formed called alt.irc.recovery.

Individuals participating in a chat create a name, known as nickname or a screen name that identifies them to others in the chat room; some chats go even further and have users create an entire identity; some such as MOOs and MUDs have users role-playing in virtual reality worlds created by the users. Newer chat worlds have users interacting and traveling in 3D environments.

Before you can participate in a chat world you will need to have a software client. For example, MOOs and MUDs require a Telnet client. Some Web sites, such as The Palace, have a link to a client program that you will need if you want to participate in their live events. Other Web sites have chats that do not require you to download any additional software. For example, Time Warner's Pathfinder Web site has a chat room for discussing news of the day. Wired magazine has a chat room open for discussion and the Discovery Channel Online has perfected online narrative making the audience part of the stories. Other requirements may include powerful multimedia PCs for 3D chats.

Conversations within chats are text-based. Users type in their message line by line. As a line is being typed, others on the channel see the message. Messages cannot be edited before they are sent to others on the channel. Anyone on the channel can respond to a message as it is revealed on their computer screen by merely typing in their response line by line.

Commercial services such as America Online, CompuServe, Prodigy, and Microsoft Network offer chat rooms for their members to communicate and meet others who have similar interests. Chat rooms with these services can be public or private. Public rooms are created by the service provider and tend to have focused discussion topics. Some of these rooms are hosted, others are not. Some of these chat rooms are available on a regular basis, others are created for special events such as a guest who is online for a forum for several hours.

Private chat rooms are created by members and can hold between 2 and 25 or more registered online users. Private chat rooms may be used for a meeting or just a casual chat between friends. There is no way as yet to see a list of private chat rooms. New interactive software for forming live interactive chat worlds makes it possible for users to create both public and private forms for communicating online.

To experience chat using the World Wide Web, explore these sites:

WEBCHAT BROADCASTING SYSTEM
http://wbs.net

DISCOVERY CHANNEL
http://www.discovery.com

CNET.COM
http://www.cnet.com

HOTWIRED
http://www.hotwired.com

TIME WARNER'S PATHFINDER
http://www.pathfinder.com

YAHOO CHAT
http://chat.yahoo.com

THE PALACE
http:www.thepalace.com

GLOBE
http://globe1.csuglab.cornell.edu/global/homepage.html

To experience 3D Chat Worlds visit these Web sites:

ALPHAWORLD
http://www.worlds.net

COMIC CHAT
http://www.microsoft.com/ie/comichat/download.htm

TIKKILAND
http://mtv.com/tikkiland

V-CHAT
http://www.msn.com/v-chat

WORLD'S CHAT
http://www.worlds.net

FREE-NETS

Free-nets provide networking services to a local community. Access to free-nets is achieved either at public libraries or by dialing in. It is also possible to access free-nets through the Internet.

Free-nets establish their own resources for users in their community. Free-nets are usually designed around a model of an electronic town. For example, you may be able to discuss local issues with the mayor or stop at an electronic school to discuss educational issues. These local networks usually have bulletin boards, electronic mail, informational resources, and educational resources. Educational resources may have local projects for classrooms or may provide information on national or international projects. Free-nets also provide links to global educational resources. Free-nets help to make finding and using Internet resources more manageable for educators who frequently do not have the time to explore cyberspace for classroom resources.

You may use a free-net as a guest; however, your access privileges may be limited. You will have to register to have full access privileges. Registration is free to people within the community; for those outside the community, there is usually a nominal registration fee.

Today, there are more than 30 free-nets online in cities across the United States and Canada. You can also find a few in Europe and New Zealand. There are several excellent educational free-nets that have resources and projects available for their local communities as well as allowing access to all Internet travelers. Listed below are three worth exploring.

To connect to a free-net you will need to Telnet. Chapter 4 provides information on Telnet.

Big Sky Telegraph

This free-net is a Global Telecurricular Clearinghouse for projects running on all networks as well as downloadable lesson plans. Also available are online courses, opportunities for exchange of information with other users via e-mail, and local bulletin board access.

To connect to Big Sky Telegraph,

   1.   telnet bigsky.bigsky.dillon.mt.us

   2.   login, type **bbs**

   3.   user ID <your e-mail address>

Cleveland Free-Net

This free-net is a very comprehensive and user-friendly telnet site. It contains an enormous number of historical documents and information related to the arts, sciences, medicine, education, and business. It also has an up-to-date news service, on-line access to USA Today, and access to Academy One resources. Although this free-net is an excellent resource for new Internet travelers, it is frequently very busy and difficult to connect with.

To connect to the Cleveland Free-Net,

   1.   telnet   freenet-in-a.cwru.edu

2. login, type   **guest**

3. user ID <your e-mail address>

LA Free-Net

This free-net has some good educational areas to explore. Also use this free-net to access Academy One. You will need to pay a $10 registration fee. Register online or by mail.

To connect to the LA free-net,

1. telnet lafn.org

2. login, type   **visitor**

3. user ID <your e-mail address>

MOOS AND MUDS

MOO (Multi-User Shell, Object Oriented) and MUD (Multi-User Domain)

MOOs and MUDs put visitors into a virtual space where they are able to navigate, communicate, and build virtual environments by using computer commands. Each of these environments uses a different type of software, but they are very similar in that users Telnet to a remote computer to create, communicate, and navigate in a text-based environment. Some MOOs and MUDs offer alternative learning environments such as Diversity University; others, fantasy role-playing games. New identities are created and experimented with.

MOOs are very similar to MUDs, but use a more sophisticated programming language than MUD. A MOO lets users build things in a simulated environment by creating objects that are linked to a parent object. MUDs and MOOs are interactive systems suited to the construction of text-based adventure games and conferencing systems. The most common use, however, is multi-participant, virtual reality adventure games with players from all over the world.

Listed below are Internet sites to visit to explore MOOs and MUDs.

http://www.butterfly.net/~pyro/moo_page.html
http://www.bushnet.qld.edu.au/~jay/moo/
http://www.io.com/~combs/htmls/moo.html

DIVERSITY UNIVERSITY
http://www.academic.marist.edu/duwww.htm
telnet://moo.du.org:8888

LAMBDA MOO
telnet://lambda.parc.xerox.com:8888/

HtMUD (a graphical MUD)
http://www.elf.com/~phi/htmud/

Hypertext MUD Lists provides links to MUDS all over the world.
http://www.eskimo.com/~tarp3/muds.html

INTERNET PHONES

The Internet has made possible the global transmission of text, graphics, sound, and video. Now, a new service has come upon the Internet shore making the real-time transmission of voice possible. Products known as Internet phones let you use your computer as a telephone. Internet phones are the hottest new Internet service to talk with another person anywhere in the world at no more than the cost of your local Internet access. Internet telephones can operate over cable, satellite, and other networks.

However, Internet phones are still in their infancy and not yet a substitute for conventional phones. At this stage in their development, they are still a novelty and far from practical to use as a business tool or for routine communication. Many Iphones require both parties to be running the same software and be online at the same time when the call is made, otherwise the phone won't ring. Currently, most Internet phone software is similar to Internet Relay Chat programs that help users running the same program find and communicate with each other.

Part of the appeal of the Internet phone is the capability to talk to anyone in the world without the cost of a long distance phone call. For the monthly cost of an Internet account two people anywhere in the world can talk for as long and as often as they choose. When one compares this to the cost of national and international phone calls, many are willing to overlook the current limitations and difficulties imposed on its users by this new technology.

How Do I Talk to Someone Using an Internet Phone?
There are two ways that you can communicate with Internet users on Net phones:

- through a central server, similar to an Internet Relay Chat server
- connect to a specific individual by using their IP (Internet Protocol) address

Some Internet users have their own IP addresses; others are assigned an IP address every time they log on. Check with your Internet provider for information on your IP address.

What Do I Need to Use an Internet Phone?

Hardware
Before you can chat using Internet phones you will need the following hardware:

- a sound card for your Macintosh or Windows system
- speakers on your computer
- a microphone for your computer

Sound Card

To have a conversation where both parties can speak at the same time, you will need to have a sound card that supports full duplexing. Many Macintosh computers (including the Power Macs) support full-duplex sound. If you are using a PC, check your existing sound card. Full-duplex drivers are available if your sound card does not support full duplexing.

Speakers

The speakers that come with your computer are adequate for the current Net phones. The audio quality of this new technology is not yet what you are accustomed to with traditional telephones.

Microphone

Many computers come with microphones that will be suitable for use with the Internet phones. If you need to purchase a microphone, do not spend more than $10 to $15 on a desktop microphone.

Software

Netscape 3.0 and 4.0 incorporate an Internet Phone into its software. Microsoft Internet Explorer 4.0 also has an Internet Phone built in.

EXPEDITION EXPERIENCE

Communicating with other Teachers

Educational Listservs Resources

Listed below are Web sites you can visit to find information on educational listservs and other online resources for communicating with teachers and K12 schools on the Internet. In some cases, you will find that you can subscribe to the listserv from the Web site.

HOT LINKS EDUCATIONAL LISTSERVS

http://www.ucalgary.ca/~jross/List.html
Visit this site to learn about the listserv and then signup on the Web page.

WEB 66

http://mustang.coled.umn.edu/teacherscom.html
Links to resources to assist teachers with communicating with other teachers over the Net.

ASK ERIC

gopher://ericir.syr.edu/11/Listservs
A list of listservs and archived messages from lists.

EMAIL DISCUSSION GROUPS AND LISTS RESOURCE

http://www.webcom.com/impulse/list.html
Resources to assist you with learning about listservs—commands, how to subscribe and unsubscribe and links to other Web sites for finding lists are among the services that you will find useful.

Educational Listservs

Listed below are a few educational listservs.

COSNDISC (CONSORTIUM FOR SCHOOL NETWORKING DISCUSSION LIST)

1. To subscribe, send a message to:

    listproc@yukon.cren.org

2. Leave the Subject field blank

3. In the first line of the body of the message enter:

    subscribe cosndisc YourFirstName YourLastName

To post or send a message to the list use this email address:

    cosndisc@yukon.cren.org

EDNET

1. To subscribe, send a message to:

    listserv@nic.umass.edu

2. Leave the Subject field blank

3. In the first line of the body of the message enter:

    subscribe ednet YourFirstName YourLastName

To post or send a message to the list use this email address:

    ednet@nic.umass.edu

KIDSPHERE

1. To subscribe, send a message to:

    kidsphere-request@vms.cis.pitt.edu

2. Leave the Subject field blank

3. In the first line of the body of the message enter:

    Type any message asking to be added to the list.

To post or send a message to the list use this email address:

    kidsphere@vms.cis.pitt.edu

KIDS-95/KIDLINK

1. To learn about KIDLINK projects, subscribe to the news service by sending a message to:

    stserv@vm1.nodak.edu

2. Leave the Subject field blank

3. In the first line of the body of the message enter:

    subscribe KIDLINK YourFirstName YourLastName

To receive a file of general information on KIDLINK, send email to

the same listserv address, leave the Subject field blank, and in

the first line of the body of the message enter: get kidlink general

K12ADMIN
A list for K-12 educators interested in educational administration.

1. To subscribe, send a message to:

    listserv@suvm.syr.edu

2. Leave the Subject field blank

3. In the first line of the body of the message enter:

    subscribe k12admin YourFirstName YourLastName

To post or send a message to the list use this email address:

    k12admin@suvm.syr.edu

LM_NET
A list for school library media specialists.

1. To subscribe, send a message to:

    listserv@suvm.syr.edu

2. Leave the Subject field blank

3. In the first line of the body of the message enter:

    subscribe LM_NET YourFirstName YourLastName

To post or send a message to the list use this email address:

    LM_NET@suvm.syr.edu

ONLINE EDUCATOR
http://www.ole.net/ole/
A resource for teachers focusing on learning how to use the Internet in the classroom. Subscription available or visit their Web site for weekly updates.

SIGTEL-L
A list for the Special Interest Group for Telecommunications, a service of the International Society for Technology in Education.

1. To subscribe, send a message to:

    SIGTEL-L@unmvma.unm.edu

2. Leave the Subject field blank

3. In the first line of the body of the message enter:

    subscribe SIGTEL-L YourFirstName YourLastName

To post or send a message to the list use this email address:

SIGTEL-L@unmvma.unm.edu

TIPSHEET
Computer help and tip exchange.

1. To subscribe, send a message to:

    listserv@wsuvm1.csc.wsu.edu

2. Leave the Subject field blank

3. In the first line of the body of the message enter:

    subscribe tipsheet YourFirstName YourLastName

Usenet Newsgroups

Connect to this Web site to link to these newsgroups or to subscribe
http://www.asd.k12.ak.us/Other_Ed/Education/EdNEWSGROUPS.html

Listed below are Usenet newsgroup of interest to educators.

alt.education.disabled
alt.education.distance
alt.education.email-project

alt.kids-talk
can.schoolnet.chat.teachers
comp.security.announce
k12.chat.elementary
k12.chat.junior
k12.chat.senior
k12.chat.teacher
k12.ed.art
k12.ed.business
k12.ed.comp.literacy
k12.ed.health-pe
k12.ed.life-skills
k12.ed.math
k12.ed.music
k12.ed.science
k12.ed.soc-studies
k12.ed.special
k12.ed.tag
k12.ed.tech
k12.edu.life-skills (especially for school counselors)
k12.euro.teachers (in Europe)
k12.lang.art
k12.lang.deutsch-eng
k12.lang.esp-eng
k12.lang.francais
k12.lang.russian
k12.library
k12.sys.projects
misc.education
misc.education.language.english
misc.education.multimedia
misc.education.science
misc.kids
misc.kids.computer
news.announce.newusers

The Internet Landscape

CHAPTER CONTENTS

The Internet Landscape

GOPHER, FTP, TELNET

The World Wide Web is only a few years old—the first Web browser, Mosaic, was introduced in 1993. Prior to that time there was electronic mail, newsgroups, Telnet, FTP, and Gopher. Although the Web is in the center of Net activity, there are many different and useful non-Web resources available. Before browsers were available, access to these resources were done with software programs called *clients*. Today, all these resources can be accessed using your browser.

In this chapter you will learn how to use your browser—Netscape Navigator or Internet Explorer—to

☞ connect to Gopher servers to access information.
☞ explore FTP sites and transfer files (FTP) between two networked sites.
☞ access and communicate with remote computers using Telnet.

Before You Begin...

Listed below are several points to remember as you begin your travels.

- The addressing information that defines the transfer protocol for accessing, viewing, and downloading information is different for each of these Internet tools.

- When you access this information using Netscape or Explorer, remember that you are working within the World Wide Web environment. Information access to files, data, and directories is by use of hyperlinks. Access these informational resources by clicking on the highlighted words.

- Navigate forward and backward using your browser's navigational tools: buttons and pull-down menus (including the history list).

- Save your favorite resources as bookmarks or favorites.

- Files that you download will be saved to your computer's hard drive.

- To travel outside the World Wide Web, just change the URL format.

For example,
This Gopher address	cwis.usc.edu
becomes	gopher://cwis.usc.edu
This FTP address	ftp explorer.arc.nasa.gov
becomes	ftp://explorer.arc.nasa.gov

GOPHER

What Is Gopher?

Gopher n.
1. Any of various short tailed, burrowing
mammals of the family Geomyidae, of North America.
2. (Amer. colloq.) Native or inhabitant of Minnesota:
the Gopher State. **3.** (Amer. colloq.) One who runs
errands, does odd-jobs, fetches or delivers documents
for office staff. **4.** (computer tech.) Software following
a simple protocol for tunneling through a TCP/IP Internet.

Before the World Wide Web there was Gopher. Gopher was developed and released by Paul Lindner and Mark P. McCahill at the University of Minnesota—home of the "Golden Gophers"—in 1991. Gopher was developed as a tool to help locate information and resources on the Internet. Gopher uses a hierarchical menu system for finding and accessing information. When you select a menu item, Gopher will "go for" it. The Gopher outline format is an easy way to find information.

Telnet or a Gopher client such as TurboGopher for the Macintosh and Gopher for Windows was used to connect to Gopher servers when Gopher was introduced in 1991. Once connected users were presented with a menu (see Fig. 4.1). Commands were used to navigate in gopherspace.

Today Netscape Navigator and Microsoft Internet Explorer can be used to travel to Gopher sites. To connect to a Gopher site, you enter the Gopher's URL in the browser's location or Netsite field as you would do with any URL.

Gopher can become one of your travel guides to the Internet. Once you have logged onto a Gopher site you can easily move from one Gopher site to another.

FIGURE 4.1
The University of Minnesota Gopher site using a Gopher client without a graphical interface

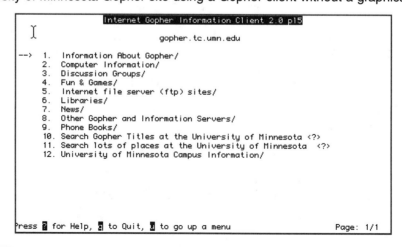

NOTE

If you are not using a Web browser to access Gopher you will need to know a variety of commands for navigating in gopherspace. Listed below are a few of the more important ones.

To display HELP information, type a ? (question mark).

To stop your Gopher client, type q (quit).

To quit immediately, without being asked for confirmation, type Q (uppercase "Q").

If you have trouble retrieving a directory, COMMAND (apple key on the Macintosh) K (kill or suspend the current job).

Gopher Conventions using a nongraphical clients—Netscape and Explorer— include:

a slash (/): Gopher menu items that end with a slash (/) indicate that there is another level of menu items beneath this level.

a question mark <?> : Menu items ending with <?> indicate that you can search for information within the menu's index.

a dot <.>: Menu items ending with a dot <.> indicate that this item of the menu is a file. After you have selected and displayed the file, you can download it to your computer.

Gopher sites lack the rich formatting that you are accustomed to on the Web (see Fig. 4.2). Notice the menu is a list of hyperlinks. Each link is preceded by a small icon indicating the type of resource with which the link connects. Gopher links connect with

- submenus
- text files
- images
- indexes
- movie and binary files

FIGURE 4.2

The University of Minnesota Gopher site using a Web browser

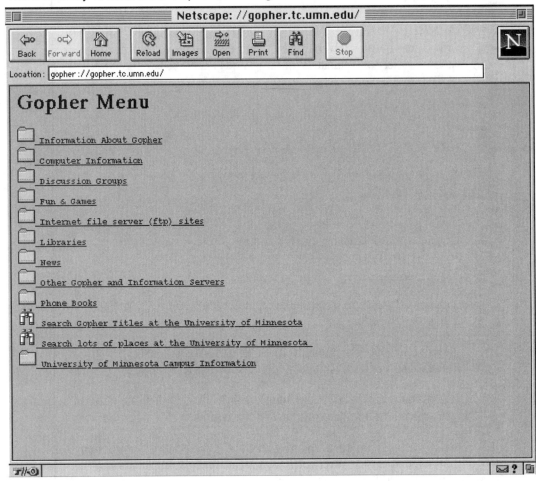

The folder icons are links that connect to more folders icons or submenus. Eventually you will link to files represented by page icons.

Guided Tour 1
Using a Browser to Connect to a Gopher Server

In this Guided Tour you will

- connect to the ERIC (Educational Resource Information Center) Gopher server at Syracuse University.
- travel to ERIC's online lesson plan resources.

STEP 1

Login to your system.

STEP 2

Open your browser—Netscape Navigator or Internet Explorer

STEP 3

Type in this Gopher URL for the ERIC Gopher: **gopher://ericir.syr.edu**.

NOTE

The Gopher address of

ericir.syr.edu

becomes this URL

gopher://ericir.syr.edu.

STEP 4

When you first connect to the ERIC server you will see this main menu.

FIGURE 4.3
The main menu for the ERIC Gopher server.

Gopher Menu

About AskERIC

Map of the Library

Search AskERIC Menu Items

AskERIC Toolbox

Frequently Asked Questions (FAQ's) about ERIC & AskERIC

AskERIC InfoGuides

Lesson Plans

Education Listservs Archives

ERIC Clearinghouses/Components

ERIC Digests File

ERIC Bibliographic Database (RIE and CIJE)

STEP 5

Now, let's look at ERIC's online Lesson Plans. Double-click on the Lesson Plan folder (see Fig. 4.3).

STEP 6

You will now see this Gopher menu.

FIGURE 4.4
ERIC's Gopher server displaying online lesson plan resources

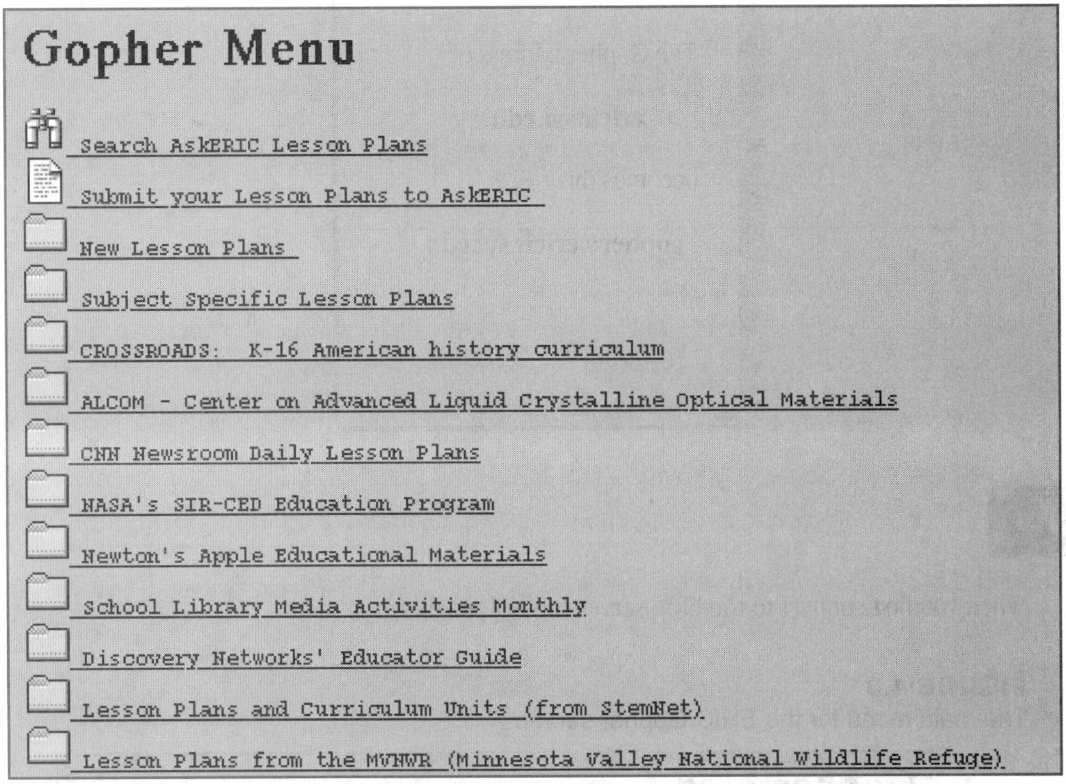

Explore the ERIC lesson plans. Use the **Back** and **Forward** button to move around in gopherspace just as you do on the Web.

Guided Tour 2
Traveling in Gopherspace

In this guided walk you will

- connect to the ERIC Gopher server.
- travel down many pathways to explore Gopher resources.

STEP 1

Login to your system.

STEP 2

Open your browser.

STEP 3

Connect to the ERIC Gopher server by entering in this Gopher URL in your browser's location field.

gopher://ericir.syr.edu

STEP 4

When you first connect to the ERIC Gopher server you will see a hierarchical menu consisting of folder icons which are text-based links to online resources. When you double-click on a folder you are taken to a submenu with more folders and files.

Double-click on the folder called Other Educational Resources.

FIGURE 4.5
Gopher menu for Other Educational Resources

Gopher Menu

📁 U.S. Department of Education

📁 State and Regional Education Information

📁 Internet Projects for K-12

📁 Adult Literacy Resources

📁 Vocational Education Resources

📁 Access the Regional Educational Laboratory Gophers

📁 American Library Association (ALA)

📁 Association for Educational Communications & Technology (AECT)

📁 CICNET gopher server

📁 Consortium for School Networking (CoSN)

📁 Discovery Learning Community

📁 Education Gopher at Florida Tech

📁 Goals 2000

STEP 5

Next, double-click on the folder called Internet Projects for Kids. You should have this Gopher menu on your screen.

FIGURE 4.6
Gopher menu for Internet Projects for Kids

```
Gopher Menu

📁  Arkansas Public School Computer Network

📁  CICNet Select K-12 Internet Resources

📁  Carleton University

📄  Engaging Students in a Global Study of Wildlife Migration

📁  Internet for Minnesota Schools Gopher

📄  MathMagic (a K-12 telecommunications project)

📁  NCEET

📁  NYSERNet: New York State Education and Research Network

📄  Southern College Gopher

📁  University of Massachusetts K12
```

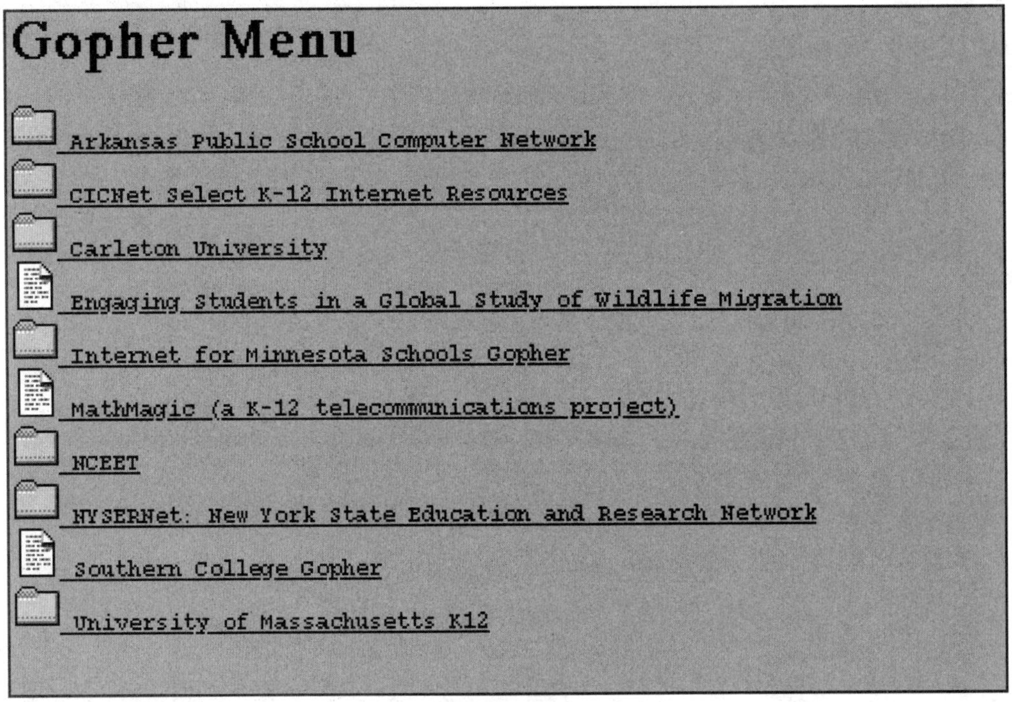

Explore the projects in this menu.

STEP 6

When you have finished exploring the Internet Projects for Kids go back to the main ERIC Gopher menu by either using your **Back** button or your browser's history list. You can also type in the ERIC Gopher URL: **gopher://ericir.syr.edu.**

We are now going on a journey to explore and learn about Gopher pathways. As you explore gopherspace you will find a series of hierarchical menus or pathways. Double click on a folder icon to travel to a submenu.

STEP 7

When you are at ERIC's Gopher main menu, double-click on the Other Educational Resources folder icon. Next click on the University of Massachusetts K12 Gopher folder.

FIGURE 4.7

Gopher Menu

- About Gopher
- Books, Dictionaries, Language Arts, Languages, Magazines, Thesaurus
- Educational Gophers, Policies
- Five Colleges/Public School Partnership
- Government, History, UN, Social Studies, Women's Studies
- Internet Information, Policies; Gopher Jewels, Subject Guides
- Libraries - UMass, Five Colleges, Massachusetts, and Others
- News Services - Press reviews, newspapers
- Other Gopher and Information Servers
- Science, Agriculture, Ecology, Math, Space, Weather
- Telecommunications Projects
- UMass, Five Colleges, Amherst College Information
- UMassK12, and Kidlink, Informtion
- 4-H Energy Education Resources Database

University of Massachusetts K12 Gopher menu

STEP 8

From the University of Massachusetts K12 Gopher menu, double-click on the Books, Dictionaries folder. Notice the files with information on citing electronic media. There are also submenus for electronic books and magazines.

STEP 9

Open the Virtual Reference Desk folder (see Fig. 4.8).

STEP 10

Open the CIA World Factbook (see Fig. 4.9).

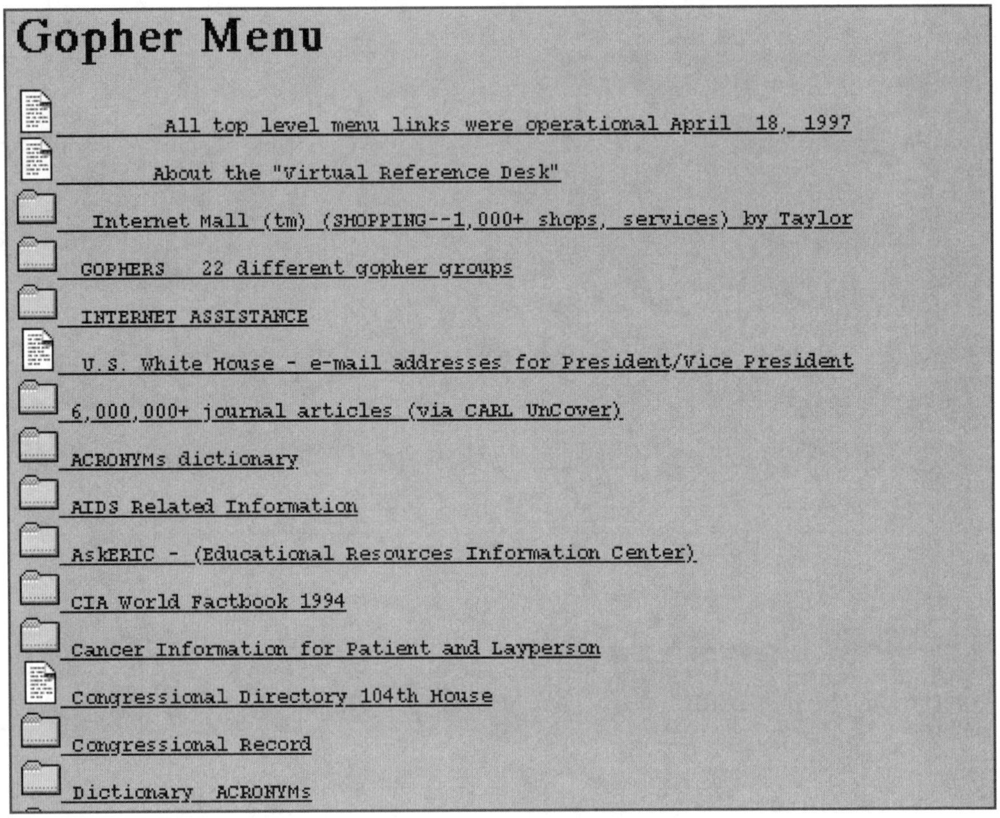

Gopher Menu

All top level menu links were operational April 18, 1997

About the "Virtual Reference Desk"

Internet Mall (tm) (SHOPPING--1,000+ shops, services) by Taylor

GOPHERS   22 different gopher groups

INTERNET ASSISTANCE

U.S. White House - e-mail addresses for President/Vice President

6,000,000+ journal articles (via CARL UnCover)

ACRONYMs dictionary

AIDS Related Information

AskERIC - (Educational Resources Information Center)

CIA World Factbook 1994

Cancer Information for Patient and Layperson

Congressional Directory 104th House

Congressional Record

Dictionary ACRONYMs

FIGURE 4.8
Virtual Reference Desk Gopher menu

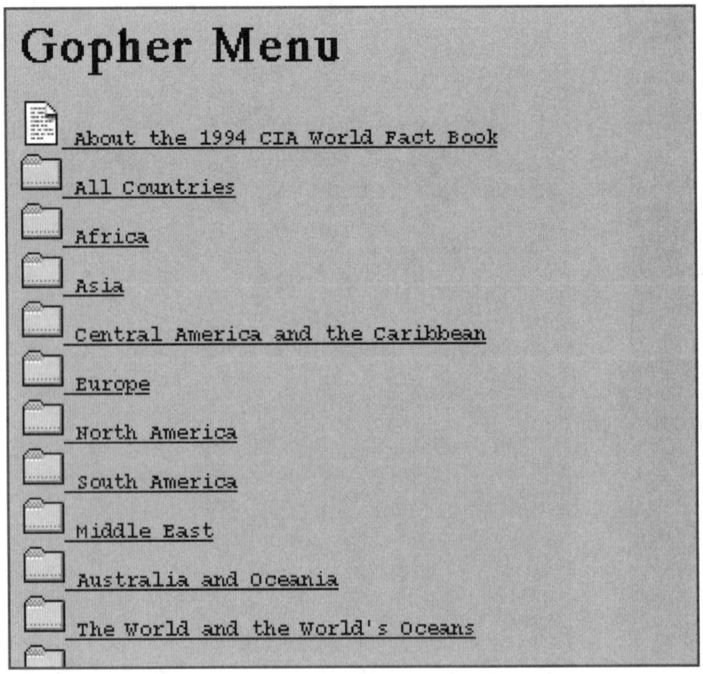

Gopher Menu

About the 1994 CIA World Fact Book

All Countries

Africa

Asia

Central America and the Caribbean

Europe

North America

South America

Middle East

Australia and Oceania

The World and the World's Oceans

NOTE

What you have just done is to travel down Gopher pathways. First you connected to the Gopher server, then followed links from one menu to a submenu until you finally found the resource you were looking for. This journey through menus and submenus is called a *pathway*. The pathway that we just took from the ERIC main menu to the CIA World Factbook would be:

Other Educational Resources / University of Massachusetts K12 Gopher / Books, dictionaries... / Virtual Reference Desk / CIA World Factbook

When you reference a Gopher site, be sure to include the Gopher URL and the pathway. It is often difficult to find a particular resource at a Gopher site if the pathway is not given.

FIGURE 4.9
Gopher menu for CIA World Factbook.

Continue Exploring. Use your browser's navigational aids to explore resources that you viewed in previous Gopher menus.

EXPEDITION EXPERIENCE

Exploring Gopher Holes

Now that you have learned how to navigate gopherspace, here are some Gophers for you to explore.

AMNESTY INTERNATIONAL
This gopher contains a database about Amnesty International: mission, techniques used to battle capital punishment, torture and "disappearances" around the world.

gopher://gopher.igc.apc.org:70
Path: /Organizations on the IGC Network Gopher/Amnesty International

ARIZONA STATE UNIVERSITY
This Gopher site contains links to many excellent educational Gophers. Here you will find connections to the following sites: ASU College of Education; AskERIC; Exploratorium Science Museum; National Center for Adult Literacy; New York State Department of Education; The Chronicle of Higher Education; The Holocaust: A Guide for Teachers; The Hub; UNICEF; United States Department of Education; Eisenhower National Clearinghouse; many colleges and universities; federal agencies; journals and publications; higher education Gophers; K-12 school districts; resources for K-12 education, and much more.

gopher://info.asu.edu

ARMADILLO
Visit Texas and learn more about the state; investigate projects, library services and resources.

gopher://riceinfo.rice.edu
path: /Other Gophers and Information Servers/Armadillo/Super Projects

check these paths:
/Library Services & Resources
/Other Gophers with Texas Twist
/Technology Help & Multimedia Software & Lessons

ART: NEW YORK ART LINE
The New York Art Line (NYAL) is being developed in a search for art and art resources on the Internet. NYAL is primarily a connection to these resources, as well as connections to one-stop shopping. Arts organizations, New York City artists, and artists who work with technology post information here. This site connects you to the following art resources: Arts Wire (art news and information network); online art magazines; design (architecture, interior, fashion, and more); online galleries; images and imaging software; museums and schools, inter netic art; media arts; The Neo Internet Roadside Diner; technology and art resources; other art Gophers; Wet Paint.

gopher://gopher.panix.com
path: /New York Art Line

CICNET K-12 GOPHER
CICNet is funded in part by the National Science Foundation and supports cooperative academic programs among the Midwest's major research institutions.

gopher://gopher.cic.net
path: /Other CICNet Projects and Gopher Servers/K-12/Classroom Activities & Projects

CIVICS AND GOVERNMENT ARCHIVE
This site is maintained by Internet Wiretap. Here you will find many excellent documents and resources. Many have been taken from different places; many are controversial. You will also find information on copyright, bills before Congress, historical documents, speeches and addresses, reports, treaties, NATO, and miscellaneous world documents.

gopher://wiretap.spies.com
Path: /Government Docs

DEPARTMENT OF EDUCATION
Visit the Department of Education Institutional Communication Network Gopher server for an extensive collection of documents and other educational information. The primary function of this site is to communicate and share information among educational institutions.

gopher://gopher.ed.gov

K12 GOPHER SERVERS
Links to K12 Gophers.

gopher://winnie.fit.edu:70/11/gophers/k12

DIRECTORY OF GOPHER SERVERS
A categorized listing of Gopher servers.

gopher://ds2.internic.net:70/11/dirofdirs/gophersite

FLORIDA TECH EDUCATION GOPHER
This Gopher site links to many educational resources including electronic texts, libraries, a reference desk, search tools, FTP sites, and many educational Gophers.

gopher://sci-ed.fit.edu:70/1

GLOBAL COMMUNICATION NETWORK
The Institute for Global Communications (IGC) runs four computer networks known as PeaceNet, EcoNet, ConflictNet, and LaborNet. IGC is the U.S. member of the Association for Progressive Communications, a 16-country association of computer networks working for peace, human rights, environmental protection, social justice, and sustainability.

gopher://gopher.igc.apc.org:70
path for environmental education programs & projects: /EcoNet-Environmental Education

path for International Arctic project: /Education & Youth/International Arctic Project

Investigate this menu item: /Education & Youth/Education & Youth Projects on the Internet, or /Global Rivers Environmental Education Network

path for PeaceNet projects
/PeaceNet — Peace, Human Rights and Social Justice

GOPHER JEWELS
This excellent Gopher site contains a searchable catalog of outstanding gopher sites.

gopher://cwis.usc.edu:70/11/Other_Gophers_and_Information_Resources/Gopher-Jewels

GROWING CURRICULUM
This Gopher is managed by the Consortium for School Networking. The pathway leads to directories that focus on how the Internet can enhance learning environments. Curriculum areas include language arts, mathematics, science, and social studies.

gopher://digital.cosn.org
path: /CoSN Activities/COSNDISC/CoSNDISC/Topics/Growing Curriculum

HOLOCAUST
This directory contains information on school curricula for teaching about the Holocaust. In some instances, the full text of the curricula appear here.

gopher://gopher://info.asu.edu:70/11/asu-cwis/education/other/k12resources/holocaust

HORTICULTURE
Or visit the Master Gardener and learn more about flowering plants, fruits and vegetables.

gopher://leviathan.tamu.edu
path: /Master Gardener Information

INDIANA DEPARTMENT OF EDUCATION— IDEANET
IDEAnet contains education data from Indiana's 294 school districts and general purpose Bulletin Board services. In addition, IDEAnet serves as a distribution medium for a variety of curricular materials.

gopher://ideanet.doe.state.in.us

KIDLINK
KIDLINK is a project whose goal is to get as many children from ages 10 to 15 involved in a global dialog. At this site you will find many projects, and pen pals from around the world. The cost of admission is to answer four questions about yourself, your life, future plans, and your hopes for the planet. In return, you will receive KIDCAFE newsletter by e-mail.

gopher://global.kidlink.org
path:/explore on your own

KIDART
The KIDLINK GALLERY Of Computer Art is a place where children can express themselves in graphic form. The Gallery is primarily for works that were created on computers. These works often are not reproduced well on the commonly available printers. Distribution as computer files maintains

the graphic qualities of the originals and allows them to be seen by a wider audience.

gopher://global.kidlink.org:70/11/kidart

LIBRARY WITHOUT WALLS
North Carolina State University houses this excellent virtual library. Here you will find links to Internet resources by category: astronomy and astrophysics; biology; chemistry; earth science; economics and business; education; engineering; environmental science; fine arts; geography; government and law; health science; language and literature; marine science; mathematics; physics; religion; social sciences.

gopher://dewey.lib.ncsu.edu
Path: /Library Without Walls/Study Carrels

MERIT NETWORK
Merit Network, Inc. is a non-profit consortium of state-supported universities in Michigan. Merit also works with the National Science Foundation. Some of the resources at this site include: K-12 in Michigan; Merit Software Archives; National Science Foundation Network; information on how to connect to the Internet; and links to other Gopher servers.

gopher://nic.merit.edu

MOTHER GOPHER
Make a bookmark of this Gopher server as a starting point for Gopher exploration.

gopher://gopher.tc.umn.edu

Explore this Gopher server at Washington and Lee University in Virginia. This excellent Gopher site links you to other Gopher resources, libraries and information access, and links to help you explore and find Internet resources such as mailing lists, people, information by subject, and more. There are also links to Internet Guides and Tutorials.

gopher://liberty.uc.wlu.edu

NON-GOVERNMENTAL AGENCIES
This gopher server provides links to many non-governmental organizations such as PeaceNet, EcoNet, ConflictNet, and Labor Net.

gopher://gopher.igc.apc.org:70/11/orgs

SMITHSONIAN
This Gopher server houses data from the Smithsonian's natural history and anthropology collection.

gopher://nmnhgoph.si.edu

UNITED NATIONS
gopher://nywork1.undp.org

UNIVERSITY OF ILLINOIS — COLLEGE OF EDUCATION
Resources at this Gopher site include K-12 Learning Resources; Teacher Education Resources; Higher Education Resources; and General Internet Resources.

gopher:// gopher.ed.uiuc.edu

UNIVERSITY OF MASSACHUSETTS

This Gopher server has many excellent links to resources such as books, dictionaries, magazines, thesaurus, educational Gophers, government, history, images and fine arts, Internet information, libraries, news services, science, ecology, math, space, weather, and much more.

gopher://k12.ucs.umass.edu

VIRTUAL REFERENCE DESK

This excellent resource connects you with frequently sought information sources and tools. The coverage of the desk is encyclopedic.

gopher://ericir.syr.edu
path: /Other Educational Resources / University of Massachusetts K12 Gopher / Books, dictionaries... / Virtual Reference Desk / CIA World Factbook

VIRTUAL SCHOOL

Visit this virtual school and visit the computer labs, library, arts floor, English floor, environmental studies room, French floor, Life Studies floor, math floor, science and engineering floor, social studies floor, and the staff room.

gopher://gopher.schoolnet.carleton.ca
path: /SchoolNet Gopher /The Virtual School

WHITE HOUSE

gopher://gopher.tamu.edu:70/11/.dir/president.dir

YANOFF'S LIST

Scott Yanoff maintains a list of useful and interesting sites on the Net, sorted by subject.

gopher://gopher.uwm.edu
Path: /Remote Information Services/Special Internet Connections

FILE TRANSFER PROTOCOL (FTP)

Transferring Files With FTP

FTP is a special method used to transfer files between two Internet sites. Files or data can be sent to another site—uploading a file—or can be retrieved from a remote site—downloading a file. Many servers that make files available to Internet users are known as *anonymous FTP* sites. Any Internet user can log onto these sites and retrieve files. Before Web browsers, users would connect to an FTP site and login using anonymous as their username, and their email address as their password. When using a Web browser such as Netscape or Explorer, this login procedure is taken care of by the browser software.

FTP resources include computer software, databases, updates to most retail software, electronic texts, technical reports, journals, magazines, news summaries, books, images, and sound. One of the most widely used FTP services is to travel to FTP servers to download the most current versions of software such as Netscape, Explorer, Eudora, Helper Applications, or plug-ins such as Shockwave and RealAudio. Using a browser to FTP makes file retrieval easy. Enter in the URL for the FTP site or the Web site that has a link to the FTP server, and just follow the links.

NOTE

One disadvantage of using a Web browser to access FTP sites is that the browser automatically logs you in as anonymous and uses your email address as your password. Most FTP sites use this login for unregistered visitors. However, some FTP sites may require different login information. Consequently, you will need to use FTP software. Visit software sites such Jumbo (http://www.jumbo.com) and Tucows (http://www.tucows.com) for FTP software.

GUIDED TOUR 1
Traveling to an FTP Site

In this guided tour we will travel to the FTP site for Project Gutenberg. At this site you will find many archived books, including the classics.

STEP 1

Type this URL in your browser's Location field **ftp://uiarchive.cso.uiuc.edu**

> # NOTE
>
> To visit a FTP site using a browser, type in the URL information. The format will be **ftp://address**
>
> Some FTP servers are accessed using the World Wide Web and the **http://** address is used. You will have an opportunity to travel to an FTP Web site in Guided Tour 2.

FIGURE 4.10
Netscape link to the Gutenberg FTP site

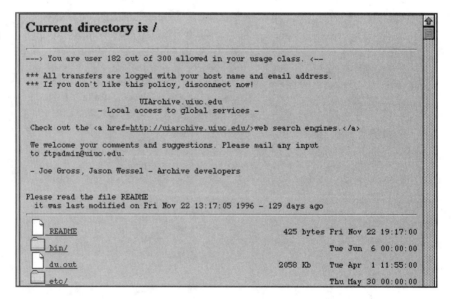

```
Current directory is /

---> You are user 182 out of 300 allowed in your usage class. <--

*** All transfers are logged with your host name and email address.
*** If you don't like this policy, disconnect now!

                    UIArchive.uiuc.edu
               - Local access to global services -

    Check out the <a href=http://uiarchive.uiuc.edu/>web search engines.</a>

    We welcome your comments and suggestions. Please mail any input
    to ftpadmin@uiuc.edu.

    - Joe Gross, Jason Wessel - Archive developers

Please read the file README
  it was last modified on Fri Nov 22 13:17:05 1996 - 129 days ago

    README                              425 bytes Fri Nov 22 19:17:00
    bin/                                          Tue Jun  6 00:00:00
    du.out                                2058 Kb Tue Apr  1 11:55:00
    etc/                                          Thu May 30 00:00:00
```

Notice that the FTP directory and content pages have minimal formatting. When possible, the browser displays the type, size, date, and a short description of each file in a directory. The directory is presented as a list of links, each link preceded by a small icon indicating whether the link is a directory or a file. Clicking on a directory link brings you to another subdirectory.

Scroll down the list and notice the "README." files. These are text files with information about the FTP server. To read any of these text files, click once on the file's underlined name.

The icons that look like folders have an underlined name next to them followed by a slash (/). This indicates a link to a subdirectory. Follow this pathway to Project Gutenberg **/pub/etext/gutenberg** where each segment pub, etext, and gutenberg are displayed.

FIGURE 4.11
FTP directory for Project Gutenberg

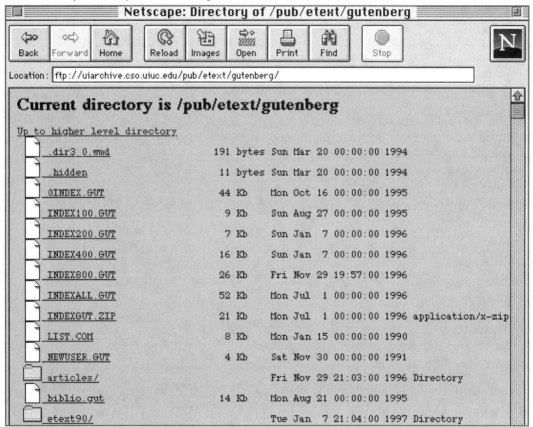

Notice the hyperlinks that access text files, software, images, and other subdirectories.

FTP Survival—Understanding Compression

Before you begin downloading files, it will be helpful to learn about compression. An important concept to understand is that any computer file that is going to be made available to other computers around the world needs to do two things.

- Be in a format that can be transmitted quickly from one computer to another.

- Be in a format that can be read by all computers (i.e., Macintosh, Windows, etc.).

To understand how this is accomplished you need to understand compression and helper applications because before you can view or use many multimedia files you may have to uncompress them and/or use a helper application to see or hear them.

Large files are compressed to save disk space and to make it faster to transmit them between computers. Software applications (that is, Internet browsers, Helper Applications, and compression programs) are examples of large files that you will be downloading to your computer from remote computers. More than likely these files will be compressed. Some of these files will be self-extracting, which means that the program will decompress by just double-clicking on it. If the file is not self-extracting, you will need a decompression program to open them. Likewise, if you are going to send large files, use a decompression program to make them smaller. Software applications are available to make your compressed files self-extracting.

The type of compression method used on a file is indicated by an extension added to the end of the filename. For example, many compressed Macintosh files end with .sea. A filename compressed using this method may look like this

Eudora2.1Fat.sea

Files ending in .sea are self-extracting archives and can be decompressed by double-clicking on the program icon.

Files compressed for the PC also have extensions to indicate the type of compression.

Most decompression software programs can be downloaded from the Internet for free.

Macintosh Extensions and Compression

Macintosh compressed file extensions include

.cpt	A file compressed using CompactPro. CompactPro is a shareware program available on the Internet.
.hqx	A file compressed using the BinHex compression program. You must use BinHex, CompactPro, or Stuffit to decompress it.
.sea	A self-extracting archive. To open the file, double click on the file.
.sit	A file compressed using Stuffit. Use Stuffit Expander to decompress it.
.txt	An ASCII text file that can be read by virtually any computer using a simple text program.

One of the most commonly used decompression programs for Macintosh is Stuffit Expander. There are many Internet sites where you can find a copy of Stuffit Expander and download it to your computer by double-clicking on the Web link. After you obtain a copy of Stuffit Expander, place a copy on your desktop. When you receive files that need to be decompressed, drop them onto the Stuffit icon. Two World Wide Web sites you can visit to search for compression software are

JUMBO
http://www.jumbo.com

TUCOWS
http://www.tucows.com)

The All-In-One Search page is another site to visit for links to freeware and shareware. **http://www.albany.net/allinone.** When you connect to this page, scroll down and select the Software option.

PC Extensions and Compression

Some of the more common file extensions for the PC include

.asc	A simple ASCII text file that can be read by all computers.
.doc	A text file or a Microsoft word document.
.exe	A file that can be run by double-clicking on the file icon or from the Windows 95 Run command.
.zip	A file that has been compressed using the PKZIP compression program. To open or extract these files use PKUNZIP or WinZip.

The best Web site to find copies of compression/decompression software for the PC is TUCOWS— **http://www.tucows.com**. WinZip is frequently mentioned as the best for file compression/decompression. WinZip also makes an application for creating self-extracting archives.

Guided Tour 2
Downloading Files

When files are downloaded to your computer, you are using FTP. FTP can be done in two ways

- enter in the FTP address for the FTP site.
- go to a Web site that has links to FTP servers.

In this guided tour we will visit a World Wide Web site with links to FTP servers for downloading the popular PC decompression program, WinZip.

STEP 1

Connect to the Internet.

STEP 2

Double-click on the Navigator or Explorer icon to launch the program.

STEP 3

Enter in the URL for the Web site—in this example, Tucows. Type Tucows's URL
http://www.tucows.com in the Location field or click on the **Open** button. Hit Enter.

NOTE

If you are only looking for
the WinZip utility, you may
want to connect directly to
their Web site at
http://www.winzip.com

STEP 4

When you have connected to the software site, follow the links to the Windows utilities. You might
want to take some time to look around at the other PC applications and utilities available from
Tucows.

FIGURE 4.12
Tucows Compression Utilities page

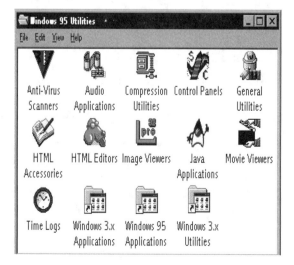

STEP 5

Click on the Compression Utilities link.

FIGURE 4.13

The Compression Utilities page for downloading compression software

STEP 6

Click on the WinZip for Windows 95 link.

STEP 7

After your browser makes contact with the remote FTP site, you will be asked for a location to download the file to. Select a location on your hard drive, then click the Save button. The file will now begin to download to the designated location on your computer. As the file downloads you will see a dialog box showing the status and progress of the file transfer.

NOTE

This example is for obtaining a
copy of WinZip for Windows 95.
If you are using Windows 3.1
follow the Tucows links to the
Windows 3.1 page. If you are
using a Macintosh, use the
same procedure, but connect to
a site with Macintosh software.
In Chapter 7 you will find additional Web sites for software
and shareware.

FTP Survival—

Helper Applications for Viewing Images

Graphics images can be saved in as many as 50 different formats. These formats are merely different
ways to preserve images. However, you will find that most images have one of these extensions
GIF, JPEG, XBM.

GIF (Graphics Interchange Format) was created by CompuServe; JPEG (Joint Photographic Experts
Group) is named for the group that invented it; XBM refers to X Bit Map format. Regardless of the
format, images can only be seen by using an image viewer. Netscape Navigator and Explorer have
the built-in capability to view images saved in these formats. You can also use these browsers to
view images when you download them to your computer's hard drive.

Two popular image viewers for the Macintosh are GIFConverter and JPEGView. Obtain copies of
these applications by visiting Jumbo and All-In-One sites. There are several image viewing programs
for the PC: LVview Pro, Paint Shop Pro, Thumbs Plus, and VuePrint, and WebImage. Visit the
TUCOWS Web for your PC viewers.

To see a listing of helper applications required to view image, video, and sound files, go Netscape's
Option menu, select **General Preferences** and open the panel for **Helpers**. Find the name of the
helper application for viewing the desired multimedia file.

Helper Applications for Sound and Video Files

Movie viewers allow users to view and manipulate movie files such as Quicktime or MPEG. Several
of the more popular movie players for the PC are QuickTime Player, VMPEG Lite, and MPEG Movie
Player. QuickTime is the most widely used movie player for the Macintosh.

Many sound files are heard using RealAudio. RealAudio makes it possible to hear sound immediately
after clicking on a sound link. There is little or no time used to download the sound file. Visit the
Web site **http://www.realaudio.com** for a copy of RealAudio. Visit the National Public Radio site
http://www.npr.org to experience RealAudio.

EXPEDITION EXPERIENCE

Traveling to FTP Sites

Now that you have taken several FTP guided tours, it is time for you to begin exporing FTP sites. Listed below are FTP sites for you to visit.

BERKELEY ARCHIVE
Visit this site to find many interesting documents: Shakespeare, poetry, song lyrics, and much more.

ftp://ftp.ocf.berkeley.edu/
path: /pub/library

BIOLOGY
This site contains biology software, data, and news. It also includes items to browse, search, fetch, and links to information sources in biology.

ftp://ftp.bio.indiana.edu

FTP SITES
Travel to these sites and find a listing of all the FTP sites on the Internet.

ftp://ftp.virginia.edu/pub/FTP.sites

ftp://ftp.virginia.edu
path: /pub/FTP.sites

ftp://rtfm.mit.edu/
path: /pub/usenet/news.answers/ftp-list

HISTORY ARCHIVE
This site at Mississippi State contains historical documents and links to other historical databases.

ftp://msstate.edu
path: /pub/docs/history

KYBER-K-12 ARCHIVE
Travel to this site to find K-12 resources.

ftp://byrd.mu.wvnet.edu/
path: /pub/estepp/kyber-12

MAILING LISTS FOR EDUCATORS
Download a listing of current mailing lists for educators.

ftp://nic.umass.edu/
path: /pub/ednet

MIT MEDIA LAB
Visit the MIT Media Lab server to read papers and programs written by members of the MIT Media Lab.

ftp://cecelia.media.mit.edu

NEWSGROUP LIST
This site has an updated listing of the currently active newsgroups.

ftp://rtfm.mit.edu/
path: /pub/usenet/news.announce.newsgroups

PROJECT GUTENBERG
Project Gutenberg makes electronic books available. Visit this site to select your book. Other directories include: kites, mac stuff, MUDs, and more.

ftp://mrcnext.cso.uiuc.edu/
path: /pub/etext

NASA
Visit the Goddard Space Flight Center's FTP archive site. Here you will find great images of bodies in space and much more.

ftp://dftnic.gsfc.nasa.gov/
path: /images/gifs/

SOFTWARE ARCHIVES
This site at Stanford makes personal computer software available.

ftp://sumex-aim.Stanford.edu

Another site at the University of Michigan has a huge collection of freeware and shareware.

ftp://archive.umich.edu

Washington University has a large collection of freeware and shareware.

ftp://wuarchive.wustl.edu

WEATHER SATELLITE IMAGES
This site contains weather satellite images from all parts of the globe.

ftp://wuarchive.wustl.edu/
path: /multimedia/images/wx

TELNET

Telnet is one of the oldest Internet technologies that allows users to log onto another computer and run resident programs. Although Telnet is not as visually interesting as the World Wide Web, it is essential to Internet travel. Telnet is a text-based environment requiring commands to navigate. Some Telnet access sites automatically link you to Web pages. Many Telnet sites, such as libraries, allow anyone to login without having a special account. Others require users to have a valid account before accessing many of the resident programs. Basic instructions for using Telnet can be found at these Web sites

> http://www.w3.org/hypertext/WWW/FAQ/Bootstrap.html
> http://www.web.com. com/~futures/telnet.html

There are things on the Internet that Telnet can do better. For example, when you Telnet to a remote computer, frequently a mainframe supercomputer, you are working on another machine and are using that machine's speed and power. College students and business travelers dial a local Internet service provider and then Telnet to their college or business accounts to get their e-mail. Telnet saves them the cost of a long distance phone call.

Telnet also provides direct access to Internet services not always available from your Internet provider. Many of these services are exciting and interesting. Some open doors to alternative learning environments.

Some of the Internet services available using Telnet include

- databases (such as earthquake, weather, special collections)
- libraries (public, academic, medical, legal, and more)
- Free-Nets (noncommercial, community-based networks)
- interactive chats
- MOOs, MUDs
- bulletin boards

Databases
Many of the databases that you access with Telnet have the latest information on many topics like severe storms and weather conditions. Others, such as the Library of Congress, have archive collections.

Libraries
Telnet makes it possible to access libraries all around the world. Each library will vary on how much online help they make available to you.

Free-Nets
Free-nets provide networking services to a local community. Access to free-nets is achieved either at public libraries or by dialing in. To connect to a free-net, you will need to Telnet.

Free-nets establish their own resources for users in their community and are usually designed around a model of an electronic town. For example, you may be able to discuss local issues with the mayor or stop at an electronic school to discuss educational issues. These local networks usually have bulletin boards, electronic mail, informational resources, and educational resources.

Educational resources may have local projects for classrooms or may provide information on national or international projects. Free-nets also provide links to global educational resources. They make finding and using Internet resources more manageable for educators who frequently do not have the time to explore cyberspace for classroom resources.

You may use a free-net as a guest, but your access privileges may be limited. You will have to register to have full access privileges. Registration is free to people within the community. For those outside the community, there is usually a nominal registration fee. Today, there are more than 30 free-nets online in cities across the United States and Canada. You can also find a few in Europe and New Zealand.

Chats

Chats are programs that allow you to talk to many people at the same time from all over the world. Internet Relay Chat (IRC) is the most widely used program. Many Internet access providers make IRC available to new subscribers. Some World Wide Web sites will have chat rooms for interactive discussion of topics of interest. For example, Time Warner's Pathfinder Web site has a chat room for discussing news of the day. Wired magazine has a chat room open for discussion.

MOO (Multi-User Shell, Object Oriented) and MUD (Multi-User Domain).

MOOs and MUDs put visitors into a virtual space where they are able to navigate, communicate, and build virtual environments by using computer commands. Each of these environments uses a different type of software, but they are very similar in that users Telnet to a remote computer to create, communicate, and navigate in a text-based environment. Some MOOs and MUDs offer alternative learning environments such as Diversity University; others, fantasy role-playing games. New identities are created and experimented with.

MOOs are very similar to MUDs, but use a more sophisticated programming language than MUD. A MOO lets users build things in a simulated environment by creating objects that are linked to a parent object. MUDs and MOOs are interactive systems suited to the construction of text-based adventure games and conferencing systems. The most common use, however, is multi-participant, virtual reality adventure games with players from all over the world.

Bulletin Boards

Usenet newsgroups are examples of bulletin boards (BBS). BBSs are places where people with similar interests can exchange information and share their thoughts with others without being logged on at the same time. Additionally, users can upload and download files and make announcements.

Telnet Software

If you are using Windows 95 the Telnet application is built in, but if you are using another platform you will need to visit a Web site and download the Telnet appliction.

The reason why the Telnet application is required and not included with Netscape Navigator or Internet Explorer is that Web browsers and Telnet work the Internet in different ways.

If you are using Netscape Naviagator you will need to follow these steps before you can begin a Telnet session.

> ## NOTE
>
> You will need to have a copy of the Telnet application before you begin a Telnet session.
>
> Telnet programs are usually included with your TCP/IP software from your Internet provider. If you do not have a Telnet client program visit one of the Web software sites such as Tucows (**http://www.tucows.com**) or Jumbo (**http://www.jumbo.com**).

Using the Telnet Application with Netscape Navigator

STEP 1

Open Netscape Navigator.

STEP 2

Go to the **Options** pull-down menu and select **General Preferences**.

STEP 3

Click the **Apps** tab.

STEP 4

Enter the name of the Telnet application in the Telnet application field. If you are using Windows 95 just type "telnet."

STEP 5

Click on the **Browse** button to find where it is located on your computer.

STEP 6

When you have found where the Telnet application resides on your hard drive, click O.K.

NOW YOU ARE READY FOR A TELNET SESSION.

GUIDED TOUR
Traveling to a Telnet Site

In this guided tour you will

- travel to the Smithsonian Institute's Telnet site.
- learn how to find resources at a Telnet site.

STEP 1

Type in this URL for the Smithsonian   **telnet://siris.si.edu**

> # NOTE
>
> To visit a Telnet site using a browser, type in the URL information. The format will be **telnet://address**

FIGURE 4.14
Smithsonian Welcome screen

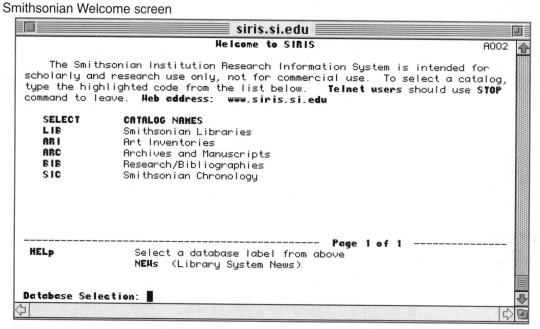

```
╔══════════════════════════ siris.si.edu ══════════════════════════╗
                      Welcome to SIRIS                        A002  ▲

     The Smithsonian Institution Research Information System is intended for
  scholarly and research use only, not for commercial use.  To select a catalog,
  type the highlighted code from the list below.  Telnet users should use STOP
  command to leave.  Web address:  www.siris.si.edu

        SELECT         CATALOG NAMES
        LIB            Smithsonian Libraries
        ARI            Art Inventories
        ARC            Archives and Manuscripts
        BIB            Research/Bibliographies
        SIC            Smithsonian Chronology




  --------------------------------------------------- Page 1 of 1 ----------------
  HELp                 Select a database label from above
                       NEWs  (Library System News)


  Database Selection: █
```

Select the Art Inventories Catalog and type in the code ARI next to Database Selection.

Notice that you no longer have hyperlinks for navigation. Read all the information to find the command you must use for navigating at the site. This screen informs visitors to select the Smithsonian archive that they would like to visit.

FIGURE 4.15

Art Inventories Catalog, Smithsonian

```
------------------------------------------------------------------
               WELCOME TO THE ART INVENTORIES CATALOG
The database, maintained by the National Museum of American Art, contains over
300,000 records describing American paintings and sculpture.  This information
is compiled from reports supplied by museums, historical societies, special
survey projects, public art programs, published catalogs, and private
collectors.  Reports are recorded as given and are not certified as accurate
or complete.  Inclusion of a painting or sculpture in the database does not
imply a recommendation of its aesthetic merit, historic significance, or
authenticity.
Copyright 1994 Smithsonian Institution.  Data may be used solely for non-
commercial study or research purposes.  Commercial use of information obtained
through the Inventories is prohibited without the express written consent of
the Smithsonian Institution.
For more information on the Art Inventories, press ENTER .
Type CHOOSE  to switch to other catalogs on SIRIS.
-----------------------------------------------   + Page 1 of 4  ------------
STArt over        Enter search command                <F8>  FORward page
                  NEWs

NEXT COMMAND: █
```

Read the Welcome screen for information on what command to enter to continue your exploration. In this case, we press the ENTER key.6

FIGURE 4.16

The Art Inventories Catalog

```
                    THE ART INVENTORIES CATALOG
The Art Inventories database contains over 300,000 records from two ongoing
projects -- The Inventory of American Paintings Executed before 1914 and
the Inventory of American Sculpture.   You may limit your search to a
specific Inventory, or search both Inventories together.

To choose one of the inventory catalogs, type SET CAT .
To search both inventory catalogs together, use a command from list below.
              COMMAND:         TO SEARCH BY:
                 A=            Artist
                 T=            Title
                 S=            Subject
                 K=            Keyword
                 C=            Record number
For more information on searching commands, press ENTER.
-----------------------------------------------   + Page 2 of 4  ------------
STArt over        Enter search command                <F8>  FORward page
                  NEWs                                 <F7>  BACK page
```

STEP 4

Search for information on Native Americans. The screen indicates to type in the command K=name of keyword. In this case we type K=native americans.

FIGURE 4.17

The result searching for Native Americans

```
Search Request: K=NATIVE AMERICANS                    ART INVENTORIES
Search Results: 23 Entries Found                         Keyword Index
---------------------------------------------------------------------
      DATE  TITLE:                                    AUTHOR:
   1  1993  Touching Souls <3-dimen>                  Kaufman, Mico
   2  1992  Intersect <3-dimen>                       Canneto, Stephen
   3  1992  River Scenes at the Tennessee Aq <3-dimen> Nivola, Claire
   4  1989  Buffalo Dance <3-dimen>                   Goodacre, Glenna
   5  1988  Maui Pohaku Loa <3-dimen>                 Toth, Peter
   6  1987  Prelude <3-dimen>                         Cunningham, Robert
   7  1985  The Immigrants <3-dimen>                  Hopen, W. D
   8  1985  The Future <3-dimen>                      Houser, Allan
   9  1982  Bodark Ark <3-dimen>                      Puryear, Martin
  10  1981  Trail of Tears <3-dimen>                  Toth, Peter
  11  1976  Native American <3-dimen>                 Toth, Peter
  12  1973  Cherokee Chieftain <3-dimen>              Toth, Peter
  13  1957  Ten O'Clock Line Monument <3-dimen>       Hollis, Frederick L
  14  1935  Hoover Dam Elevator Tower Relief <3-dimen> Hansen, Oskar J. W
---------------------------------------------- CONTINUED on next page ----
STARt over          Type number to display record     <F8>  FORward page
HELp                MARK
OTHer options

NEXT COMMAND: ▮
```

STEP 5

To find information on the first title, type the number 1.

FIGURE 4.18

Information on Touching Souls

```
Search Request: K=NATIVE AMERICANS                    ART INVENTORIES
ARTWORK -Record 1 of 23 Entries Found                    Brief View
---------------------------------------------------------------------
ARTIST:       Kaufman, Mico, 1924-     , sculptor.
TITLE:        Touching Souls, (sculpture).
DATE:         Dedicated June 13, 1993.
MEDIUM:       Sculpture: bronze; Base: concrete.
DIMEN:        Sculpture: approx. H. 27 in. x W. 8 ft. 3 in.; Base: ranges
                 from: H. 7 1/2 in. to H. 3 in. x Diam. 9 ft. 9 in.
OWNER (outdoor site):
              Tewksbury United Methodist Church, South Street, Tewksbury,
                 Massachusetts 01876
---------------------------------------------------------------------
FILE:                RECORD NUMBERS:        CATALOGED
Sculpture Inventory  MA000015              Circ. info not available
(Non-Circulating)

------------------------------------------- Page 1 of 1 ---------------
STARt over          LONg view              <F6>  NEXt record
HELp                INDex
OTHer options       MARK
```

EXPEDITION EXPERIENCE

Traveling via Telnet

Now that you have taken a Guided Tour using Telnet you are ready to being to explore Telnet resources.

The following Web sites have links to Telnet sites.
>http://www.nova.edu/Inter-Links/start.html
>http://www.magna.com.au/bdgtti/bdg_92.html#SEC95

Bulletin Boards

>SBI LINKS TO BULLETIN BOARDS
>http://dkeep.com/sbi.htm

>GUIDE TO SELECT BBSS ON THE INTERNET
>http://dkeep.com/sbi.htm

Chats

>WEBCHAT BROADCASTING SYSTEM
>http://wbs.net

>HOTWIRED
>http://www.hotwired.com

>THE PALACE
>http:www.thepalace.com

>GLOBE
>http://globe1.csuglab.cornell.edu/global/homepage.html

Free-Nets

>COMMUNITY COMPUTER NETWORKS AND FREE-NETS
>http://freenet.victoria.bc.ca/freenets.html

>INTERNATIONAL FREE-NET COMMUNITY LISTING
>This page is a listing of Free-Nets and Community Nets around the world.
>http://www.uwec.edu/Info/Freenets/

>GOPHER LINKS TO FREE-NETS
>gopher://info.asu.edu:70/11/other/freenets

MOOs and MUDs

>http://www.butterfly.net/~pyro/moo_page.html
>http://www.bushnet.qld.edu.au/~jay/moo/
>http://www.io.com/~combs/htmls/moo.html

Diversity University

>http://www.academic.marist.edu/duwww.htm
>telnet://moo.du.org:8888

Lambda MOO

>telnet://lambda.parc.xerox.com:8888/

Internet Research

CHAPTER CONTENTS

Internet Research Tools

Search Directories

Search Engines

Internet Collections

Reference Collections

Virtual Libraries

Using Internet Sources for Research

INTERNET RESEARCH

Searching for information is like a treasure hunt. Unless a researcher has knowledge of all the resources and tools available, then the search for useful information may be a time consuming and frustrating process. In this chapter you will learn about resources on the Internet that will facilitate the search for information of interest to you, your career, and your field of study. Careful thought about the desired knowledge sought, where the best place is to begin to look for that knowledge, and extensive exploring and searching in layers of Web links, usually provides the desired reward—the gold nugget Web site.

The tools that you will learn about and use to conduct research include

- search directories
- search engines
- Internet collections
- Reference resources
- Virtual libraries

You will also learn

- how to evaluate information you find on the Internet as to its content validity;
- how to record Internet information sources; and
- how to reference electronic media.

INTERNET RESEARCH TOOLS

The Internet contains many tools that speed the search for information and resources. Research tools called "search directories" and "search engines" are extremely helpful.

Search Directories

Search directories are essentially descriptive subject indexes of Web sites. They also have searching options. When you connect to their page, you will find a query box for entering keywords. The search engine at these sites searches only for keyword matches in the directories' databases. Directories are excellent places to begin your research.

Search Engines

Search engines are different from search directories in that they search World Wide Web sites, Usenet newsgroups, and other Internet resources to find matches to your descriptor keywords. Many search engines also rank the results according to a degree of relevancy. Most search engines provide options for advanced searching to refine your search.

Basic Guidelines for Becoming a Cybersleuth

Search directories and search engines are marvelous tools to help you find information on the Internet. Search directories are often the best places to begin a search, as they frequently yield more relevant returns on a topic than a search engine, which may produce a high proportion of irrelevant information.

Search engines can be frustrating to use and may not be the best Internet resources to begin with, often supply thousands of links on your keyword search. Although these search tools have advanced options for refining and limiting a search, researchers may discover that finding the desired information is not easy and that search results frequently offer a high percentage of irrelevant and useless information. For example, using a search engine for a search with the keywords business management returned 500,000 occurrences (hits) of the words "business" and "management." Many of the occurrences of these words were in job listings or companies that were advertising their services. This is why search directories are frequently an excellent resource to begin with when starting your research. The search directory may lead you to the goldmine collection of electronic resources you are searching for.

Research Guidelines

When researching information on the Internet, it is essential that you use several search tools. The basic approach to finding information involves the following steps:

STEP 1

Use the following search directories to search for information under a related topic or category.

YAHOO
http://www.yahoo.com

EXCITE
http://www.excite.com

GALAXY
http://galaxy.einet.net/galaxy.html

MAGELLAN
http://magellan.mckinley.com

INFOSEEK
http://guide.infoseek.com

Explore the links that seem relevant to your topic, and make bookmarks of the ones you would like to investigate further. Look for one site that has a large collection of links on your topic. This is the resource goldmine that you are looking for.

STEP 2

Use search engines to further research your topic by determining one or more descriptive words (keywords) for the subject. Enter your keywords into the search dialog box.

STEP 3

Determine how specific you want your search to be. Do you want it to be broad or narrow? Use available options to refine or limit your search. Some search engines permit the use of Boolean operators (phrases or words such as "AND," " OR," and "NOT" that restrict a search). Others provide HELP for refining searches, and some have pull-down menus or selections to be checked for options.

STEP 4

Submit your query.

STEP 5

Review your list of hits (a search return based on a keyword).

STEP 6

Adjust your search based on the information returned. Did you receive too much information and need to narrow your search? Did you receive too little or no information and need to broaden your keywords?

STEP 7

Use several search directories and search engines for your research. No one search tool will provide a complete resource list.

Search Directories

Yahoo

Yahoo is one of the most popular search tools on the Internet and is an excellent place to begin your search. Although Yahoo is more accurately described as a search directory, this Web site has an excellent database with search options available. There are two ways to find information using Yahoo: search through the subject directory, or use the built-in search engine.

Yahoo can be accessed from your browser's Search button or by entering this URL:
http://www.yahoo.com.

Follow these steps to use Yahoo to search for information:

STEP 1

Begin by browsing the subject directory. For example, if you were searching for information on environmental online resources you would first select the Society and Culture directory, then follow the Environment and Nature category. Explore categories and see if the information you are searching for can be found under the categories (see Fig. 5.1).

STEP 2

Yahoo's search engine can also be used to find information. Enter a descriptive keyword for your subject, one that uniquely identifies or describes what you are looking for. It is often helpful to do a broad search first, though results often present the need to change descriptive keywords or to refine your query.

Perhaps you are looking for information on recycling and were not able to find it easily under one of the Environment categories. Enter the keyword, in this case recycling, in Yahoo's query box (see Fig. 5.1).

STEP 3

Click on the Search button and review your query results (see Fig. 5.2).

FIGURE 5.1

Yahoo's Environment and Nature subject index search form in which the keyword recycling has been entered

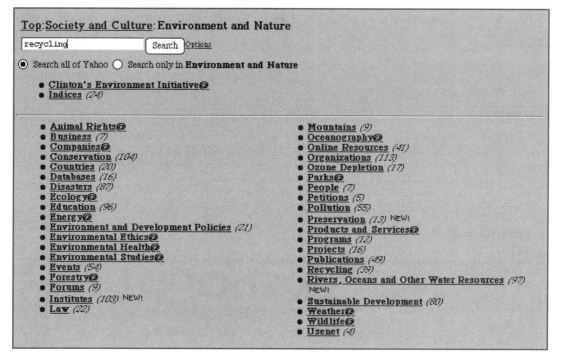

Top:Society and Culture:Environment and Nature

recycling | Search | Options

○ Search all of Yahoo ○ Search only in **Environment and Nature**

- **Clinton's Environment Initiative@**
- **Indices** *(24)*

- **Animal Rights@**
- **Business** *(7)*
- **Companies@**
- **Conservation** *(104)*
- **Countries** *(20)*
- **Databases** *(16)*
- **Disasters** *(87)*
- **Ecology@**
- **Education** *(96)*
- **Energy@**
- **Environment and Development Policies** *(21)*
- **Environmental Ethics@**
- **Environmental Health@**
- **Environmental Studies@**
- **Events** *(54)*
- **Forestry@**
- **Forums** *(9)*
- **Institutes** *(103)* NEW!
- **Law** *(22)*

- **Mountains** *(9)*
- **Oceanography@**
- **Online Resources** *(41)*
- **Organizations** *(113)*
- **Ozone Depletion** *(17)*
- **Parks@**
- **People** *(7)*
- **Petitions** *(5)*
- **Pollution** *(55)*
- **Preservation** *(13)* NEW!
- **Products and Services@**
- **Programs** *(12)*
- **Projects** *(16)*
- **Publications** *(49)*
- **Recycling** *(39)*
- **Rivers, Oceans and Other Water Resources** *(97)* NEW!
- **Sustainable Development** *(80)*
- **Weather@**
- **Wildlife@**
- **Usenet** *(4)*

FIGURE 5.2

Yahoo search results from the keyword recycling

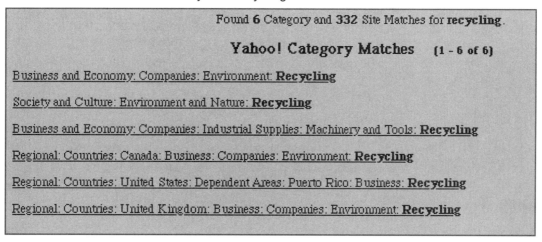

Found 6 Category and 332 Site Matches for **recycling**.

Yahoo! Category Matches [1 - 6 of 6]

Business and Economy: Companies: Environment: **Recycling**

Society and Culture: Environment and Nature: **Recycling**

Business and Economy: Companies: Industrial Supplies: Machinery and Tools: **Recycling**

Regional: Countries: Canada: Business: Companies: Environment: **Recycling**

Regional: Countries: United States: Dependent Areas: Puerto Rico: Business: **Recycling**

Regional: Countries: United Kingdom: Business: Companies: Environment: **Recycling**

STEP 4

You may now want to refine your search. Most search engines have options for advanced searching using Boolean logic or more carefully constructed database queries. Review the search page for **Options** or **Advanced Options**. When using Yahoo, click on the **Options** button.

If you are using two or more keywords, do you want Yahoo to look for either word (Boolean OR), both keywords (Boolean AND), or all words as a single string? For example, to refine your recycling search for information only on commercial recycling select Boolean and because you want to find resources that contain the words "commercial" and "recycling" in their titles (see Fig. 5.3). Otherwise the search would be too broad and would find all resources that contained any of the keywords "commercial" or "recycling."

TIP

Yahoo suggests putting a phrase in quotes, such as "commercial recycling."

FIGURE 5.3
Yahoo Options for refining a search

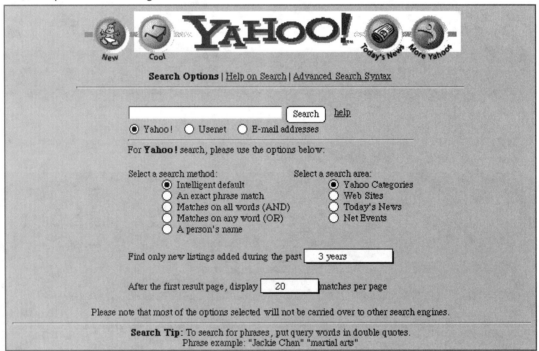

STEP 5

Further limit or expand your search by selecting a search method, search area (Yahoo categories, Web sites, Today's News, or Net Events), a period of time for the listing to have occurred, and the number of results returned per page.

STEP 6

Submit your query.

STEP 7

Review your return list of hits and adjust your search again if necessary.

STEP 8

Review your return list for other descriptive words that have been used when summarizing search results. For example, when using the keyword "recycling," search result summaries produced other important descriptive words such as "recycling consumer," "pollution," or "waste management in the home."

STEP 9

Conduct a search using other descriptive words.

Other Search Directories

Explore the subject directories listed below. You will find that their subject categories vary; most have advanced search options for refining your search and several (Infoseek and Excite) have powerful search engines built-in.

> MAGELLAN
> http://magellan.mckinley.com
>
> GALAXY
> http://galaxy.einet.net/galaxy.html
>
> EXCITE
> http://www.excite.com
>
> INFOSEEK
> http://guide.infoseek.com

FIGURE 5.4
Home page for Infoseek showing search directory

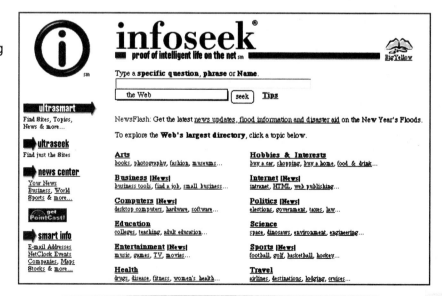

Notice the option in Figure 5.4 for connecting to its powerful search engine—Infoseek Ultra.

Other Subject-Oriented Directories

In addition to search directories, subject-oriented directories are excellent sources to find information on a topic. These directories are usually compiled by individuals rather than a search service such as Yahoo.

THE ARGUS CLEARINGHOUSE

Links to Internet directories, search tools, and virtual libraries. Select the link to The Argus Clearinghouse and you will connect to a subject-oriented research library.
http://www.clearinghouse.net/searching/find.html

ENCYBERPEDIA

The HOTTEST encyclopedia from cyberspace designed to help you find good stuff in the jungle of over two million Web Sites.
http://www.encyberpedia.com/ency.htm#menu
http://www.encyberpedia.com/ency.htm

INTER-LINKS

Inter-Links was created and maintained by Rob Kabacoff from Nova Southeastern University. Internet resources are offered in broad categories such as topical resources, fun and games, news and weather, library resources, and reference resources.
http://www.nova.edu/Inter-Links

THE INTERNET SERVICES LIST

An impressive collection of Internet resources organized in over 80 categories. This popular site is an excellent place to begin a search.
http://www.spectracom.com/islist

LIBRARY OF CONGRESS

A large and impressive collections of resources including research tools and library services to assist you with finding information.
http://lcweb.loc.gov

LOOKSMART

Don't let this simplistic interface turn you away from exploring this site that has valuable subject-oriented resources.
http://mulwala.looksmart.com

WORLD WIDE WEB VIRTUAL LIBRARY

A MUST VISIT search resource for finding Internet resources. A go to the top of the bookmark list site.
http://www.w3.org/pub/DataSources/bySubject/Overview.html

Search Engines

Search engines require a keyword(s) or phrase that is descriptive of the information you are looking for. Begin by listing keywords or phrases on your topic. When you connect to a search engine look for its Search Tips or Advanced Search Options to help you conduct a more efficient and effective search. Taking this step will save time and help to prevent information overload frustration.

Excite

Excite is one of the most widely used search engines offering a full range of services (see Fig. 5.5). Excite searches scan Web pages and Usenet newsgroups for keyword matches and creates summaries of each match. Excite also has a Web directory organized by category.

FIGURE 5.5
Excite Web page displaying services

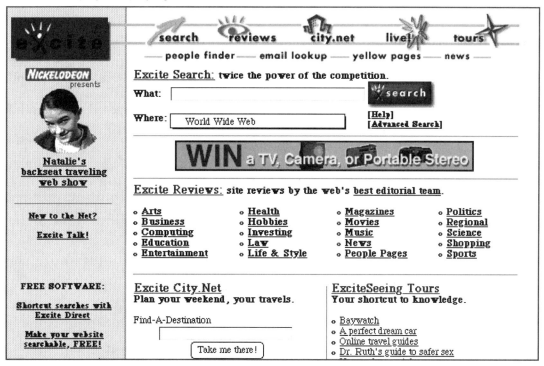

Searching With Excite

STEP 1

Type a word or phrase that fits your information need. Be as specific as you can, using words that uniquely relate to the information you are looking for, not simply general descriptive words. For example, if you are looking for information on health and healing outside of traditional medicine you might begin by using keywords such as *holistic health*. When using more than one word, read the Help information to find the best way to enter multiple words or a phrase.

STEP 2

If the search result does not contain the information you are looking for, or if the returns have too much irrelevant information, use the Advanced Search option (as shown in Fig. 5.6).

STEP 3

Advanced features include the use of a plus sign (+) in front of a search word to ensure that all the returns contain that word. Use a minus sign (-) in front of a search word and Excite will make sure that no documents contain the word. Excite also supports the use of Boolean operators (AND, OR, NOT). Search engines also may suggest the use of quotation marks around the words or phrase.

STEP 4

Excite lists 10 search results at a time in decreasing order of confidence. Each result lists a title, a URL, and a brief summary of the document. The percentage to the left of the return is the confidence rating (Fig.5.7), with 100% being the highest confidence rating attainable. To see the next listing of documents related to your phrase or keywords, click the "next documents" button. Click the "sort by site" button to view the Web sites that have the most pages relevant to your search.

FIGURE 5.6
Search query for holistic health

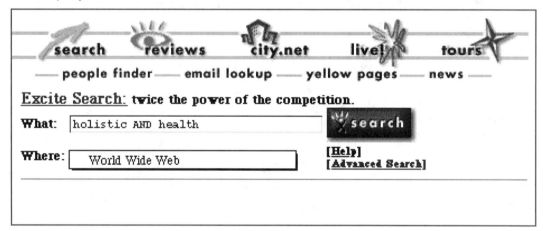

FIGURE 5.7
Search results with a percentage of confidence rating for finding relevant information

---

Excite Search found **16138** document(s) about : **holistic AND health**.
Documents **1–10** sorted by **Relevance**. Sort by Site.

84% About the American Holistic Medical Asso... [More Like This]
URL: http://www.doubleclickd.com:80/about_ahma.html
Summary: Later, associate membership was expanded to include all state-licensed holistically oriented practitioners, such as chiropractors, naturopaths, nurses, psychologists, dentists, etc. The mission of the AHMA is to support physicians in their evolving personal and professional development and to promote an art and science of health care which acknowledges all aspects of the individual, the.

82% Holistic Healing Web Page [More Like This]
URL: http://www.tiac.net:80/users/mgold/health.html
Summary: The holistic health-related information presented on this WWW page is not meant as medical advice. Environmental Issues Relating to Human & Planetary Health.

81% HOLISTIC CONCEPTS OF HEALTH AND DISEASE ... [More Like This]
URL: http://www.med.auth.gr:80/~karanik/english/vet/holist6.htm
Summary: HOLISTIC CONCEPTS OF HEALTH AND DISEASE #6. HOLISTIC CONCEPTS OF HEALTH AND DISEASE Answers.

81% Holistic Health Link [More Like This]
URL: http://www.kdcol.com:80/~daniel/prolink.htm
Summary: ....Holistic Health Services Holistic Health Care Practitioners Holistic Health Care Manufacturers, Distributors, and Suppliers. [Natural Connection] [Holistic Health Care] [Health Food Store] [Books] [E-Mail].

81% The Fosters: Holistic Health and Native ... [More Like This]
URL: http://www.blvl.igs.net:80/~bfoster/
Summary: The Fosters: Holistic Health and Native Herbs. A Homepage for Kristina and Bob Foster.

Infoseek

Infoseek provides search and browse capabilities of Web pages, Usenet newsgroups, FTP, and Gopher sites. You can even sign up for personalized news. Infoseek offers two free services: Infoseek Guide and Infoseek Ultra. Of all the search engines, Infoseek Ultra seems to find the highest number of relevant matches to keywords.

Infoseek Guide (**http://guide.infoseek.com**) is one of Infoseek's earliest services introduced in early 1996. At that time, the company also offered a subscription-based service, Infoseek Professional. Infoseek Guide integrates a browsable directory of Internet resources located on World Wide Web sites, Usenet newsgroups, and other popular Internet resource sites. Users can choose to use the search engine and enter keywords or phrases, or browse the navigational directories.

Infoseek Ultra (**http://ultra.infoseek.com**), under development for two years at Infoseek and introduced in the fall of 1996, utilizes the next generation of search technology. Ultra promises new levels of speed, accuracy, and currency unmatched by other search technologies.

Features of Infoseek Ultra include the following:

- the use of a highly accurate relevance ranking algorithm that is intended to provide highly relevant search returns;
- the ability to recognize proper names and phrases;
- permits case sensitive queries, full and partial phrase queries, and name variants;
- fast search returns for complex queries or during periods of high usage;
- an index of over 80 million URLs, with indexing of the text of over 50 million; and
- frequent updates of its Web pages' index to help ensure that you do not get a dead or obsolete link when you click on a search return URL.

FIGURE 5.8
Infoseek Ultra showing a search for more than one keyword

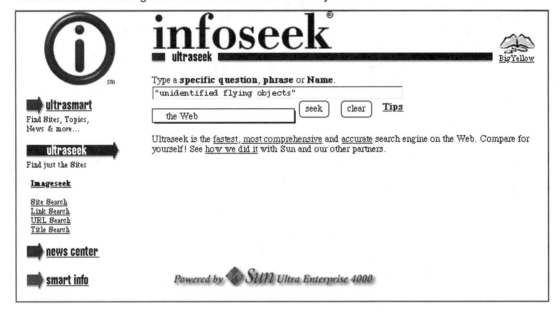

Ultra recommends using double quotes around words that must appear next to each other (see Fig. 5.8). Check the Tips link for more information on how to do efficient searches with Ultra.

Other Search Engines

There are many search engines to help you find information. You will need to use each of them at least several times before you can select the ones that best meet your needs. Listed below are additional search engines to explore.

ALTA VISTA

Alta Vista by Digital is an excellent search engine with one of the largest Web-search databases. http://altavista.digital.com

IMAGE SURFER

Image Surfer differs from most search tools in that it focuses on finding images on the Web. http://isurf.interpix.com

LYCOS

Lycos is one of the older search tools, has recently expanded its services with new search capabilities for images and sounds, information on cities, road maps, companies online, stock quotes, and an excellent link to the top five percent Web sites. Lycos (fig. 5.9) moves to the top of the bookmark list.

http://www.lycos.com

FIGURE 5.9
Lycos Home Page

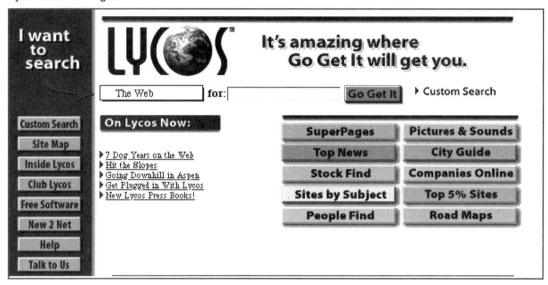

HOTBOT

HotBot is a new and very HOT search tool.
http://www.hotbot.com

INKTOMI

Inktomi is a search engine from Berkeley.
http://inktomi.berkeley.com

OPEN TEXT

Open Text has one of the most comprehensive collections of search tools and is one of the best designed search engines on the Internet.
http://www.opentext.com

WIRED SOURCE

Wired Sourcs has acollection of search engines to use for your research.
http://www.wiredsource.com/wiredsource

Internet Collections

Internet collections, compiled by an individual or group of individuals, are often goldmine resources for your research. One collection may give you all the Internet resources that you will need on a particular topic. For example, one excellent collection of business resources—Madalyn— has been compiled under a University of Delaware MBA program. Madalyn **(http://www.udel.edu/alex/mba/main/netdir2.html)** has links to accounting, corporate information, economics, entrepreneurship, ethics, finance, international business, management, marketing, quality, and more. Internet collections are your goldmine resources. If you are lucky you may be able to find your goldmine using a search directory. Listed below are some excellent collections and directories to explore.

Archeology

ARCHEOLOGY
http://www.cr.nps.gov/archeo.html
The National Park Service Archeology and Ethnography program is a leading authority on archeological and cultural resources in the United States. This site has a link to the National Archeological Database—a computerized communications network for the archeological and historical preservation community.

Art Collections

ART HOTLIST
http://sln.fi.edu/tfi/hotlists/art.html
A collection of links to art galleries, museums, and artists.

ART SOURCE
http://www.uky.edu/Artsource/artsourcehome.html
This site offers a collection on art and architecture resources on the Net including original materials submitted by librarians, artists, and art historians. For electronic exhibitions select the link to Exhibitions.

INTERNET ART RESOURCES
http://artresources.com
A complete guide to the visual arts with links to galleries, museums (over 1100 listed worldwide), art schools, artists, and much more.

Business Collections

ALL BUSINESS NETWORK
http://www.all-biz.com
The All Business Network site (Fig. 510) has a pull-down menu of business topics. Select a topic you are researching, and click the Find It button. You will then be given a list of descriptive links on the subject to explore.

FIGURE 5.10
Home page for All Business Network

GTE SUPERSITE
http://superpages.gte.net
An excellent business resource with two research services: Yellow Pages and Business Web Site Directory. The Yellow Pages have a search tool to help you find comprehensive business information from more than 11 million listings found in over 5,000 Yellow Pages directories from virtually every city in the United States. The Business Web Site Directory features links to 60,000 plus business Web sites worldwide.

I.O.M.A
http://www.ioma.com/ioma/direct.html
Links to business resources, including financial management, legal resources, small business, human resources, and Internet marketing.

MADALYN
http://www.udel.edu/alex/mba/main/netdir2.html
Maintained by the University of Delaware's MBA program, Madalyn has links to accounting,

corporate information, economics, entrepreneurship, ethics, finance, international business, management, marketing, and quality resources.

Criminal Justice

DR. CECIL GREEK'S CRIMINAL JUSTICE LINKS

http://www.stpt.usf.edu/~greek/cj.html
This award-winning Web site has one the most comprehensive listings of criminal justice resources on the Internet.

JUSTICE FOR ALL

http://www.hotsites.net/fightback/jfa
A comprehensive Web site with links to resources for victims of crime.

JUSTICE INFORMATION CENTER (NCJRS)

http://www.ncjrs.org
The National Criminal Justice Reference Service is one of the most extensive sources of information on criminal and juvenile justice in the world, providing services to an international community of policymakers and professionals. This site has many excellent links to criminal justice resources.

Environmental Collections

AMAZING ENVIRONMENTAL WEB DIRECTORY

http://www.webdirectory.com
The directory is a GOLDMINE of online environmental resources.

ENVIROLINK

http://www.envirolink.org
A virtual community that unites hundreds of environmental organizations and volunteers around the world and is dedicated to providing the most comprehensive, up-to-date environmental resources.

ENVIRONMENTAL SITES ON THE INTERNET

http://www.lib.kth.se/~lg/eindex.htm
This is the GOLDMINE site for environmental resources on the Internet. It is sponsored by the Royal Institute of Technology in Sweden. In June 1996 it was selected as the Best Comprehensive Environmental Directory by CESSE (Center for Economic and Social Studies for the Environment), Brussels, Belgium.

INDIGENOUS PEOPLES RESOURCES

http://www.halcyon.com/FWDP/othernet.html
The Internet has many other sources of information regarding indigenous peoples. This is an AWESOME list of resources.

Geography

CIA WORLD FACT BOOK

http://www.odci.gov/cia/publications/95fact/index.html

Published by the Central Intelligence Agency (CIA), The World Fact Book has a subject index for researching facts about countries.

GEOGRAPHIC NAME SERVER
http://www.mit.edu:8001/geo
Type the name of a place you want to look up and this search tool will get the information.

GEOGRAPHY RESOURCES
http://www.ipl.org/ref/RR/GEN/geography-rr.html
The Internet Public Library has a wonderful collection of geography links.

THE GREAT GLOBE GALLERY
http://hum.amu.edu.pl/~zbzw/glob/glob1.htm
This AWESOME site has links to every type of map or globe imaginable.

NATIONAL GEOGRAPHIC
http://www.nationalgeographic.com
Use the boarding pass to National Geographic's adventure travel online.

WORLD WIDE WEB VIRTUAL LIBRARY—GEOGRAPHY
http://www.icomos.org/WWW_VL_Geography.html
A collection of geography resources.

Government

FEDERAL GOVERNMENT AGENCIES
http://www.lib.lsu.edu/gov/fedgov.html
A collection of over 200 government sites.

GOVERNMENT AGENCY LINKS
http://www.fjc.gov/govlinks.html
Links to the federal courts and other government agencies.

GOVERNMENT DOCUMENT LINKS
http://thorplus.lib.purdue.edu/reference/gov.html
Purdue University has an impressive collection of online U.S. Government documents.

LIBRARY OF CONGRESS
http://www.loc.gov
Access The Library of Congress's databases, historical collections, exhibitions, publications, links to other electronic libraries, information on copyright, and much more.

PRESIDENT
http://sunsite.unc.edu/lia/president
A Web site with a collection of presidential resources and an exhibit on the First Ladies of the United States.

TEXAS A&MS WHITE HOUSE ARCHIVES
http://www.tamu.edu/whitehouse
A collection of information about the White House and those who have resided there dating back to 1992.

THE WHITE HOUSE
http://www1.whitehouse.gov/WH/Welcome.html
Visit this site and explore the virtual library for a collection of Presidential documents, speeches, and photos.

History

THE AMERICAN CIVIL WAR HOME PAGE
http://funnelweb.utcc.utk.edu/~hoemann/warweb.html
An AWESOME collection of Civil War resources.

THE ANCIENT WORLDS META INDEX
http://atlantic.evsc.virginia.edu/julia/AW/meta.html
A GOLDMINE of resources on the ancient world.

BYZANTINE & MEDIEVAL STUDIES
http://www.fordham.edu/halsall/med/medweb.html
Anything you ever wanted to know about Byzantine and Medieval history can probably be found in this amazing collection.

FROM REVOLUTION TO RECONSTRUCTION
http://www.let.rug.nl
This award-winning site has original source materials on American history from the colonial period until modern times.

GATEWAY TO WORLD HISTORY
http://neal.ctstateu.edu/history/world_history/world_history.html
This site features a collection of history archives and historical resources on the Internet.

Literature

AUTHOR'S PEN
http://www.books.com/scripts/authors.exe
A large collection of links with comprehensive resources to more than 625 authors. Author areas contain one or more home pages plus interviews, biographies, and complete bibliographies.

THE COMPLETE WORKS OF WILLIAM SHAKESPEARE
http://the-tech.mit.edu/Shakespeare/works.html
This site not only has an electronic version for each work of Shakespeare but also links to related resources and discussion forums.

THE GUTENBERG PROJECT
ftp://mrcnext.cso.uiuc.edu
http://www.w3.org/pub/DataSources/bySubject/Literature/Gutenberg/Overview.html
http://www.cs.waikato.ac.nz/~nzdl/gutenberg/text/query.html
A collection of great works of English-language literature. Gutenberg's goal is to make 10,000 texts available online by the year 2001.

ULTIMATE BOOK LIST AND WRITER'S PAGE
http://www.acpl.lib.in.us/information_resources/ultimate_book_list.html
A collection of book-related sites on the Internet. The ULTIMATE!

WORLD WIDE WEB VIRTUAL LIBRARY OF LITERATURE RESOURCES
http://sunsite.unc.edu/ibic/guide.html
A collection of book-related resources on the Internet.

Mathematics

EINET MATH GUIDE
http://galaxy.einet.net/galaxy/Science/Mathematics.html
A collection of mathematic resources from the search directory EINet Galaxy.

MATH AND SCIENCE GATEWAY
http://www.tc.cornell.edu/Edu/MathSciGateway
This collection of math and science resources for students in grades 9-12 is maintained by Cornell University. Resources include astronomy, biology, chemistry, engineering, medicine, physics, meteorology, mathematics, earth, ocean, and environmental resources.

MATH PAGES
http://www.seanet.com/~ksbrown
This site contains over 300 articles on a variety of mathematical topics, including number theory, combinatorics, geometry, algebra, calculus, differential equations, probability, statistics, physics, and the history of mathematics.

MATH RESOURCES
http://forum.swarthmore.edu/math.topics.html
Selected math resources by subject. Math subjects are divided into K-12, College, and Advanced.

MATHEMATICS INFORMATION SERVERS
http://www.math.psu.edu/OtherMath.html
An impressive collection of worldwide math resources.

TREASURE TROVE OF MATHEMATICS
http://www.astro.virginia.edu/~eww6n/math/math0.html
Although this collection has been compiled by an individual who provides a disclaimer at the top of his home page, the alphabetical listings are impressive.

THE VIRTUAL MATHEMATICS CENTER
http://www-sci.lib.uci.edu/~martindale/GradMath.html
Martindale's award-winning graduate and undergraduate mathematical center has an impressive collection of math resources. DEFINITELY MUST EXPLORE site.

Music

CLASSICAL NET
http://www.classical.net
The site provides an extensive collection of classical music resources—over 2,000 in all—as well as more than 1,800 links to other interesting Web sites.

INTERNET MUSIC RESOURCES
http://www.music.indiana.edu/music_resources
A collection of Internet music resources from Indiana University.

YAHOO MUSIC RESOURCES
http://www.yahoo.com/Entertainment/Music
An extensive collection of music resources.

News

ELECTRONIC NEWSSTAND
http://www.image.dk/~knud-sor/en
A collection of news publications including newspapers, magazines, radio and television stations, money and economy, sports, weather, e-zines, and much more.

Science

ASTRONOMY LINKS FROM NASA
http://quest.arc.nasa.gov/lfs/other_sites.html
An AWESOME collection of astronomy links from NASA.

CHEMISTRY RESOURCES
http://www.rpi.edu/dept/chem/cheminfo/chemres.html
A collection of resources related to chemistry and associated fields.

EARTH PAGES
http://starsky.hitc.com/earth/earth.html
Earth Pages, sponsored by NASA, is a search and index tool to help navigate the Internet for data, information, and resources related to earth science.

EINET GALAXY
http://galaxy.einet.net/galaxy/Science.html
A collection of science and math resources.

GEOLOGICAL TIME MACHINE
http://www.ucmp.berkeley.edu/help/timeform.html
Hop into this virtual time machine and experience time travel from the very early Precambrian to Quaternary present day.

INFOSEEK SCIENCE
http://guide.infoseek.com/Science
Infoseek's collection of science resources.

SCIENCE HOBBYIST
http://www.eskimo.com/~billb
This COOL site is an example of how individuals can contribute valuable information for the global universe. There are many unusual places to explore. A DEFINITELY MUST VISIT site.

SCIENCE TABLES AND DATABASES
http://www-sci.lib.uci.edu/~martindale/Ref3.html
Another Martindale site with an AWESOME collection of science tables and database resources.

VIRTUAL ASTROPHYSICS AND SPACE CENTER
http://www-sci.lib.uci.edu/~martindale/GradSpace.html
Martindale's award-winning graduate and undergraduate space center has an impressive collection of resources. DEFINITELY MUST EXPLORE site.

VIRTUAL BIOSCIENCE CENTER
http://www-sci.lib.uci.edu/~martindale/GradBioscience.html
A Martindale site with an exhaustive collection of bioscience resources including genetics, proteins, biology, botany, ecology, marine biology, genetics, and other resources such as Periodic Tables, dictionaries, and publications.

VIRTUAL CHEMISTRY CENTER
http://www-sci.lib.uci.edu/~martindale/GradChemistry.html
Martindale's graduate and undergraduate center for chemistry resources.

WINDOWS TO THE UNIVERSE
http://www.windows.umich.edu
An AWESOME astronomy collection from the University of Michigan is heavily designed with beautiful graphics. Although it seems to be designed for K-12, it is definitely worth a visit.

YAHOO SCIENCE RESOURCES
http://www.yahoo.com/Science
An extensive collection of science resources.

Reference Resources
The Internet is the newest and perhaps largest reference library. This rich source of information is available to Net users. Listed below are a few reference resources that you will find useful.

ASK AN EXPERT
http://njnie.dl.stevens-tech.edu/curriculum/aska.html
This Web site provides opportunities for you to interact with experts on topics such as computers, economics, literature, and science by sending questions via email.

BARTLETT'S FAMILIAR QUOTATIONS
http://www.ccc.columbia.edu/acis/bartleby/bartlett/index.html
Looking for a quote for your class presentation or paper? Connect to this Web site and search by keyword or choose from a list of people.

BRITANNICA ONLINE
http://www.eb.com
For a minimal fee you can subscribe to the Britannica Online and Merriam-Webster's Collegiate Dictionary. Some of the encyclopedia text is linked to Internet sites.

CIA WORLD FACT BOOK
http://www.odci.gov/cia/publications/95fact/index.html
Published by the Central Intelligence Agency (CIA), The World Fact Book has a subject index for researching facts about countries.

DICTIONARIES & THESAURI
http://www.arts.cuhk.hk/Ref.html#dt
A GOLDMINE collection of cyberdictionaries, thesauri, and other subject-oriented references.

ENCYBERPEDIA
http://www.encyberpedia.com/ency.htm
The HOTTEST encyclopedia from cyberspace designed to help you find good stuff in the jungle of over two million Web Sites.

MEGACONVERTER
http://www.megaconverter.com
MegaConverter.com is an ever-growing set of weights, measures, and units conversion/calculation modules.

MY VIRTUAL REFERENCE DESK
http://www.refdesk.com/main.html
Links to many excellent reference resources including a link to a subject directory of resources—My Virtual Encyclopedia (see Fig. 5.11).

FIGURE 5.11
My Virtual Reference Desk's link to a subject directory of resources

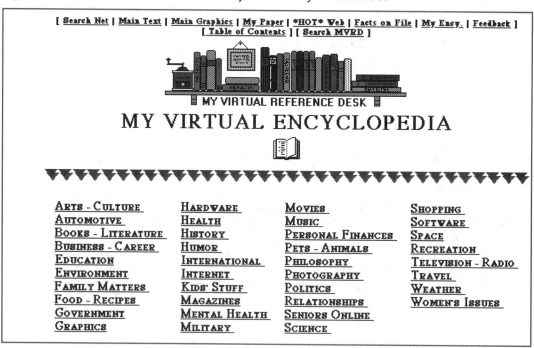

NOBLE CITIZENS OF PLANET EARTH
http://www.tiac.net/users/parallax
This dictionary contains biographical information on more than 18,000 people who have shaped our world from ancient times to the present day. Information contained in the dictionary includes birth and death years, professions, positions held, literary and artistic works, and other achievements.

ONELOOK DICTIONARIES
http://www.onelook.com
Type in a word and this search tool will look for multiple definitions from a variety of online dictionaries: computer/Internet dictionaries, science, medical, technological, business, sports, religion, acronym, and general.

REFERENCE CENTER
http://www.ipl.org/ref
This virtual library helps to make finding valuable information online easy. Click on a reference shelf and be linked to resources (see Fig. 5.12).

FIGURE 5.12
Online Reference Center Home Page

REFERENCE DESK
http://www-sci.lib.uci.edu/~martindale/Ref.html
This GOLDMINE site has won multiple awards for its SUPERB resource collection. A go to the top of the bookmark list site.

REFERENCE INDEXES
http://www.lib.lsu.edu/weblio.html
Links to online references such as dictionaries, library catalogs, newsstand, and subject collections.

REFERENCE SHELF
http://gort.ucsd.edu/ek/refshelf/refshelf.html
The University of California, San Diego, sponsors this collection of online reference resources.

RESEARCHPAPER.COM

http://www.researchpaper.com/directory.html

This award-winning online research tool offers an archive of thousands of magazines, newspapers, books, and photographs.

THE VIRTUAL REFERENCE DESK

http://thorplus.lib.purdue.edu/reference/index.html

Purdue University's links to an AWESOME list of valuable online resources.

WIRED SOURCE

http://www.wiredsource.com/wiredsource

A collection of search engines to use for your research.

Virtual Libraries

Libraries from around the world can be accessed for research. Some libraries require a Telnet connection and use of commands to find and retrieve information. Some libraries provide Help menus to assist you; others do not. Many libraries now have World Wide Web access, thus eliminating the need for commands to find information. Listed below are library resources on the Web.

ELECTRIC LIBRARY

http://www.elibrary.com

The Electric Library is a virtual library where you can conduct research online. Submit a question and a comprehensive search is launched of over 150 full-text newspapers, 800 full-text magazines, two international newswires, two thousand classic books, hundreds of maps, thousands of photographs, as well as major works of literature and art.

INTERNET PUBLIC LIBRARY

http://www.ipl.org

The Internet Public Library is the first public library of the Internet created by librarians committed to providing valuable services to that world. The goal of this project is to provide library services to the Internet community, to learn and teach what librarians have to contribute in a digital environment, to promote librarianship and the importance of libraries, and to share interesting ideas and techniques with other librarians. Their mission directs them to serve the public by finding, evaluating, selecting, organizing, describing, and creating quality information resources.

LIBCAT

http://www.metronet.lib.mn.us/lc/lc1.html

An AWESOME guide to library resources on the Internet.

LIBRARY OF CONGRESS

http://www.loc.gov

http://lcweb.loc.gov

Access the Library of Congress databases, historical collections, exhibitions, publications, links to other electronic libraries, information on copyright, and much more (see Fig. 5.13).

FIGURE 5.13
Library of Congress Home Page

LIBWEB
http://sunsite.Berkeley.EDU/Libweb
A collection of online libraries worldwide.

SMITHSONIAN INSTITUTION
http://www.si.edu/newstart.htm
A valuable online research service, the Smithsonian Institution features over one million resources. Click on the link to Resources and Tours to begin your journey.

WEBCHATS
http://library.usask.ca/hywebcat
Library catalogs on the Web.

USING INTERNET SOURCES FOR RESEARCH

Internet resources provide valuable information that you can use for class presentations, papers, research, dissertations, and theses. However, the Internet should never be your sole source of information but rather another resource that you use to find information on a topic. The Internet can access

- information collections and databases,
- government documents,
- exhibitions,
- research papers,
- publications,
- news,
- online educational events,
- the latest and most current information on a topic, and
- communication with experts on your topic.

In this section you will learn

- how to evaluate Internet information sources.
- how to record information sources.
- how to reference Internet sources.

Evaluating Internet Information

The Internet is analogous to a wilderness frontier that is wild and untamed. With an estimate of 20 to 50 million pages of data created from a variety of sources—individuals, businesses, corporations, non-profit organizations, schools, special interest groups, or illicit if not illegal sources—it is inherent that not all the information is accurate, unbiased, reputable, scientifically valid, or up-to-date. Unlike scholarly publications, there is no editorial board for most Internet information. It is therefore essential that you understand how to evaluate information you research on the Net.

How strict you are with your evaluation will depend on your purpose. For example, if you are writing a factual report, dissertation, thesis, or paper that others will rely on for accurate content, it will be essential that you are judicious in choosing what information will be reported from the Net.

The first thing you must do when using the Internet for your studies is to determine which resources to use. The following guidelines will assist you with evaluation.

Information Source

Where does the information come from—an individual, organization, educational institution, or other source? One way to quickly determine the source of the information is to look at the URL—Net site address. The first address protocol often will give you the source of the information—name of institution and domain. For example, an address such as **http://gort.ucsd.edu** tells the name of the institution—University of California, San Diego—and the **edu** ending indicates an educational institution. An educational institution has a good chance of being a reputable source. Other address endings that are highly likely to be reputable are **gov** for government or **mil** for military. Naturally, you will want to evaluate the information further. Just because the information is from an educational institution, government, or military source does not ensure that the content is factual and reliable.

Check to see if the document resides in an individual's personal Internet account or is part of the organization's official Internet site. This information can often be determined by looking at the URL address pathway.

Is the organization that publishes this document recognized in the field you are studying? Is the organization qualified to be an expert in this topic?

Authorship

Closely related to the information source is the reputation of the data and the reliability of its source. Information on an educational institution Web site may be compiled by a student or graduate student who is not as yet an authority on the subject and may enter in written errors or present incorrect data without realizing it. The content may not have been reviewed for accuracy and reliability.

Who is the author? Does the author have credentials to be an expert on the topic? Consider educational background, experience, and other published writings. Have you encountered the author's name in your reading or in bibliographies?

Does the Internet document furnish information on the author such as institutional affiliation, position, experience and credentials? If none of this is provided, is there an email address or a mailing address from which you can request biographical information? Correspond with the author to obtain more information about the source of his or her content.

Accuracy

Is the data accurate? Check to see if there is a reference for the information. Where does the information come from—a published research paper or report, historical document, news publication, or is it a personal viewpoint? Does the document include a bibliography? Does the author acknowledge related sources?

Although information may be written from a personal view point, don't invalidate it. Bias is to be expected especially if one is a participant in an event. If the writing seems biased, look for inconsistencies or incorrect thinking. Does the author acknowledge that his treatment of the subject is controversial? Are there political or ideological biases? Can you separate fact from opinion? Do any statements seem exaggerated or overly simplified? Has the author omitted any important details? Is the writer qualified to be authoritative?

One example of inaccuracy in Web writing is the use of the words *endangered species* when referring to animals that may in fact be only threatened or vulnerable. Many authors loosely use the words *endangered species.* To cross check this information, a reliable source such as the Convention on International Trade and Endangered Species (CITES) and the International Union for the Conservation of Nature (IUCN) must be used. These international organizations keep the working lists of which species are categorized as either extinct, endangered, threatened, vulnerable, indeterminate, or out of danger.

Verifiable

Can the data be verified? Does it appear to be well-researched? Does the author make generalizations without proof or validation? Always be thinking "Show me why or how." In some instances you may need to ask if the data has statistical validity—supported by statistical testing. Watch for errors or omissions.

When numbers or statistical information is reported, it is critical that the data be cross checked with a reliable publication source. For example, some Web factual data contain errors due to carelessness in copying and transposing numbers from a print version to a Web site. Reporting that 17,000 areas of rain forest are destroyed daily when the correct number is 700 acres is an inexcusable error in sloppy copy.

Consistency of data

Is the data consistent or does it reflect contradictions with other information on the topic? Are definitions used consistently throughout?

For example search for reputable Web sites on the rain forest led to the discovery of Public Broadcasting System (PBS) and the Rain Forest Action Network as excellent online references to cross check the consistency of data.

Quality

Is the text error free; is it well organized and grammatically correct? Check for the misspelling of names or carelessness and lack of attention to details in other areas. Information that contains these types of careless errors probably should not be relied on.

Is the tone scholarly, technical, factual, authoritative, or personal?

Currency

Is the information current and up-to-date? Does the document include a publication date or a date of copyright? Does it appear to be appropriate and relevant for today? Information that was reported in 1985 is probably not valid today. Look for the most current information unless currency is not an issue.

Bonus guidelines— other important suggestions

- ✍ Whenever possible, check online information against other sources.

- ✍ Never use information that you cannot verify.

- ✍ Question everything that you read. Learn to be critical and skeptical.

- ✍ Information found on the Internet should complement information from traditional research resources. Never use Internet information as your sole source of knowledge.

- ✍ "When in doubt, leave it out."

If you don't know where to find a reliable source to cross check your information, talk with a resource librarian, teacher, or professor. These individuals can be excellent resources for finding publications to verify your data. You can also call a reputable organization.

Recording Internet Information Sources

As you browse the Internet reviewing resources that are informative and valuable, it is important to make note of where these resources can be found. You will need this information for referencing your work. In your writing you may want to indicate to your readers that information has come from the Internet by making a reference note.

When you find an Internet resource that you think you would like to use in a class paper or project, make note of where this information can be found and make a bookmark within your browser. You may want to create a special browser folder for your URLs that you will be using for the paper or project.

The following information should be recorded as you select Internet information resources.

- title of the Internet document or resource (located in the title bar at the top of your browser's page)

- author (if no author is listed look for an email address at the bottom of the page)

- Internet address (URL) including all pathways

- date of publication (this date may be listed as the date of the latest revision or modification)

- date you accessed the Internet site (this indicates to readers that on this date the Internet document you are referring to was available at the given URL)

Remember—the purpose of referencing items is to provide the necessary information so others can find your resources. It is therefore critical that you record this information accurately. When recording a URL, check and double check the electronic address to be sure it is correct.

TIP

One way to be sure that you have copied the URL exactly is to have a word processing program open at the same time you are working within your Internet browser. Go to the Address location field in your browser, highlight the URL, then use the **Copy** command to copy the URL. Next, go to your word processing program and in an open file paste in the URL. This ensures that you have the exact URL to record in your reference notes or bibliography.

Referencing Electronic Media

As with any published reference, the goal of an electronic reference is to credit the author and to enable the reader to find the material. The International Standards Organization (ISO) continues to modify a uniform system of citing electronic documents. The following guidelines and examples have been compiled from The American Psychological Association (APA) Publication Manual, MLA-Style, and The Chicago Manual of Style.

- Be consistent in your references to online documentation or information.

- Capitalization follows the "accepted practice for the language or script in which the information is given."

- Use your discretion for the choice of punctuation used to separate elements and in the use of variations in typeface or underscoring to distinguish or highlight elements.

- If a print form is available and the same as the electronic form, referencing of the print form is preferred.

Include the following in your reference:

- The author's name if it is available or important for identification.

- The most recent date of publication or a modification date if document undergoes revision.

- The date you accessed the document on the Internet.

- Title of the document, file, or World Wide Web site.

- Specific protocol: Telnet, Gopher, FTP, World Wide Web.

- Internet address or retrieval path for accessing the information including the file name, directory, and pathway. Do not end a path statement with a period, because it is not part of the Internet address and may hinder retrieval if used.

- If the information is available via a listserv mailing list, provide subscription information.

> ## NOTE
>
> The examples provided in this section use APA style. Although the type of information required for referencing is similar, the format for the references varies between the APA, MLA, and the Chicago styles. Refer to the style manual for the reference format.

The following is the format for referencing online information in the APA style.

> Author, I. (date of work). Title of full work [online] . Available: Specify protocol and path (date document was accessed).

> Author, I., & Author, I. (date). Title of full work [online]. Specify protocol and path (date document was accessed).

Examples of APA Style

World Wide Web

The World Wide Web provides many types of information you may want to reference: text, images, video, or sound. To reference these information sources include the following:

- author's name (if known)
- date of Web site information (if known or different from date you accessed)
- title of the page or article
- additional information such as version or edition
- the URL for the page you are referencing
- date you accessed this page

EXAMPLE 1
Referencing World Wide Web site
The first reference is from CNET.COM, a computer network that integrates television programming with a network. CNET's Web site takes advantage of the Web's interactive capabilities to deliver valuable information on computer technology, the Internet, and the future of technology in a well-designed, creative, and rich multimedia environment (see Fig. 5.14).

FIGURE 5.14
World Wide Web page to be referenced

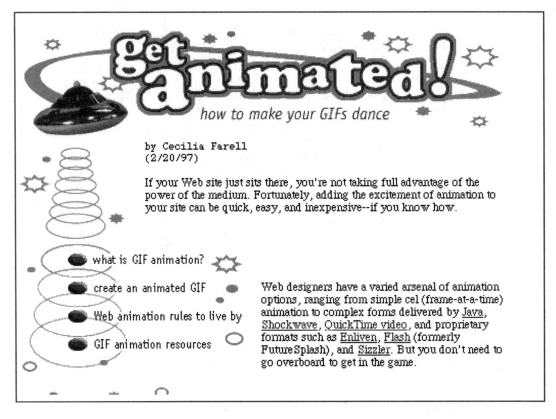

World Wide Web Reference #1
> Farell, C. (1997, February). Get animated: How to make your GIFs dance [Online].
> Available: http://www.cnet.com/Content/Features/Howto/Webanim/index.html
> (March 1997).

EXAMPLE 2
World Wide Web Reference
The second example, is an excellent Web site for helping students with career planning and finding a job. The Home Page for this site (**http://www.jobtrak.com/jobguide**) supplies much of the needed information for the reference.

FIGURE 5.15
World Wide Web site for a reference

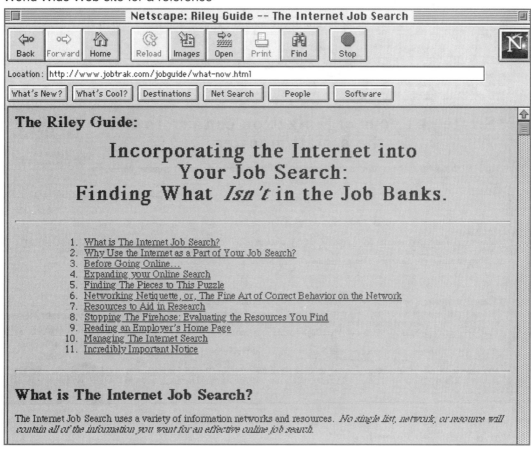

World Wide Web Reference #2
　　Riley, M. F. (1996). Incorporating the Internet into your job search [Online]. Available:
　　　　http://www.jobtrak.com/jobguide/what-now.html (March 1997).

EXAMPLE 3
World Wide Web
References an article on Netscape World's site.

FIGURE 5.16
Article from Netscape World

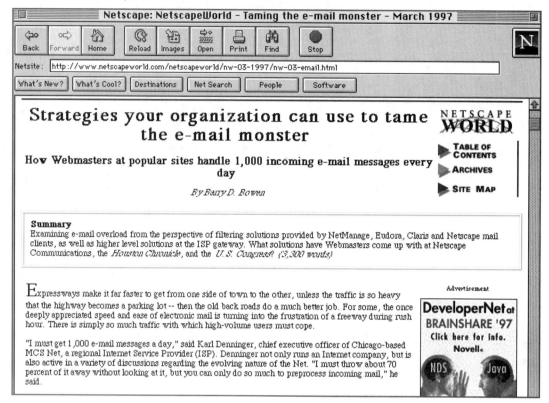

World Wide Web Reference #3

> Bowen, B. D. (1997). Strategies your organization can use to tame the e-mail
> monster [Online]. Available : http://www.netscapeworld.com (March 1997).

Gopher

When referencing Gopher sites, include the following information.

- author's name (if known)
- date of publication
- title of the page, article, or file
- additional information such as version or edition
- the URL for the page you are referencing and the pathway to this information
- date you accessed this page

EXAMPLE 1
Gopher Reference
The Library of Congress has information on copyright. To reference this information visit their Gopher server.

FIGURE 5.17
Library of Congress document at their Gopher site

```
Circular 1

                          COPYRIGHT BASICS


WHAT COPYRIGHT IS

Copyright is a form of protection provided by the laws of the
United States (title 17, U.S. Code) to the authors of "original
works of authorship" including literary, dramatic, musical,
artistic, and certain other intellectual works.  This protection
is available to both published and unpublished works.  Section 106
of the Copyright Act generally gives the owner of copyright the
exclusive right to do and to authorize others to do the following:

   --  To reproduce the copyrighted work in copies or phonorecords;

   --  To prepare derivative works  based upon the copyrighted work;
```

Gopher Reference #1
> Library of Congress. (updated 9/95). Copyright Basics [Online]. Available:
> gopher://marvel.loc.gov:70/00/.ftppub/copyright/circs/circ01 (March 1997).

EXAMPLE 2
Gopher Reference
The second example is a NASA Gopher site. Figure 5.18 shows the first page for this site (**gopher://naic.nasa.gov**). For this page numerous pathways (links) must be taken to find the information on the M.U.S.E report. It is essential that this information be provided for others to find this article.

NOTE

Gopher Reference #1 lists the server pathway as part of the URL. In Gopher Reference #2, the server pathway is very long and is therefore listed as a pathway separate from the URL. One factor to consider in determining whether to make the the pathway part of the URL is its length. If you list the server pathway separate from the URL it may be easier to find a site that has changed one part of its pathway links.

FIGURE 5.18

The opening menu for NASA's Gopher server

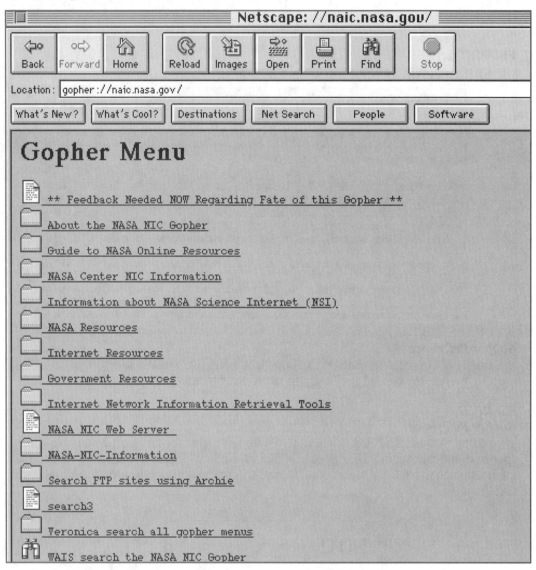

Gopher Reference #2

Part I - M.U.S.E. Report (1993, December). [Online]. Available Gopher:
gopher://naic.nasa.gov/   Pathway: /Guide to NASA Online Resources/
NASA Scientific, Educational, and Governmental Resources/
Government Resources/Americans Communicating Electronically/
Electronic Mail Issues for the Federal Government/ Unified Federal
Government Electronic Mail Users Support Environment Report
(November 1996).

File Transfer Protocol

When referencing documents that you have accessed using FTP, include the following:

- author's name (if known)
- date of publication (if available)
- title of the document, article, or file
- the address for the FTP site, along with the pathway to this information
- date you accessed this site

EXAMPLE 1
FTP Reference

Figure 5.19 is an article with information on how to use email to access Internet resources.

FIGURE 5.19

Internet By E-Mail document at NASA's FTP site

```
                Accessing The Internet By E-Mail
                   2nd Edition - August 1994


            Copyright (c) 1994, "Doctor Bob" Rankin

   All rights reserved.  Permission is granted to make and distribute
   verbatim copies of this document provided the copyright notice and
            this permission notice are preserved on all copies.


How to Access Internet Services by E-mail
-------------------------------------------------

If your only access to the Internet is via e-mail, you don't have to
miss out on all the fun!  Maybe you've heard of FTP, Gopher, Archie,
Veronica, Finger, Whois, WAIS, World-Wide Web, and Usenet but thought
they were out of your reach because your online service does not provide
those tools.  Not so!  And even if you do have full Internet access,
using e-mail servers can save you time and money.
```

FTP Reference #1

Rankin, B. (1994, August). Accessing the Internet by e-mail, 2nd edition [Online]. Available: ftp://dftnic.gsfc.nasa.gov/general_info/internet.by-email (March 1997).

EXAMPLE 2
FTP Reference

Figure 5.20 is from Project Gutenberg's FTP site. The article to be referenced is on the history and philosophy of Project Gutenberg.

FIGURE 5.20
Article on an FTP site to be referenced

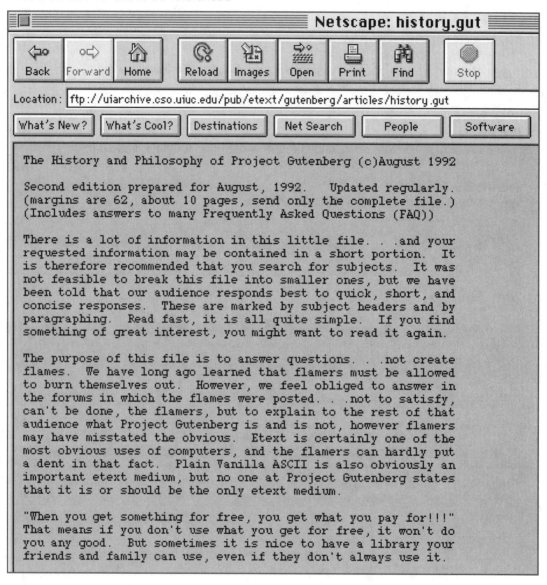

FTP Reference #2

History and pilosophy of Project Gutenberg (1992, August). In Gutenberg Archives
[Online]. Available FTP: ftp://uiarchive.cso.uiuc.edu
Directory: /pub/etext/gutenberg/articles/history.gut (April 1997).

Telnet

When referencing Telnet sites, include the following:

- author's name (if known)
- date of publication (if available)
- title of the work or the name of the Telnet site
- the address for the Telnet site
- directions for accessing the publication when connected
- date you accessed this site

EXAMPLE 1
Telnet Reference
The first example, is from the Smithsonian Institution's Telnet site.

FIGURE 5.21
Abstract on the history of the Smithsonian founder, James Smithson

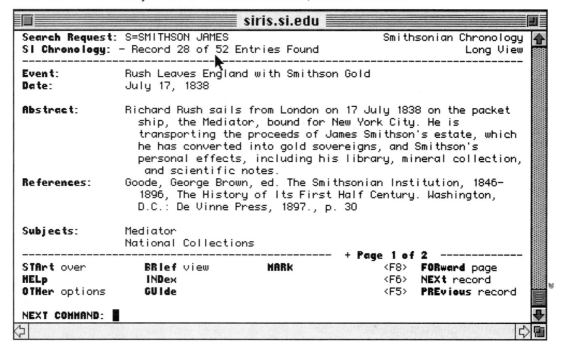

Telnet Reference #1
S1 Chronology (Record 28). Rush leaves England with Smithson gold [Online].
Available: telnet://siris.si.edu (March 1997).

EXAMPLE 2
Telnet Reference
Figure 5.22 is from the MOO, Diversity University.

FIGURE 5.22
Information on navigating within Diversity University's text-based virtual environment

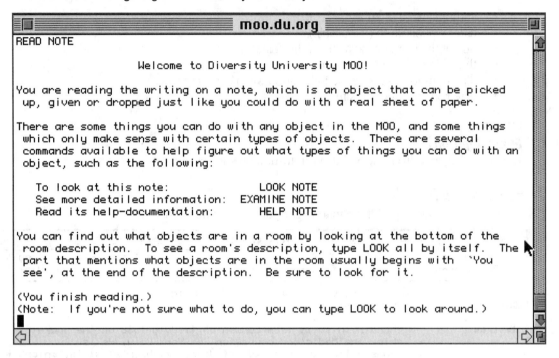

Telnet Reference #2
> Diversity University_Guest. Welcome to Diversity University MOO [Online].
>   Available: telnet://moo.du.org:8888 (March 1997).

Email, Listserv Mailing Lists, and Usenet Newsgroups

Information from email, listservs, and newsgroups is both timely and personal, often representing an individual's point of view. This information must also be referenced. Do not reference personal email. Email references will mainly come from listservs and newsgroups. To reference these information sources, provide the following:

- author's name (if known)
- date of the email message, listserv message, or Usenet posting
- subject
- name of the listserv or newsgroup
- address of the listserv or newsgroup
- information on how to find the group's archives, if available
- date accessed

EXAMPLE 1
Email Reference
The latest document on how to use email to access Internet resources is available by using email (see Fig. 5.19).

Email Reference #1

Rankin, B. (1994, August). Accessing the Internet by e-mail [Online]. Available
Email: LISTSERV @ubvm.cc.buffalo.edu: GET INTERNET BY-EMAIL
NETTRAIN F=MAIL

EXAMPLE 2
Listserv Mailing List Reference

The example in Figure 5.23 has been taken from a listserv for NASA's Galileo expedition.

FIGURE 5.23

NASA's listserv with updates on the Galileo mission

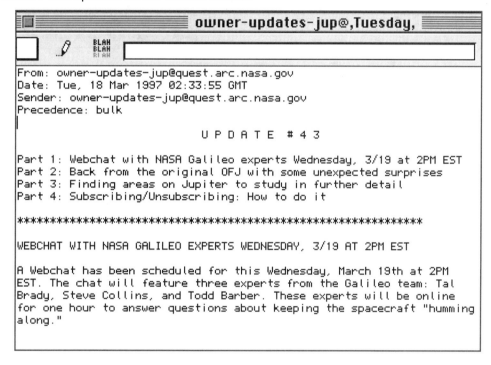

Listserv Reference #1

Orton, G. (1997, February). Back from the original OFJ with some unexpected
surprises [Online]. Available Email: listmanager@quest.arc.nasa.gov: subscribe
updates-jup. Also available http://quest.arc.nasa.gov/galileo/people.html

EXAMPLE 3
Usenet Newsgroup Reference

The example shown in Figure 5.24 was taken from an environmental newsgroup.

FIGURE 5.24

Newsgroup discussion on solar energy viewed from Netscape's news reader

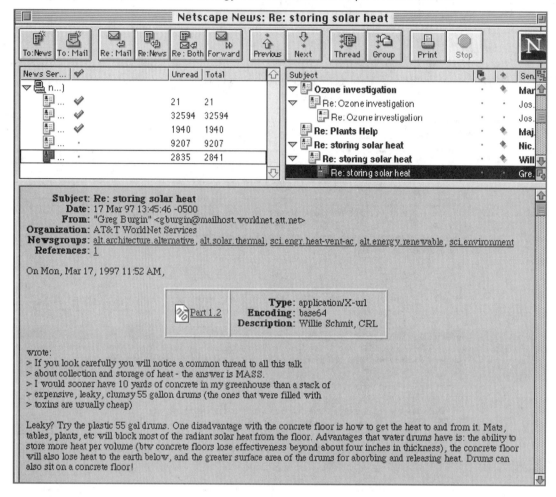

Newsgroup Reference #1

Burgin, G. (1997, March). Storing solar energy [Online]. Available Newsgroup:
sci.environment (March 1997).

For more information on referencing Internet resources visit the following Web sites:

MLA REFERENCE
http://www.cas.usf.edu/english/walker/mla.html

BEYOND THE MLA HANDBOOK: DOCUMENTING ELECTRONIC SOURCES ON THE
INTERNET
http://english.ttu.edu/kairos/1.2/inbox/mla_archive.html

MLA'S HOME PAGE DISCUSSES PROBLEMS RESEARCHERS ENCOUNTER IN CYBER-
SPACE:
http://www.smpcollege.com/online-4styles~help

Internet-Based Learning Expeditions

CHAPTER CONTENTS

LEARNING EXPEDITIONS

This chapter helps educators learn how the Internet can be used as a tool for teaching and learning. Three thematic units offer online and off-line interdisciplinary activities that encourage an active approach to learning and help minimize lines of division among content areas. These units offer many opportunities for students to analyze information, distinguish between fact and opinion, and identify cause and effect as they learn about

- Oceans
- Ancient Civilizations—Greece and Rome
- The Rain Forest

All the curriculm for these thematic units was researched and created by Gail Hartman—a former teacher, educational consultant, and curriculm design expert.

The article on Performance-Based Assessment by Jay McTighe from the Maryland Assessment Consortium and Steven Ferrara of the Maryland State Department of Education was printed by permission from the National Education Association's Center for Innovation. The article is taken from NEA's book *Assessing Learning in the Classroom*, © 1994.

PERFORMANCE-BASED LEARNING

Introduction

Performance-based learning and assessment has become an important part of the educational reform movement of the 1990s. This reform movement defines new standards for national curriculum and perhaps most importantly, emphasizes learning goals outside the traditional content domains. There are many factors that have contributed to the direction of educational reform. Several that are relevant to this chapter include:

- research in cognitive psychology
- changes in the workplace
- the information age
- differences in individual styles—generational, learning, intelligence

Research in Cognitive Psychology

Research from cognitive psychology has greatly contributed to educational reform. In the past learning was viewed as a linear process where basic facts had to be mastered and memorized. The role of the teacher was that of a subject matter expert whose job was to dispense facts and content. Learning was believed to occur from drill and practice and memorizing information for tests.

Cognitive psychology has demonstrated that learning is a complicated and highly individualistic process. When information is memorized it is not retained in the minds of learners for very long. And, perhaps most importantly, not available for use outside the classroom to solve problems or to use in a meaningful way. Cognitive psychologists have investigated how information taken into the minds of learns is transformed into knowledge—knowledge which is available for use in the real world. What we now know is that learners gain understanding when they construct knowledge and make connections between new information and their prior knowledge. Therefore, each of us constructs our own understanding of the world we live in—of the information we take in. We make sense of the world by interpreting new information in terms of what we already know.

The learning process, therefore, involves the taking in of information, the synthesis of information based on prior knowledge and experiences, and the creation of new cognitive maps interconnecting the new and old information.

These theories of learning provide new challenges to educators to rethink the teaching and learning process. Several important considerations for developing environments conducive to learning and the transformation of information into knowledge include:

- providing problems and opportunities for creating relevance;
- providing learning activities where new information can be related to prior knowledge and experience in a meaningful way;
- providing learning opportunities where students use higher-level thinking skills such as compare, contrast, classify, evaluate, analyze, create, abstract, deduct, or solve a problem;
- provide learning tasks that encourage decision making, problem solving, investigation, experimental inquiry, invention, design, creation;

- provide opportunities for students to think about and evaluate how they learn;
- provide a positive learning environment where individual differences, differences in learning styles, and differences in thinking is valued and respected.

Changes in the Workplace

The workplace has been changed and transformed over the last twenty years. No longer do individuals join a company and stay with that company until retirement. The words "job security" have vanished from vocabulary of the corporate world. Buzzwords such as total quality management (TQM), re-engineering, re-defining, reinventing, revitalizing, or transforming the corporation have given new direction to companies often leading to reorganization and the loss of jobs. Morphed from these new "theories of business" has come reorganization, restructuring, work teams, quality teams, training and development, mentoring, and coaching.

Emerging hand in hand with these new work environments has been the development of new competencies for workers. The Department of Labor has identified competencies necessary for today's workplace:

- creative thinking
- decision making
- problem solving
- learning to learn
- collaboration
- self-management

These competencies clearly define the skills and capabilities that students should have upon graduation from school to be competitive in finding and keeping a job. These competencies have also been a stimulus to change schools standards and the curriculum, with new emphasis on performance-based learning and assessment.

Living in the Information Age

"Living in the information age" is not a new or unfamiliar concept for most of us today. Not only do we see and hear this phrase spoken continually but many of us are experiencing the information age first hand as we stagger to support the weight of information overload. In response to the information age and information overload, new concepts, services, and jobs have arisen. Companies offer services to help find and manage information; tools are constantly being designed for helping us to find information; new information design processes are being developed for solving problems, conveying complex information, and creating clarity of meaning.

Information is not only growing exponentially, but the sources of information continue to grow and become a necessary and important part of our lives. Traditional sources of information such as newspapers, books, magazines, and the television continue to be for many of us the place we look to for our important. Added to these media are new technologies that now have become powerful mediums for communication and information exchange and sharing. The World Wide Web, electronic mail, bulletin boards, Usenet newsgroups, chats, and most recently push technologies are new and up-to-date sources of information. Additionally, through our electronic networks we now have access to thousands of databases, libraries, and museums all over the world.

Some of the challenges that the information age provides for educators include:

- teaching students to become infocritical;
- teaching students how to reference and document online information;
- teaching students about becoming responsible netizens;

- teaching students about inappropriate information and what to do when it is encountered;
- helping students to understand copyright issues related to the easy access of information, multimedia, and resources;
- providing opportunities for students to interact with the information in a meaningful, thoughtful, and critical way;
- helping students to understand how electronic information resources fit with traditional sources of information in books, periodicals, and newsletters;
- helping students to appreciate diversity as expressed in information exchange and sharing;
- helping students learn to find the latest and most valuable information when then they need it;
- helping students learn to manage information;
- providing opportunities for students to integrate new information into existing knowledge;
- helping students to realize that the information age requires each of them to become life long learners.

Differences in Style

Much as been written about the Generation Xers and the need to understand "where they are coming from" if one is to work with, educate, or train them. What is known is that Generation Xers have different values, communication styles, and learning styles that have come about as a result of their life experiences. The styles of these Xers are so different from those of baby boomers that many view them as a national curse or a symbol that America is in a decline.

Even in the field of education, there seems to be a lack of understanding of this young generation. The authors of the *Nation at Risk* even charged that for the first time in the history of our country, the "educational skills of one generation will not surpass, will not equal, will not even approach, those of their parents." Additionally, there have even been studies to show what facts our young do not know. Are we evaluating this and other generations in terms of what we understand the term "educational skills" to mean? If one asks Xers what "educational skills" means to them, one would hear a very different definition. Generation Xers tend to resist information being forced onto them. They prefer a sense of control over their learning and respond well to experiences that are meaningful, relevant, fun, memorable, and provide choices.

Generation Xers are but one part of a population demonstrating styles that are diverse, unfamiliar, uncomfortable, and at times difficult to understand. Today the diversity of our student bodies has never been greater—not just in ethnicity, but also in attitudes, values, interests, communication, and learning styles.

Another type of diversity was introduced in the 1980s when Bernice McCarthy introduced educators to diversity in learning styles. McCarthy's 4MAT system was based on research in right and left brain dominance, creativity, learning styles, management, art, and dance focused on the diverse way in which people learn. Today, many educators value, accept, and recognize in their classroom differences in learning styles.

The 1980s also introduced educators to Howard Garner's theory of multiple intelligences. Gardner— a Harvard psychologist—challenged the common belief about intelligence. In his theory of multiple intelligences, Garder broadens the scope of human intelligence outside the realm of the IQ test. He believes that intelligence has more to do with an individual's capacity to solve problems or create a product. Gardner's seven intelligences are:

- linguistic—capacity to use words effectively
- logical-mathematical—capacity to use numbers effectively
- spatial—ability to perceive the visual-spatial world accurately
- bodily-kinesthetic—using one's body to express ideas or feelings
- musical—expression of musical forms
- interpersonal—sensitivity and perception to the feelings, moods, motivations, and intentions of others
- interpersonal—self knowledge and the ability to act based on that knowledge

Diversity in style provides many challenges to educators. However, mere acceptance of differences is style is the first step to providing and designing learning environments that take into account diversity. The above discussions on theories of learning and their application to teaching and learning are highly relevant and valuable when considering diversity. For example, cognitive psychology supports the presentation of information using several different mediums—instead of just presenting information in text form, consider visual media. Research indicates that people tend to remember more from text-based information when the information can be related to an associated image. Upon recall, these individuals use the image as a cue to assist with information recall often remembering significantly more information than subjects who used no image for the learning or recall of information.

Dual coding theory (Paivio, 1986) supports this research. According to dual coding theory what appears to happen is that the text content is semantically organized and stored in the mind along with the spatial structure of the image. If learners fail to retrieve the target information using verbal cues, then they may resort to recalling the image. The image is believed to assist the learner in the search process for information stored in memory.

Performance-Based Learning and Assessment

Advances in communication technology add to the educational challenges we have just discussed. However, instead of adding to the complexity of these changes we should view these new technologies as bringing in new tools to support and enhance educational change. Computer networks such as the Internet offer new tools for information access, information sharing, and communication. Traditional teaching and learning practices cannot be used with these new sources of information. Students must become active in the learning process, as they go out onto the networks and search for information sources. On their journey students have opportunities to interact, communicate, and collaborate with many different individuals of all ages. These new information sources eliminate passive learning and open new doors for teaching and learning from global resources. No longer is the teacher the sole source of information. The teacher's role changes from the dispenser of information to a learning guide.

The challenge now is to understand this new information and communication medium—its capabilities as well as its limitations. We must help our learners to understand these new sources of information. As we continue to explore how to use these sources of information in our classroom, new doors seem to easily open for using and applying this information in meaningful and useful ways. These opportunities provide a natural transformation to performance-based learning and assessment.

Performance-based learning and assessment is built on theories of learning, differences in learning styles, and perhaps most importantly the need to prepare the learner for life outside the classroom. Performance-based learning provides opportunities for students to acquire knowledge, skills, and mental habits that will be of value to them in the world of work in the information age.

Central to performance-based learning and assessment are standards. The national educational reform movement uses the word "standards-based education" to define and clearly identify what students should know and be able to do. There are two types of standards: curriculum standards—the goals of classroom instruction; and content standards—the knowledge and skills specific to a discipline. Content standards therefore have two parts, the knowledge required in discipline and the skills related to the application of that knowledge.

In this chapter you will find examples of both curriculum standards and content standards. Three thematic units of instruction have been selected based on curriculum standards that many districts and states require their teachers to teach: rain forest, ancient civilizations, and the oceans. Within each of these thematic curriculum units you will find content standards. These thematic units provide examples of how the Internet can used as a resource to support teaching and learning as well as a new opportunity to convert existing curriculum into performance-based learning. As you go through the thematic units try to identify the content standards. It might be easier to separate the content standards into two different types of learning outcomes: knowledge outcomes and skills or performance outcomes.

Knowledge outcomes is the essential knowledge that a student must know in a specific discipline. Also known as declarative knowledge, knowledge outcomes is the information necessary for the understanding of subject or discipline—facts, concepts, principles, events, individuals.

Performance outcomes, also known as procedural knowledge, are the skills or competencies needed for use of that knowledge in the real world.

An example of a knowledge outcome come would be: Describe the events occurring in meiosis.

A related performance outcome would be: Recognize the phases of mitosis in plant and animal cell micrographs under the microscope.

Directly related to performance-based learning is performance-based assessment. Assessment is the tool used to evaluate the content standards. Using the Internet as a communication and information source for teaching and learning lends itself to the creation of performance-based assessment. You will notice that many of the classroom activities could be used as assessment measures.

To help you better understand performance-based assessment you will find an excellent article written by Jay McTighe and Steven Ferrara at the end of this chapter.

The following references are excellent resources for a more in-depth discussion and excellent examples of performance-based learning and assessment.

Blum R. E., and Arter, J.A. (editors). (1996). A handbook for student performance assessment in an era of restructuring. Association for Supervision and Curriculum Development: Alexandria, VA.

Educators in Connecticut's Pomeraug Regional School District 15 (1996). Performance-Based Learning and Assessment. Association for Supervision and Curriculum Development: Alexandria, VA.

Marzano, R. J., Pickering, D., & McTighe, J. (1993). Assessing Student Outcomes—Performance assessment using the dimensions of learning model. Association for Supervision and Curriculum Development: Alexandria, VA.

THEMATIC UNIT—OCEANS

Oceans Introduction

The oceans cover more than 70 percent of the Earth's surface—about 139 million square miles. Oceans are home to plants, fish, and animals. They are a main source of food for many people around the world and a major source of the oil and gas that we use for fuel and energy. Some medicines even come from natural chemicals found in ocean plants and animals. Oceans are vital to the support of life on the planet. They help regulate the Earth's temperature and rainfall, and to dilute toxic materials in the atmosphere and in fresh and salt waters.

And yet, oceans have become the dumping ground for toxic chemicals. Tankers are spilling oil. Ocean food chains, of which humans are a part, are becoming poisoned. Forever gone from our oceans are stellar sea cows, Biscayan right whales, and Panamanian fire coral, just to name a few species that have become extinct in recent years.

Since the mid-19th century, scientists have been studying the oceans, the role they play in our lives, and the creatures living in them. There is still much we don't know. Oceanographers work alongside such professionals as meteorologists, geologists, paleontologists, archaeologists, botanists, zoologists, and geographers to uncover the mysteries of the deep.

This issue of **Internet Adventures** takes a look at ocean life from seashores to the abyss. Topics include the natural history and physical geography of the world's oceans, early ocean explorers, careers in oceanography, farming the sea, the conservation of coastal and ocean resources, and current scientific research. Thrown in for good measure are such topics as undersea shipwrecks, sea chanties, mythical sea creatures in literature, art of early explorers and island cultures, and even piracy on the high seas!

In this unit, students will have the opportunity to:

- examine ocean ecosystems, including the coast, sea floor, and deep-sea life;
- discover how marine organisms can interact with one another in producer/consumer, predator/prey, or parasite/host, scavenger/decomposer relationships;
- recognize the diversity of life in our seas and how all living things in the oceans depend on each other for food;
- determine that the studies of oceanography, geology, and meteorology are interconnected;
- learn about the ways in which humans interact with oceans, including food, recreation, travel, research, mining resources, and dumping waste materials;
- examine the effect of oceans on our weather;
- examine the water cycle, tides, waves, and currents;
- understand how islands are formed;
- learn about the travels of ancient sailors and discover how geography and archaeology are applied to interpret the past;
- view current ocean research being conducted around the world;
- interpret and create maps, tables, and other graphic representations to depict problems and/or data;
- discover how humans' actions modify the physical environment;
- consider the use, distribution, and importance of renewable and non-renewable resources.

Start the unit by identifying on a world map the five largest oceans in order of size (Pacific, Atlantic, Indian, Antarctic, and Arctic). You might also want to identify other large bodies of water such as seas and gulfs.

Invite students to create a cluster map on a large piece of butcher paper. Start by encircling the word "oceans" in the middle of the paper and then ask students to brainstorm words or phrases that describe what they know about oceans. Encourage them to think about marine animals and fish, as well as how we farm and explore the seas. Each category should branch out from the center circle. Students can add to this map as they learn more throughout the unit. Use the cluster map to help you determine what students know and don't know about oceans, as well as what they would like to learn.

Social Studies Connections

1. Steering with only the aid of the sun, stars, winds, and ocean currents, early explorers sailed the oceans trading food, tools, and other materials with the people they met on their journeys. Learn about the travels of the ancient Polynesian sailors who explored a vast area of the Pacific from Hawaii to New Zealand to Easter Island. **http://www.tahiti-explorer.com/history.html**

2. The Polynesian Voyaging Society has a wonderful site full of information about ancient voyages, canoe-building, and the art of wayfinding. **gopher://gopher2.hawaii.edu/11/PVS**

3. Where exactly are the Cook Islands? Find out at **http://www.ck/geog.htm** The history of the Cook Islands, including pre-European and post-European contact can be found at **http://www.ck/history.htm**

4. Take a virtual field trip to the Islands of the Bahamas and Culture site. **http://www.interknowledge.com/bahamas/bscul01.htm**

Christopher Columbus

5. Learn about early explorers: *Pacific Ocean*, including Vasco del Balboa, Ferdinand Magellan, and Captain James Cook; *Atlantic Ocean*, including the Vikings, Leif Erikson, and Christopher Columbus; *Indian Ocean*, including Marco Polo, Vasco da Gama, and Captain James Cook. The A&E Television site offers excellent biographies. Search by typing in the name of the explorer. **http://www.biography.com** Then have students create Venn diagrams to compare and contrast these explorations.

6. Two other sites with information about early explorers are Social Studies Sources **http://www.halcyon.com/howlevin/social.studies.html** and Kathy Schrock's Guide for Educators: Social Studies. **http://www.capecod.net/Wixon/history.htm**

7. Visit the Norwegian Explorers page for histories of the ocean explorations of the Vikings, Fridtjof Nanse, and Roald Amundsen. **http://odin.dep.no/html/nofovalt/depter/ud/nornytt/uda-299.html**

8. The Vikings explored the seas around Iceland, Greenland, and Northeastern North America in the 11th Century. They designed a ship that had a keel—a long plank of wood at the bottom—that kept the ship from rolling and made it easier to steer. Learn about their travels and trades. **http://www.nls.no/viking/e/ehome.htm**

9. Twenty-four ancient Hawaiian plants were carried on many early Polynesian voyages. Find out which they were, why they were carried, and also find good pointers to native Hawaiian resources on the Web. **http://hawaination.org/nation/canoe/canoe.html**

10. The Library of Congress has good information on Columbus. Visit 1492: An Ongoing Exhibit. **http://sunsite.unc.edu/expo/1492.exhibit/Intro.html**

11. Before steam-powered ships came on the scene, the flow of ocean currents and atmospheric winds shaped worldwide trade and travel routes. Early explorers had to be keenly aware of the weather at

all times. Invite students to research and map ancient trade and travel routes. Then look at weather maps to see current weather patterns. The Space Science and Engineering Center (SSEC) posts real-time weather data on the Web.
http://www.ssec.wisc.edu/data/index.html
Students can also visit the WWWebVirtual Library: Meteorology page with links to many weather-related sites around the world.
http://www.met.fuberlin.de/DataSources/MetIndex.html

12. How did ancient cartographers view the oceans and continents of the world? Discover ancient maps at Mapping the World and the Heavens, the British Library's Online Information Server.
http://portico.bl.uk/exhibitions/maps

13. The 1912 sinking of the Titanic remains an intriguing story around the world. See the historical Peoria Herald front page story.
http://pjstar.com/titanic.htm Learn about the Titanic at GTE's site.**http://www.im.gte.com/titanic** Select the *Resources* link. The Discovery Channel site has the latest updates on the most recent attempts to raise the Titanic.
http://www.discovery.com/DCO/doc/1012/world/specials/titanic/titanicopener.html

The Sinking of the Unsinkable Titanic site is a little slow, but well worth a look.
http://johnson.alfred.edu/ces121/student/Winter-Titanic/page

14. The Guide to Historic Wrecks site was compiled by the University of St. Andrews.
http://www.cru.uea.ac.uk/ukdiving/misc/deswreck.htm Have students find the points of latitude and longitude of each wreck and mark them on a world map.

15. Another terrific site for students interested in shipwrecks is the Nautical Archaeology page which contains pointers to many wonderful sites, including shipwrecks, treasure hunts, and cultural and historical information.
http://pc-78120.udac.se:8001/www/Nautica/Pointers/ Nautical_Archaeology.html

16. The Texas Historical Commission has created a site with regular updates on the La Salle Shipwreck, the final resting place of the historic 17th century French ship, Belle, which sank in Matagorda Bay in 1686. This is a busy site, but well worth a look. Tell students to keep trying if they can't get through the first or second time.
http://www.thc.state.tx.us/belle/index.htm

17. Learn about the Monte Cristi, a 17th Century ship that lies on the north coast of the Dominican Republic. See what the Pan-American Institute of Marine Archeology (PIMA) has discovered on the shipwreck.
http://www.wbm.ca/users/nfisher/pipe_wreck.html

18. Visit the Underwater Archaeological Preserves site to view shipwrecks off Florida's coasts.
http://199.44.58.12/dostate/dhr/bar

19. Not all old ships sank! Climb on board the Queen Mary, now harbored in Long Beach, California, to find out about its history.
http://www.rmplc.co.uk/eduweb/sites/sterling

Submersible

To find links to other historical ships that survived, visit John's Nautical Links. Select *Links to Other Nautical Sites* and then the *Museums and Historical Sites link* . **http://www.cyber-dyne.com/~jkohnen/ nautical.html**

20. For students interested in the history of submarines, visit this site for historical and modern submarines around the world. **http://www.sealion.com/weblinks.html**

21. Salem's Maritime Heritage is an interesting site with beautiful pictures of historical sailing ships and information on Salem's history, 1776 to 1812, and after. **http://www.star.net/salem/maritim1.htm**

22. Maritime History on the Internet offers links to ships, museums, nautical archaeology, and more. **http://ils.unc.edu/maritime/#resource**

23. The Smithsonian Institution has an exhibit of the Hall of American Maritime Enterprise that focuses on three centuries of ocean and river commerce. **http://www.si.edu/organiza/museums/nmah/ homepage/docs/marit19.htm**

24. Students will enjoy reading the journal of a Finnish sailor from 1859 to 1869. **http://www.sheldonbrown.com/biz/hub/ anders_ junnila.html**

25. Read another journal at the Life and Times of Captain Adams Dodd (1836-1922), compiled by his granddaughter. Select the *Journal* link. **http://www.oakvalley.com/adams**

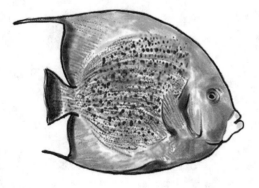

26. Early steamships were driven by paddle wheels until 1840 when John Ericsson developed screw propellers. The Steamboat and Paddle Wheeler Information site has photos and answers to frequently asked questions. **http://www.acy.digex.net/~capnmark/steampg. html**

27. Immigrants often traveled in cheap steerage aboard steamships. Visit a 4th/5th grade classroom's study of immigration and read their fictional journals about travels on ships to America at The Immigration Story site. **http://www.mth.mtlib.org/LCLHomepage/Main List/SchoolInfo/Henson-CentralLibrary.htm/ Veroulis.html** (See Language Arts Connections for a follow-up activity.)

28. "The main idea behind all my expeditions is the common origin of true civilizations from the moment man started to build ships." In 1947, Thor Heyerdahl traveled from Peru to Polynesia on a balsa raft called the Kon-Tiki. Find out more about the man and his travels from this site created by the Norwegian Broadcasting Co. It includes a slideshow with audio and a biography of his life. **http://www.nrk.no/undervisning/ heyerdahl** For more information about Heyerdahl's travels, have students go to **http://www.gyldendal.no/gyldendal/ kon-tiki/maske.htm**

29. Voyager Publishing offers some demonstration Quicktime movies to download, depicting the Kon-Tiki's construction and voyages. These clips are from their Kon-Tiki Interactive CD-ROM. (See recommended software list.) **http://www.voyagerco.com/catalog/ kontiki/indepth**

30. Since 1802, when Napoleon's engineer started making plans, they'd been talking about it. In 1994 they finally did it! What in the world is a "Chunnel" and what does it do? Students can read all about it at the Chunnel Tunnel and Eurostar site. **http://www.eurail.com/eurail/articles/ chunnel.htm**

Have students plan a fictional trip through the Chunnel by using passenger information. **http://www.starnetinc.com/ eurorail/eurostar.htm#Chunnel**

31. The Age of Sail Page has good links to such things as global nautical museums, shipwrecks, photographs of historical ships, and even clip art. **http://www.cs.yale.edu/homes/sjl/sail.html**

32. The Franklin Institute Science Museum has a link to *Shipbuilding on the Delaware*. Select it to go to the exhibit and try some related hands-on activities. **http://sln.fi.edu/tfi/exhibits/ex-summ.html**

33. This site has excellent resources, even though its title may not give any hint of it! Check out the Transshipments and General Cargo site to learn about ships, seafarers, ports, harbors, submarines, and submersibles. **http://www.pacifier.com/~rboggs/LANES.HTML**

34. The field of oceanography has four main branches: physical, chemical, biological and geological. Have interested students research careers in oceanography. **http://wwocean.tamu.edu/Careers/careers.html** Learn more at the Woods Hole Oceanographic Institute. **http://www.whoi.edu/k12/ k12resources.html#Careers** Older students may wish to find out about careers in marine mammal science. **http://www.rtis.com/nat/user/elsberry/marspec/ mmstrat.html**

35. Challenge older students to discover what a hydrologist, malacologist, mammalogist, conchologist, and ichthyologist do! Encourage them to use such search engines as Yahooligans **http://www.yahooligans.com** Infoseek **http://www.infoseek.com** and Excite **http://www.excite.com**

36. During the 1996 Jason Project VII: Adapting to a Changing Sea, students joined Dr. Robert Ballard to investigate the ocean waters of southern Florida. All of the expedition journals and results are still on-line. **http://seawifs.gsfc.nasa.gov/JASON/HTML/ JASON.html**

37. Encourage students to check another interactive project, geared toward 9th and 10th graders, called The Living Ocean: Studying Ocean Color Form. **http://seawifs.gsfc.nasa.gov/SEAWIFS/ LIVING_OCEAN/LIVING_OCEAN.html**

38. Older students may wish to learn about The Law of the Sea Treaty, drafted in 1973 by representatives from more than 15 countries. Ask them to discover why the U.S. has not signed it. Learn about this issue and other maritime interests of the U.S. **http://www.ndu.edu/ndu/inss/strforum/forum41 .html** To see an overview of the Treaty, visit **http://www.clark.net/pub/diplonet/ los_guide.html** Go to the Public International Law site to learn about all the sea-related policies and treaties that have been signed by nations around the world. **http://www.ecel.uwa.edu.au/law/links/fauburn/ law-sea.htm**

39. The National Geographic site has wonderful maps of the oceans' floors! **http://www.nationalgeographic.com.** Click on the graphic of the passport and then on the *Map Machine* link. Follow the *Physical Map* link.

40. What's a study of the oceans without some pirates? Older students will enjoy the Pirates of the Caribbean site with lots of fun facts about piracy on the seas, particularly the Caribbean. There is much information here, including facts, myths, and legends of piracy. (NOTE: Teachers will want to evaluate this site before asking students to explore all the links. There is some mention of pirates' not-so-nice behaviors...but, after all, they *were* pirates!) **http://tigger.cc.uic.edu/~toby-g/pirates.html**

41. Go to The World's Lighthouses site to visit lighthouses across the globe. Some of the pointers at this site will connect students to lighthouses with their own Web sites. **http://www.maine.com/lights/www_vl.htm**

42. Teachers will find interesting lesson plans on map-making at the What Do Maps Show site. Select the *Reading a Topographic Map* link and have students try these warm-up activities before creating their

own topographic maps.
http://info.er.usgs.gov/education/teacher/what-do-maps-show/index.html

43. Ask students to make their own globes from balloons. Directions can be found at the ERIC (Educational Resources Information Center) site. **gopher://ericir.syr.edu:70/0R0-2617-/Lesson/Subject/ SocialStudies/cecsst.134**

44. Learn about modern day shipping lanes and how ships passing through the Panama Canal in Central America make shortcuts that save thousands of miles. Learn the history and importance of the Panama Canal.
http://gcunix.gc.maricopa.edu/~2dts000/cis133/962/962046.htm

45. The Perry-Casteñada Library Map Collection has wonderful historic world maps.
http://www.lib.utexas.edu/Libs/PCL/Map_collection/Map_collection.html

46. The I*EARN (International Education and Research Network) Global Projects site joins students together to make a difference in the health and welfare of the planet. There are environmental and cultural projects waiting for student volunteers. Join other classes who are interested in learning about our oceans.
http://www.iearn.org/iearn/projects.html

Math Connections

1. Sea levels are on the rise in Florida and global warming is suspected as the cause. Older students can view some of the algebraic formulas used in the Projecting Sea Level Rise in Sarasota Florida Project where scientists are trying to predict the levels for the 21st century. Before visiting the site, review the mathematical definitions of *mean* and *median*.
http://www.marinelab.sarasota.fl.us/SEARISE.HTM

2. Estimate the high and low tides of the oceans and then go check the actual numbers. **http://www-ceob.nos.noaa.gov/tideframe.html** Discover how scientists use the concept of means or average to determine the results. Review the Tide Glossary at NOAA.
http://www-ceob.nos.noaa.gov/tidegloss.html

3. Look at some samples of oceanographers' graphs at the Ocean Atlas of Hawaii site.
http://satftp.soest.hawaii.edu/atlas

4. Have students keep track of sea level measurements for one week, then graph their findings. Global sea level measurements can be found at the TOPEX/Poseidon site **http://topex-www.jpl.nasa.gov**
Then graph and compare high and low tides around the world at the Tidal Information Page.
http://www.catalina.org/goodies/tides.htm

5. The Georgy Girl's Ocean Links site has weekly updates about hurricanes, tsunamis, and math challenges for older students, related to oceans and weather. Students who enjoy a mathematical challenge will like this site.
http://www.uslink.net/~nienaber

6. Encourage students to use linear measures to determine distances on a map as they create a fictional travel plan. Visit The Virtual Tourist World Map. **http://www.vtourist.com/webmap**

7. Learn about weather and atmosphere and how it relates to the oceans at the Athena Project. Students will find activities to practice measuring and charting weather.
http://inspire.ospi.wednet.edu:8001/curric/weather/index.html

8. Greenwich Mean Time was originally developed to aid sailors navigating the New World in the 15th Century. Learn all the fascinating history and see what mathematicians and scientists are thinking about for the Millennium. Visit Greenwich2: Home of Greenwich Mean Time site.
http://greenwich2000.com Select the *Time* link.

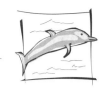

9. The International Dateline is exactly 180 degrees in either direction from the prime meridian. Have students create word problems about ships that cross the International Dateline.

10. Teachers will find good resources and many lessons at the Explorer Home Page, a network database system which documents curriculum on the Net. Select any of the mathematics folders to browse through the curricula. **http://server2.greatlakes.k12.mi.us** Most of the available lessons can be downloaded for Adobe Acrobat or ClarisWorks formats.

11. Teachers may want to check out The Globe Program which links students and teachers with scientists around the world who are working on projects to study and understand the environment. Students do experiments, compile data, and record it to be shared with researchers and then archived. **http://www.globe.gov**

12. Introduce or review the concept of sets (members of a set; equal sets; subsets, intersection or union of sets, and null or empty sets). Then ask students to classify into sets information they are learning about marine mammals. Visit the Electronic Zoo/NetVet: Marine Mammal site. **http://netvet.wustl.edu/marine.htm**

13. Make a list of all the ways an oceanographer uses math. Visit the Woods Hole Oceanographic site. **http://www.whoi.edu/k-12/ k12-resources.html#Careers**

14. There are more than 13,000 different species of fish in the oceans! Have students create original word problems using fish trivia. Go to the Fish FAQ: A Bouillabaisse of Fascinating Facts. **http://www.wh.whoi.edu/ homepage/faq.html**

15. Visit the Ancient Mathematics site and select *Ptolemy's Geography* link. Learn of his calculations (and miscalculations) and learn how his work influenced Columbus' ocean travels. Be sure to look at the amazing photographs of Ptolemy's maps and tables. **http://www.ncsa.uiuc.edu/SDG/Experimental/vat ican. exhibit/exhibit/d-mathematics/ Mathematics.html**

16. Create a sunken treasure map, using lines of latitude and longitude. For example, "Start at Anchorage, Alaska. Move 20 degrees west longitude. Then go ...." Go to the Xerox PARC map site **http://mapweb.parc.xerox.com/map** Divide students into small groups to create a treasure hunt map using points of latitude and longitude on the school yard. Then have groups exchange the maps and try to find the hidden "treasure."

17. The Grave of the Titanic site at the Gulf of Maine Aquarium is an excellent resource for math activities. Teachers won't want to miss this site. **http://octopus.gma.org/space1/titanic.html**

18. Scientists can map the ocean floor by using ultrasound echoes. The research vessel produces sound waves which reflect off the ocean's floor and are re-received at the surface. The following formula is used to determine the exact distance of the ship to the ocean floor at any given point: $D = 1/2 \, t \, x \, v$ (D = the depth of the ocean, t = the time for the vibrations to make a round trip, and v = the velocity of sound in water, which is 1500 meters per second.) Have older students create

Seagull

Whale

word problems using this formula to map fictional finds on the ocean floor. Older students can learn how marine acoustics are used for mapping the sea floor. **http://lthgt.tg.lth.se/coe/coe_lth.html**

19. Daniel Bernoulli's (1700-1782) work included understanding the basic properties of fluid, pressure, density, and velocity. He won many awards for his work with ocean tides and currents and the behaviors of ships at sea. Read his biography at **http://wwwgroups.dcs.stand.ac.uk/~history/Mathematicians/Bernoulli_Daniel.html**

20. Determine the meter and rhythm patterns of sea chanties! (See Language Arts and Arts Connections.)

21. To help students visualize the enormous size of whales, have them design a simple measurement scale, such as 1 inch = 1 foot. Then use chalk or take string on the schoolyard to measure and mark the exact length of an average whale, humpback, sperm whale, etc. Visit Sea World's Animal Information Database. Select the *Animal Bytes* link or the *Animal Resources* link to gather information on whale sizes. **http://www.bev.net/education/SeaWorld** Follow-up the activity by having students create a pie graph representing the average weights of six marine mammals.

22. Economics plays an important role in the farming and mining of our seas. Mariculture (the farming of ocean resources) is big industry around the world. Visit Reefscapes Unlimited to see what ocean resources they sell. **http://www.reefscapes.com/company.html** Older students may wish to read How Bountiful are Our Ocean Fisheries? Be sure they view the table of economically-important species. **http://www.gcrio.org/CONSEQUENCES/winter96/oceanfish.html**

23. What does the state of oceans have to do with economics and politics? Older students can find out by reading the articles and editorials at Splash. **http://www.ibb.com/splash.htm**

24. Discover how ancient explorers used sextants and the North Star to determine their location at sea. Go to the Newton's Apple site to do the *Ahoy, There Mate* activity. Students will make a sextant to determine how far they are from the equator. **http://ericir.syr.edu/Projects/Newton/13/lessons/equat.html**

25. Make and use a sundial as early sea explorers did at the Sundials on the Internet site. **http://www.sundials.co.uk/index.htm**

26. Help younger students to improve classification skills by having them sort a variety of seashells by size, color, length, design, etc. Older students can use a balance and sets of gram masses to measure each shell's mass in grams. If you don't have shells in the class, just log onto the Seashell Pictures site. **http://www.mindspring.com/~bearl/gashell/shell**

pic.htm Want more resources on shells? Go to the Internet Resources for Conchologists. **http://fly.hiwaay.net/~dwills/shellnet.html**

27. The How Far Is It site lets students type in two areas of the world to get the longitude and latitude measurements as well as the distance between the two places. **http://www.indo.com/distance** Invite students to design a creative board game using the information.

28. How did ancient Polynesians use mathematics to navigate? Find out at **gopher://gopher2.hawaii.edu/11/PVS** Select the *Wayfinding* folder and follow links to how the Wayfinder determines latitude, locates land, etc.

29. Throughout history, cartographers have been faced by some big map-making challenges. The Mathematics Behind Maps at the MegaMath site provides some puzzlers for students who like a challenge. **http://www.c3.lanl.gov/mega-math/workbk/map/mpbkgd.html**

30. An interesting site for older students is the Web's First Animated Guide to Marine Navigation. **http://www.marinedata.co.uk/ref/buoyage/navpt1.html**

31. What's a nautical league, a knot, and a nautical mile? Learn about all about it at UC Berkeley's Common Weights and Measures site. **http://www.cchem.berkeley.edu/ChemResources/Weights-n-Measures/weights-n-measures.html**

32. Project Athena has pointers to many sites using statistical information about the oceans. Encourage students to explore the many links on the page. **http://inspire.ospi.wednet.edu:8001/curric/oceans/index.html**

33. Ocean currents move in a clockwise direction in the Northern Hemisphere, but counterclockwise in the Southern Hemisphere. Learn how oceanographers measure ocean currents using drifter buoys. Students can participate in a spreadsheet activity to chart the Gulf Stream, just as Benjamin Franklin did. (He was, in fact, the first person ever to do so.) **http://inspire.ospi.wednet.edu:8001/curric/oceans/drifters/index.html**

34. Archimedes discovered that an object will float in liquid if it displaces a volume of the liquid equal to its own weight. Help students see this principle of buoyancy by adding 6 raisins to a 6 oz. cup of ginger ale or 7-Up. The raisins will sink and then, slowly rise as the CO_2 bubbles—which are lighter than the soda—cling to them. When the bubbles break at the surface, the raisins now weigh more than the liquid they're displacing and will sink again. Ask students how they think this principle allows submarines to float and dive. How can a steel ship weighing thousands of tons float on the seas? Try the buoyancy experiment at the Franklin Institute Science Museum to answer these and other questions. **http://sln.fi.edu/tfi/activity/ocean/oc-2.html**

35. Experiment with volume, density, and mass at the MathMol site. **http://cwis.nyu.edu/pages/mathmol/modules/water/density_intro.html**

36. Create a graph showing diving depths of humans (with and without SCUBA gear or submersibles) and marine animals. Visit the How Deep Can They Go? site. **http://seawifs.gsfc.nasa.gov/OCEAN_PLANET/HTML/oceanography_how_deep.html**

Science Connections

1. Antarctica is the driest, windiest, highest, and coldest continent on earth. When ice forms on the surface of the sea there, the sea's salt is pushed into the water below and spreads throughout the world's oceans. Want to know more? Visit Amazing Antarctica.
   http://www.antdiv.gov.au/aad/p&p/is/amaz_ant/amaz_ant_toc.html

2. Newton's Apple has good activities for students of all ages related to learning about Antarctica.
   http://ericir.syr.edu/Projects/Newton/10/lessons/AntarcticI.html
   http://ericir.syr.edu/Projects/Newton/10/lessons/AntarcticII.html

3. Invite students to visit TerraQuests: Virtual Antarctica to learn about the ecology, animals, and geology of the region.
   http://www.terraquest.com/va/index.html

4. Another Antarctic site, Gateway to Antarctica, has links to the history and ecology of the region.
   http://www.icair.iac.org.nz Barb's Travel Journal: Antarctica is another great resource. It's a personal account of one woman's journey to the region.
   http://www.gowild.com/barb/antarctica/index.html

5. A Guide to the Arctic on the Web has discussions of arctic explorations, Inuit culture and history, and environmental issues facing the seas, including the melting rate of Arctic Sea ice.
   http://coos.dartmouth.edu/~lizzy/arctic.html
   Find out about the status of marine mammals and the fight over oil reserves and mining at the Arctic National Wildlife Refuge site.
   http://www.igc.apc.org/refuge

6. Woods Hole Oceanographic Institute is a must-see for any study of the oceans. **http://www.whoi.edu** Select the *K-12 Resources Link* or just go straight to **http://www.whoi.edu/k-12/k12-resources.html** to find ocean-related links galore.

7. Learn about Jacques Cousteau, the Cousteau Society and their role in preserving our oceans.
   http://www.math.clemson.edu/~rsimms/cousteau.html
   The Calypso, Cousteau's research vessel, sank on Jan. 6, 1996 after being hit by a barge. Learn about what happened to the vessel.
   http://www2.nando.net/newsroom/ntn/world/011496/world5_8548.html

8. In 1994, The Cousteau Society drafted the "Bill of Rights for Future Generations" and submitted it to the United Nations General Assembly. Read the entire document at
   http://www.math.clemson.edu/~rsimms/cs/wf8.1 Discuss with students what impact, if any, they think this document might have.

9. Jacques Cousteau said, "My dream is that, like dolphins, we can intelligently join together and work together to save our planet and ourselves." What does he mean? Learn all about dolphins at the Dolphin FAQ, a great site.
   http://www.ping.be/~ping1081/eghtm/egdolfaq.htm

Jacques Cousteau

Dolphins

10. If your students can't get enough of dolphins, have them visit E Cards—Common Dolphins **http://www.e-cards.inter.net/writeups/dolphin.html** and Project Pod Dolphin Research, to learn what's happening with bottlenose dolphins in Florida. **http://members.aol.com/projectpod/index.html** The Dolphins in Crisis site tells about past and current dangers to dolphins. **http://www.bev.net/education/schools/pfork/pfefifth/dophins.htm** Finally, don't miss the Dolphin Picture Gallery. **http://www.dolphin-synergy.com/predolphin.html**

11. The Earth and Sky site is a daily science radio series that should not be missed. Be sure to select the *Past Shows* link to discover excellent information on oceans and use their search engine. You might wish to assign students the task of sorting through this comprehensive site to read and share findings with their peers. **http://www.earthsky.com**

12. There are literally hundreds of Web sites with information about whales. Following are some of the best sites:
   • The WWWeb Virtual Library—Whale-Watching. **http://blues.helsinki.fi:80/whale**

   • Watery World of Whales in Australia. **http://whales.magna.com.au/home.html**
   • The Virtual Whale Museum created by a third grade class. **http://www.shs.org/whales/home.html**
   • The Virtual Whales Project focuses on feeding behaviors of Pacific humpback whales. **http://www.sfu.ca/~michaec/whales.htm**
   • Whales—A Thematic Web Unit **http://curry.edschool.virginia.edu:80/~kpj5e/Whales**
   • WhaleNet **http://users.aol.com/yorspecial/starfish/tell-tail.html#oceans**

Whale Breaching

13. Even more whale sites:
   • Tirpitz, a Norwegian site.
   http://tirpitz.ibg.uit.no/wwww/ss.html
   • Whale and Dolphin pictures.
   http://elpc54136.lboro.ac.uk/pictures
   • The Killer Whale Adoption Project in British Colombia offers beautiful photographs and information about how to help and protect killer whales. **http://www.zoology.ubc.ca/~adoption**
   • California Gray Whale information.
   http://www.slocs.k12.ca.us/whale/whale0.html
   • Invite a whale to class! Well, sort of. Download sounds of orcas at Sea World
   http://www.ccsr.uiuc.edu/~gmk/ Projects/Orcas-SW
   • Whale Adoption Project: International Wildlife Coalition **http://www.webcom.com/~iwcwww/ whale_adoption/waphome.html**
   • Whales and Dolphins
   http://longwood.cs.ucf.edu/~MidLink/ whale.html

14. Whale Corps, sponsored by the Santa Barbara Museum of Natural History, has lots of information on whales and whale sightings off the coast of Santa Barbara, California. **http://www.rain.org/~inverts/ WHALECORP/whlcorp.htm**

15. The state of Vermont has a whale named Charlotte, but she doesn't live in an aquarium. Discover who Charlotte is and how she is helping in the study of geology and history of the area.
   http://www.uvm.edu/whale/whalehome.html

16. The Tale of the Whales site has some interesting links and information including dolphin safety, shark fossils, and the recent manatee deaths in Florida caused by red tide. Click each of the embedded links to explore.
   http://whales.prodigy.com/index.html
   Learn more about manatees at the Save the Manatee Club site.
   http://www.objectlinks.com/ MANATEE/homepage.htm?54,75

17. WhaleNet at Wheeler College, Boston, has excellent educational resources, links, and research vessel reports. Students can even ask a scientist questions

and become keypals with students around the world who are studying a similar unit. **http://whale.wheelock.edu**

18. The Whale and Dolphin Conservation Society site in England offers information on these majestic creatures and on the status of commercial fishing and whaling around the world. **http://www.glen.co.uk/wdcs**

19. The first Voyage of the Mimi is an adventure not to be missed. Created by the Bank Street College of Education, students are introduced to a scientific expedition to study whales. Learn more about the Mimi program at the Sunburst Communications site. **http://www.nysunburst.com/mimi.html** Fans of the Mimi Voyages will also want to visit The Mimi Connections site hosted by Peter Marston (aka Captain Granville) **http://www1.shore.net/~nya/MIMI.html** and The Mimi for Landlubbers Telecommunications Project. **http://www.voicenet.com/~bdolton/ mimi96.html**

20. Ocean water is salty because freshwater rains wash salt from soils and carry it to the seas. (About three percent of sea water is salt.) Invite students to download an experiment to determine why the sea is salty. **gopher://ericir.syr.edu:70/0R0-2339- /Lesson/Subject/ Science/cecsci.166**

Seahorse

21. Oceans contain important minerals. Besides salt, they contain magnesium, bromine, and manganese. Visit the Periodic Table of Elements on-line to discover more about these minerals and how we use them in our everyday lives. Students have their choice of several interactive tables.
    • **http://www.shef.ac.uk/uni/academic/A-C/chem/web-elementsweb-elements-home.html**
    • **http://steele.isgs.uiuc.edu/pt**
    • **http://www.cs.ubc.ca/elements/periodic-table**

22. EcoNet provides information on and many links to the status of oceans, rivers, and seas. **http://www.igc.apc.org/igc/www.water.html**

23. The U.S. Geologic Survey has maps of the U.S. sea floor as well as many links to marine geology resources. Select the *Learning Web* link for some interesting activities. **http://www.usgs.gov**

24. Older students may be interested in the ATOC (Acoustic Thermometry of Ocean Climate) site at UC San Diego. Select the *Marine Mammal Research* and *Climate Research* links to see what's currently being studied. **http://atoc.ucsd.edu**

25. The American Oceans Campaign works to protect the seas. Find out why they are not happy with the practices of Sea World. **http://www.ibb.com/aoc.htm**

26. Teachers should not miss EnviroLink, one of the best environmental education servers on the Internet. **http://www.envirolink.org**

27. Coral reefs have been called the "rain forests of the sea." Ask students to think about why that might be so. Visit the How to Save Coral Reefs site. **http://www.stf.ycg.org/starcora.htm**

28. Coral reefs in different parts of the world are endangered by pollution. Sewage from cities and factories eventually makes its way to the sea. Chemicals from sewage, brought by ocean tides and currents, and oil from accidental spills harm the plants and animals in the reefs. As with any food chain, chemically altered seaweed (which grows in the reefs) harms the animals that feed on it and the humans who harvest it. The Coral Reef page is

loaded with information and links.
http://planet-hawaii.com/sos/coralreef.html

29. Students may be interested to know that coral has recently been implanted in some people to spur the growth of new bone. Harvesting coral from fragile reefs is not a problem as long as it is done in ways that sustain the reefs as living structures. Learn more about coral at the Coral Forests site.
http://www.blacktop.com/coralforest

30. Did you know that seaweed is just a common name for kelp? Learn many facts about seaweed at the Seaweed Information Server and even pick up a recipe or two for some tasty seaweed treats!
http://seaweed.ucg.ie/seaweed.html

31. Tide pools are located in areas where waves pound rocky shores continuously, and changes in water level and temperature are constant. Ask students to create a chart showing the physical characteristics of seaweed that allows it to endure such harsh conditions. Visit the Tidepool site.
http://octopus.gma.org/katahdin/tidepool.html

32. Older students will enjoy the Deep Sea Research site to view pictures and videos of undersea submarines and laboratories.
http://www.jamstec.go.jp/jamstec/deepp.html

33. Activities relating to various marine mammals can be found at Sea World's site.
http://www.bev.net/education/SeaWorld/teacher guides.html After researching animals, have

Coral

students create a chart or mural classifying the creatures by the ocean zones in which they live: sunlight, twilight or abyssal zones.

34. Sea turtles are in danger of extinction. Visit the Earth Island Institute and select the *Sea Turtle Restoration Project* link to learn more. **http://www.earthisland.org** Additionally, everything you need to know about dolphin-safe tuna and turtle-safe-shrimp can be found at this site.

35. In 1989, the Exxon Valdez ran aground and spilled almost eleven million gallons of oil into Prince William Sound, Alaska. Learn details of what happened at **http://www.alaska.net:80/~ospic** Select the *What Happened on March 24, 1989* link to get started. After researching the Valdez accident, have students determine firsthand the problems of cleaning up an oil spill. Visit the Franklin Institute Science Museum for an experiment where students attempt to remove oil from water. **http://sln.fi.edu/tfi/activity/earth/earth-2.html** Another set of activities related to oil spills can be found at the Newton's Apple site. **http://ericir.syr.edu/Projects/Newton/10/lessons/Oilspill.html**

36. There's nothing like the Great Barrier Reef in Australia. It extends 1,240 miles along the Queensland coast and hosts the most complex diversity of marine life in the world. Take a virtual field trip to explore its beauty. **http://www.lonelyplanet.com/dest/aust/gbreef.htm** View beautiful underwater photographs of the Great Barrier Reef and Melbourne area. **http://werple.mira.net.au/~margaret/scuba.htm**

37. The Underwater Page in Australia has good information, photos, and links. **http://student.uq.edu.au/~s058655/contents.htm**

38. For updates on campaigns to save our oceans, visit the International Marine Mammals Project. **http://www.earthisland.org/immp/immp.html**

39. Students interested in helping protect our oceans can visit the Save Our Seas site **http://planet-hawaii.com/sos** and Ocean Awareness, a site that discusses what can be done to stop pollution of our oceans and seas. **http://www.cs.fsu.edu/projects/sp95ug/group1.7/ocean1.html**

40. Older students may wish to read an editorial, "The Politics of Extinction" by Captain Paul Watson, concerning the rate of extinction of species in the oceans. Have them respond to it orally or in a response journal. **http://envirolink.org/archives/seashep/0066.html**

41. For those students interested in SCUBA diving, visit the SCUBA site. **http://oceans.net/scuba.html**

42. The bends (decompression sickness) is a serious condition. How do divers prevent it? Find out at Newton's Apple. Download the activity to complete in class.**http://ericir.syr.edu/Projects/Newton/11/bends.html**

43. Share the excitement of an exploration with the scientists who study Antarctica. Visit Newton's Apple to download a fun, related activity. **http://ericir.syr.edu/Projects/Newton/10/lessons/AntarcticI.html**

44. How do dolphins communicate? Conduct a lesson called "Smell and Tell," available at the Newton's Apple site. **http://ericir.syr.edu/Projects/Newton/13/lessons/dolcom.html**

45. Learn about solar, wind, and water power at the Renewable Energy Education Models site. Ask students why they think people are trying to harness the power of the oceans. **http://solstice.crest.org/renewables/re-kiosk/index.shtml**

46. Pangaea, named by geologists, was the single supercontinent that broke up some 250 million years ago. Older students interested in the study of plate tectonics should visit this site: **http://www.seismo.unr.edu/ftp/pub/louie/class/100/plate-tectonics.html**

Have students use a copy of a world map, cut out the shapes of continents, and then arrange them as they may have fit together millions of years ago. Discuss support for and flaws in their theories.

47. Younger students interested in plate tectonics will find a hands-on experiment at The Franklin Institute Science Museum.
http://sln.fi.edu/tfi/activity/earth/earth-9.html

48. Ocean Odyssey Hands-on Children's Museum has links for all ages. This is a site not to be missed.
http://www.wln.com/~deltapac/ocean_od.html

49. Have students design and maintain a freshwater aquarium in your class. Visit the Fish Information Service (FINS) index for pointers to much information. **http://www.actwin.com/fish** On the lighter side, students can go to The Amazing Fish Cam to see live video shots of an aquarium. Be sure to check out their links to *Other Interesting Internet Fish Places*. And, while they're there, have students select the *Tell Time with Fish* link. It's too silly to pass up.
http://www.netscape.com/fishcam/fishcam.html

50. Winds and ocean currents largely determine our weather. What is the El Niño condition in the Pacific? Have older students find out at the El Niño Theme Page.
http://www.pmel.noaa.gov/toga-tao /el-nino/home.html

51. Teachers can download some great activities from the Tomorrow's Forecast: Oceans and Weather site.
http://educate.si.edu/art-to-zoo/oceans/cover.html

52. The Exploratorium has a Filling the Marina exhibit that talks about how water reshapes the land.
http://www.exploratorium.edu

53. The Underwater World Home page at the Monterey Bay Aquarium has plenty of good information.
http://pathfinder.com/@@4d4HzAQA3yDF2Zjx/ pathfinder/kidstuff/underwater/index.html

54. Pearl culturing is a very important industry in Japan, the Phillipines, and other countries in the Pacific.

Discover how oysters make pearls at the Monterey Bay Aquarium Q & A page.
http://pathfinder.com/@@4d4HzAQA3yDF2Zjx/ pathfinder/kidstuff/underwater/fishyq/pearl.html

55. Tsunamis are huge ocean waves, usually triggered by earthquakes or volcanic eruptions under the sea. The Welcome to Tsunami! site has great information.
http://www.geophys.washington.edu/tsunami/ welcome.html

56. Take a virtual field trip to aquariums all over the world at the Directory of Public Aquaria.
http://www.actwin.com/fish/public.cgi

57. The Oceana Project in Byron Bay, Australia, raises consciousness about whales, dolphins, and porpoises. See pictures and listen to these amazing cetacea communicate.
http://nornet.nor.com.au/users/oceania

58. The Mote Marine Laboratory in Florida is a fun site to peruse. There are many marine mammal information links, as well as good photos.
http://www.marinelab.sarasota.fl.us/Welcome.html

59. Are fish what your students want to learn about? Then check out the Electronic Zoo/NetVet's Fish links.
http://netvet.wustl.edu/fish.htm

60. What is acid rain and how does it affect the seas? Do an experiment at Newton's Apple.
http://ericir.syr.edu/Projects/Newton/9/ acdrain.html

61. ScienceWeb often has good oceanography links and information.
http://scienceweb.dao.nrc.ca/default.htm

62. Older students will find the Marine Biology Database to be very helpful. Make a selection from their list or use their search engine.
http://www.calpoly.edu:8010/cgi-bin/db/db/ marine-biology/:/templates/ index

63. Which cetaceans, fish, pinnipeds, and sea turtles are on the Endangered Species List? Go to the

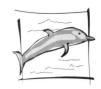

Endangered Species Act Home Page for a well-crafted chart with embedded links to each sea creature. **http://king fish.ssp.nmfs.gov/tmcintyr/esahome.html**

64. Florida's Marine Habitat is a site that gives factual information on many marine habitats including mangroves, rock and coral reefs, estuary and bay communities, and the ocean. **http://www.gorp.com/gorp/location/fl/fishing/marine.htm**

65. Students can download instructions to make a water cycle. **gopher://ericir.syr.edu:70/0R0-3063-/Lesson/Subject/ Science/cecsci.190**

66. Want to know what's happening in the ocean right now? Interactive Marine Observations offers an interactive map. Click on a specific region to get weather and ocean status reports generated by buoy marine stations around the world. **http://thunder.met.fsu.edu/~nws/buoy**

67. Ocean Planet, an exhibit at the Smithsonian, should not be missed. **http://seawifs.gsfc.nasa.gov/ocean_ planet.html**

68. Many students saw the 1993 movie, "Free Willy." Soon after the movie was made, Keiko, the killer whale "actor" of the movie, was found to be living in extremely cramped conditions in his Mexico City aquarium and was suffering from a serious skin virus. Thanks to the efforts of marine specialists and children around the world, Keiko now makes his home in far better conditions at Newport, Oregon. Keiko's health continues to improve and scientists hope one day to release him back into the ocean. Learn all the latest news about Keiko at **http://www.ohwy.com/or/k/keiko.htm** and even more at The Free Willy News site. **http://www.igc.apc.org/ei/immp/keiko.html**

69. Elephant seals were widely thought to be extinct by the end of the 19th century. But they made a remarkable recovery and now their numbers double every 4 to 5 years! Visit the Año Nuevo Island Reserve site and select the Elephant Seal link. **http://www.ucsc.edu/mb/Ano**

70. See a list of threatened or endangered animals, sorted by countries on The World Conservation Union's list at the IUCN site. **http://www.wcmc.org.uk/data/database/rl_anml_combo.html**

71. An island is born! Learn all about Hawaii's newest island, Loihi, forming 3,000 feet beneath the Pacific. Don't call your travel agent anytime soon, however. The island won't break the surface of the water for another 50,000 years or so! Read all about it at the Hawaiian Volcanoes site. **http://vulcan.wr.usgs.gov/Volcanoes/Hawaii/Loihi/framework.html** After learning about Loihi, have students learn about the area of the Pacific Ocean called the Ring of Fire because of its many active volcano eruptions. Select the *Plate Tectonics*, *Hot Spots,* and *Ring of Fire* links.

72. According to Hawaiian legend, Maui, the trickster, pulled the Hawaiian islands from the sea to bring fire to the people. So what is a volcano really and how do they form? Find out at VolcanoWorld. **http://volcano.und.nodak.edu/** Then view photographs of volcanoes around the U.S. **http://vulcan.wr.usgs.gov/Photo/framework.html**

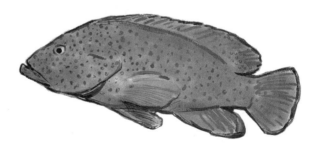

73. Download a "Make an Ocean in a Bottle" activity at the Franklin Institute Science Museum. **http://sln.fi.edu/tfi/activity/ocean/oc-1.html**

74. Visit the TerraQuest: Virtual Galápagos for a great history of the area, an atlas, photographs, education workbook for teachers, and video clips from an expedition to these islands located six miles off Ecuador's coast. **http://www.terraquest.com/galapagos/intro.html**

75. Dolphins, porpoises, and whales are all cetaceans. They breathe through "blowholes" on the tops of their heads and they use echolocation to find their way through the dark oceans. The Whale Songs site has an activity about echolocation. **http://curry.edschool.virginia.edu/~kpj5e/Whales/LessonPlans/WhaleSongs.HTML**

76. Learn more about marine mammals' behavior and communication at the Marine Mammal Acoustics site.**http://www.umassd.edu/public/people/kamaral/thesis/marinemammalacoustics.html**

Another good place to visit is the About Marine Mammals site. **http://www.marinelab.sarasota.fl.us/WMARINE.HTM**

77. Cephalopods may not have any backbones but they sure have lots of arms! Learn about octopi, squids, and other creatures at the Cephalopod Page. **http://is.dal.ca/~ceph/wood.html**

78. Not to be missed! A Treasure Hunt, sponsored by the JASON Project, tests students' knowledge of oceanography while they search for the treasure. **http://www.eds.com/jason/ecmc0000.htm**

79. Tour the NR-1 Submarine at the Jason Project site. There are photographs, sketches, and even video clips of this submarine that maps ancient coral reefs. **http://seawifs.gsfc.nasa.gov/JASON/HTML/EXPEDITIONS_JASON_7_NR1.html**

Shells

Shark

80. Shark lovers should head directly to Shark Links Galore site.
http://www.oceanstar.com/shark/links.htm

81. Want to know about mollusks? Visit the Mollusca page.
http://www.york.biosis.org/zrdocs/zoolinfo/ grp_moll.htm

82. Students interested in seashells will want to go to the Conchology site.
http://www.club.innet.be/~year0078

83. The ancient Greek philosopher Aristotle discovered that seawater levels stay pretty much the same. Although oceans lose water through evaporation, they are replenished by the same amount of water added by rainfall. Read what he had to say in his own words. Were all of his theories correct? Why or why not?
http://paul.spu.edu/~hawk/aristotle.html
Select the *Meteorology* link.

84. Older students should visit Paleontology Without Walls at UC Berkeley. Select the *Geological Time* link to see a geological time scale or the *Phylogeny* link to learn about the ancestor/descendant relationships of all organisms.
http://www.ucmp.berkeley.edu/exhibit/ exhibits.html

85. Learn all about the ships that Greenpeace uses on its voyages to protect the oceans of the world.
http://www.greenpeace.org/marine/ships.html

Language Arts Connections

1. The Cousteau Society named its research vessel "Alcyone" after the daughter of the Greek god of wind. The ship "Calypso" was named after a sea nymph in Homer's *Odyssey*. Poseidon was the Greek god of the sea and Neptune was the Roman god of the sea. Salacia is the Roman goddess of the oceans. Find out more about each deity and read myths at The Mythology and Folklore site.
http://pubweb.acns.nwu.edu/~pib/mythfolk.htm
Select the *Regional Folklore and Mythology* link to find myths and legends organized by cultural and geographic region. Select the *Special Topics* link for myths relating to meteorological and other natural events like "flood myths" from around the world. After reading myths, have students write and share their own.

2. Discover what it's like to live surrounded by the sea. Encourage students to communicate with classes whose students live on islands all over the world. Sign up for keypals at the Intercultural E-Mail

Classroom Connection.
http://www.stolaf.edu/network/iecc

3. Have students write fictional journal entries as they take on the role of an ancient ocean explorer or an immigrant coming to America by sea. (See Social Studies Connections.)

4. Write a trivia book of Fish Facts. Students can start by visiting Woods Hole Oceanographic Institute to learn (almost) everything they need to know about fish.
http://www.wh.whoi.edu/homepage/faq.html

5. The Children's Literature Web Guide is a comprehensive site with links to classic and contemporary literature, songs, poetry, folklore, myths, legends, literature reviews, parent and teacher resources and more. Find links to the books you'd like your students to read. There are many ocean-theme stories and books. Challenge students to find stories of sea monsters in literature.
http://www.ucalgary.ca/~dkbrown/index.html

6. Did you know that books like Jules Verne's *Twenty Thousand Leagues Under the Sea*, Robert Louis Stevenson's *Treasure Island*, and Herman Melville's *Moby Dick* are on the Web? Find them at Alex: A Catalog of Electronic Texts on the Internet. Type in a title of any book or author to search.
http://www.lib.ncsu.edu/staff/morgan/alex/alex-index.html

7. The Book Nook is created and maintained by and for kids of all ages. There is a comprehensive collection of book reviews written by children. All children are encouraged to write and submit their own critiques. Ask students to read some of the recommended books (see Additional Resources), write, and submit their reviews.
http://www.schoolnet.ca/english/arts/lit/booknook/index.html

8. The Reading Rainbow Home Page from PBS is a great resource for books and activities for younger children. Select the *Program Descriptions and Activity Suggestions* link.
http://www.pbs.org:80/readingrainbow/rr.html

9. Did your students know that a group of whales is called a pod or that the offspring of a fish is called a fry and the offspring of a seal is called a pup or a whelp? Create a dictionary of ocean creatures and their unusual names.

10. Many ocean-related words come from Greek and Latin roots. For example, the word plankton comes from *planktos*, meaning drifting or wandering. (Planktonic plants drift with the ocean currents.) What other words come from Greek and Roman root words? Create an Oceans glossary. Start at the Vocabulary: Britannica Online Articles related to the ocean. **http://www-pf.eb.com/cgi-bin/s?DocF=950814.cover/index.html** Students might also wish to check the Glossary of Water Resources Terms. **http://www.txdirect.net/users/eckhardt/glossary.html**

11. Have students write shape poems using themes of the sea by turning the lines of their poems into the shape of the subject matter, such as a wave, a ship, or a sea creature.

12. Haiku comes from the island culture of Japan. Have students read examples of the poems and get directions on how to write their own verses at the Haiku for People site.
http://home.sn.no/home/keitoy/haiku.html

13. At Tales of Wonder: Folk and Fairy Tales, encourage students to read ocean-related stories. This is another site that shouldn't be missed.
http://www.ece.ucdavis.edu/~darsie/tales.html

14. After learning about what's happening with Keiko, the killer whale (see Science Connections), have students write an article, advice column, song, or poem about Keiko. Then go to the Children's Writings site to find pointers to many places on the Web where students can submit writing.
http://www.ucalgary.ca/~dkbrown/writings.html Other creative writing ideas your students may wish to submit for publication: Write fictional stories about finding a treasure chest in the sea. Conduct a fictional interview with a marine mammal. Write stories about living in the deep sea. (What obstacles would have to be overcome?) Write a *porquoi*, or "why" story about why the sea is salty or how the sea

anemone, trumpetfish, viperfish, flying fish, or sea lion got its name. Write stories about sunken treasures, shipwrecks, and messages found in bottles.

15. Many cars today have personalized license plates that use letter and number codes to relay messages. Invite students to create a personalized plate for an oceanographer, a scuba diver, a whale, a mollusk, a stingray, or a bioluminescent fish! Look at a few fun examples at the KNX Radio Station site where they are running a personalized plate contest. **http://www.knx1070.com/license**

16. The Indigenous Peoples' Literature site offers a glimpse into other cultures. Read how people around the world view the sea. **http://www.indians.org/welker/natlit02.htm**

17. Have students create posters with whale facts or write a book of whale facts, cut into the shape of a whale. Visit The Whale Information Network, Australia. **http://www.webmedia.com.au/whales/whales6.html**

18. International Marine Signal Flags (semaphore flags) are used by ships at sea. Started by the British Board of Trade in 1857, there were originally 18 flags which, when combined, could communicate more than 70,000 messages. The current version has 40 flags and pennants. See the colorful flags at **http://osprey.erin.gov.au/flags/signal-flags.html**

and the signaling system at **http://155.187.10.12/flags/semaphore.html** Then have students make a set of flags (see Arts Connections) and use them to send messages.

19. SCUBA is an acronym for Self-Contained Underwater Breathing Apparatus. What other acronyms are related to the sea? Challenge students to search the Acronym Server Dictionary in the United Kingdom. **gopher://info.mcc.ac.uk/11/miscellany/acronyms** Students can type in such keywords as *underwater, ocean, nautical,* or *marine* to see related acronyms. Another site to look at is the Acronym and Abbreviation Server. **http://www.ucc.ie/info/net/acronyms/acro.html** Older students may want to view the Ocean Science-Related Acronyms site. **http://www.pmel.noaa.gov/pubs/acronym-list.html**

20. Create a dictionary of nautical terms. Visit the Nautical Pointers site and select the Dictionaries link. **http://pc-78-120.udac.se:8001/WWW/Nautica/Pointers.html**

21. Have students listen to sea chanties (see Arts Connections) and then write their own. **http://www.cco.caltech.edu/~ward/chanty/chanty.html**

The Arts (Fine, Dramatic, Music) Connections

1. In the 18th and 19th centuries, sailors on long sea voyages practiced the art of scrimshaw, carving in whalebone and ivory. In the mid-1600s, colonists killed baleen whales primarily for their oil and meat. But by the 1700s, when deep sea whaling began, sailors sought out the sperm whale and used its teeth (which baleen whales do not have) to make scrimshaw. Today, since most ivory-bearing animals are (or should be) protected, scrimshaw artists substitute such materials as ivory nuts from South American palm trees. Students can make mock-scrimshaw out of plaster of Paris. Take a look at scrimshaw examples at Ye Olde Shop Store in Kauai, Hawaii. **http://www.mixedplate.com/scrimshaw**

2. Navajo Indians, Pueblo Indians, and the Spanish all practiced the art of sand painting. It was also practiced on the Isle of Wight, a large island off the southern coast of England, where it was introduced during the reign of George III. (There, the craft is called *marmotinto*.) Students can make sand paintings using heavy cardboard and variously colored sands. Start by "painting" a picture with a mixture of glue and water. (Add only enough water to thin the glue.) Then sprinkle sand over the glued area, brushing away the excess sand as you go. Get specific directions at the Starwave site. **http://family.starwave.com/funstuff/activity/tv274.html**

3. Gyotaku (gyo＝fish, taku＝impression) is the ancient art of fish painting—literally with a fish! This Japanese art form was traditionally part of Samurai warriors' training. Each man had to record the fish he caught by inking them and pressing paper to the inked fish. Check the Hawaiian Fish Prints site to see how it's done. **http://www.mauigateway.com/~gyotaku** Your students can participate in this art form using India ink and a fresh fish. Fish with distinct scale patterns make the best designs.

4. The Japanese also create fish or carp banners to hang from bamboo poles on Children's Day each May. Have students make their own carp banners by drawing an outline of a large fish on construction paper. Cut out the outline and glue the edges together after stuffing tissue paper into the fish. Decorate with scales, fins, etc. Hang from the classroom ceiling. See carp kite models at the Sumitomo Corp. **http://www.sumitomocorp.co.jp/closer/5.html** Need some carp kite inspiration? Visit a really interesting site in Japan called Nishikigoi. You'll be welcomed by a fish and learn everything you ever wanted to know about "koi." Be sure to read the story about koi and how to appreciate one! **http://www.digitalstudio.or.jp/studiois/NISHIKIGOI.html**

5. Learn about crafts of the early Polynesians, including a quilt-making technique called *tivaevae*. Challenge students to make their own version of these interesting patchwork quilts. **http://www.ck/tivaevae.htm**

6. The Wooden Canoe Heritage Association is dedicated to disseminating information on canoeing heritage in North America. **http://www.wcha.org/toc.html** Select the *Historic Canoe Catalog* link for some interesting photographs. Then create miniature models of these historic canoes.

7. Hobby World Montreal has historical information and pictures of clippers, schooners, and other kinds of ships used to explore the world's oceans throughout history. **http://www.hobbyworld-inc.com/mainship.html** Do Viking ships interest your students? Then head to the World of the Vikings in England for pictures and information. **http://demon.com.uk/past/vikings** After looking at these pictures, have students create their own models.

8. Make origami sea creatures and boats! Lincoln Schools' Origami Links page has links to origami sites around the Web. **http://www.mind.net/music/origami.html** Jasper's Origami Menagerie has instructions on how to make mammals, birds, and insects. **http://www.cytex.com/go/jasper/origami** Joseph Wu's Origami site is another one to see. **http://www.datt.co.jp/Origami**

9. Create illustrations of tide pool filter feeding animals such as sponges or clams, and scavengers, such as snails and crabs. Why are their jobs so important in the ecosystem? How have these animals adapted to the conditions of a tidepool environment? Visit the Life in a Massachusetts Tide Pool site for an illustration and information. **http://www.umassd.edu/public/people/kamaral/ thesis/tidepools.html**
Use construction paper strips (taped or glued together to form a chain) to create a marine food chain. Hang from the ceiling. Students can also create food chains of these ecosystems: marsh, beach, kelp forest, and coral reef.

10. Visit the Marine Art Information center for many great links to galleries and museums. **http://www.marineart.com**

11. Make dioramas of tide pools or coral reefs.

12. Creatures of the sea have some very helpful appendages, including spines (starfish, sea urchin) and arms and tentacles (octopus, jelly fish). Some animals, like penguins, can camouflage themselves with protective coloration and shading. Creatures living in the abyssal zone, far below the area of light penetration in the sea, have adapted to their dark, high pressure environment. Most are small and have soft bodies with little bone structure. Others are bioluminescent. Have students visit the British Columbia Creature Page to look at pictures of hundreds of underwater creatures and marine plants.
http://clever.net/kerry/creature/creature.htm
Then make papier mâché models of some of these creatures, along with information cards telling about their special features, appendages, or behaviors. Students might also want to create their own fictional underwater creature.

13. Catch a wave at the Surfing Museum in Santa Cruz, CA. If you're lucky, you might even catch a glimpse of a surfer from their live camera stationed at Cowell Beach!
http://www.cruzio.com/arts/scva/surf.html

14. Create dioramas of the Chunnel, the tunnel connecting England with continental Europe. (See Social Studies Connections.)

15. Ask teams of students to create salt dough maps of the sea. For a recipe, head to Zia Salt Dough Models site. **http://www.zia.com/tdough.htm** Use a piece of plywood or thick, corrugated cardboard as a base. Use the salt dough clay to shape the land forms and sea. Use tempera paint to color-code the continents and ocean areas on the map.

16. Find directions to make a plankton net.
http://www.umassd.edu/public/people/kamaral/thesis/planktonnet.html

17. Have students make a set of semaphore flags (see Language Arts Connections) to use in skits or just for fun to communicate with one another. After learning the signals, demonstrate them to other classes.

18. Make such traditional aborigine crafts as boomerangs or "stone and bark" paintings after visiting the Australian Dreamtime Aboriginal Art Gallery.
http://www.mbay.net/~patricia/art/index.html
Encourage interested students to search the Internet for instructions on how to page other traditional crafts from island cultures throughout the world.

19. After learning about The Law of the Sea Treaty (see Social Studies Connections) divide students into debate teams to discuss whether or not the U.S. should sign it.

20. Divide students into teams to simulate a 1946 debate of the International Whaling Committee (IWC), the group formed to protect the future of whales.

21. What is musical or singing sand and what does it have to do with Charles Darwin? Find out at Musical Sand in Japan.
http://www.yo.rim.or.jp/~smiwa/index.html

22. What would a study of the oceans be without listening to a few tunes from the Beach Boys?! Head to Capitol Records to download some sound clips.
http://www.hollywoodandvine.com Select the *Search by Artist* link and then select the *Audio* file.

23. Listen to marine sounds, including foghorns, boat warnings, and harbor sounds, and find links to folk songs and sea chanties!
http://www.marineart.com/www.shtml#s

24. Sing along with traditional sea chanties, hosted by Caltech, and challenge students to write their own. (See Language Arts Connections.)
http://www.cco.caltech.edu/~ward/chanty/chanty.html

25. Go to the Digital Tradition Folk Song Database and search for songs using such keywords as *ship, boat, ocean, sea, whale*, etc.
http://pubweb.parc.xerox.com/digitrad

26. Listen to samples of island music from around the world at the Seventh Wave Island Music site.
http://planet-hawaii.com/7thwave

27. Culminate the unit by turning the classroom into an underwater environment! Students can make models of sea animals, coral reefs, tide pools, etc. Create marine mammals from chicken wire frames and papier mâché and hang from ceilings to represent the sea surface. (Hang blue cellophane from the ceiling.) Students may wish to build the base of a volcano as well. Finally, create snorkel masks for other students to wear as they "swim" through your classroom. Dive into Aquanaut, a site loaded with SCUBA pictures and links.
http://www.aquanaut.com

28. Thinking about creating your own class Web site? Encourage students to share what they've learned in this unit. They can post information, their writing, pictures of artwork, and links to their favorite ocean theme sites.

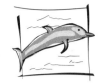

Additional Resources

Adler, David. *Our Amazing Ocean*. Troll Associates, 1983.

Ancona, George. *Turtle Watch*. Macmillan, 1987.

Arthur, Alex. *Shell* (Eyewitness Books series). Alfred A. Knopf, 1989.

Bramwell, Martin. *Oceans*. Franklin Watts, 1984.

Carr, Terry. *Spill! the Story of the Exxon Valdez*. Watts, 1991.

Carson, Rachel. *The Sea Around Us*. Oxford University Press, 1961.

Cousteau Society. *Coral, the Sea's Great Builders*. Simon & Schuster, 1991.

Doris, Ellen. *Marine Biology*. Thames & Hudson, 1993.

Epstein, Sam and Beryl. *What's for Lunch? The Eating Habits of Seashore Creatures*. Macmillan, 1985.

Freeman, Don. *The Seal and the Slick*. Viking, 1974.

Grover, Wayne. *Dolphin Adventure: A True Story*. Greenwillow Books, 1990.

Hughey, Pat. *Scavengers and Decomposers: The Clean-Up Crew*. Macmillan, 1984.

Lasky, Kathryn. *Shadows in the Water: A Starbuck Family Adventure*. Harcourt, 1992.

L'Engle, Madeline. *A Ring of Endless Light*. Dell, 1980.

Jasperson, William. *A Day in the Life of a Marine Biologist*. Little, Brown and Co., 1982.

Johnson, Rebecca. *The Great Barrier Reef: A Living Laboratory*. Lerner, 1991.

Lambert, David. *Seas and Oceans* (Our World series). Silver Burdett Press, 1988.

Macquitty, Miranda. *Ocean* (Eyewitness Books series). Alfred A. Knopf, 1995.

Mallory, Kenneth and Andrea Conley. *Rescue of Stranded Whales*. Simon & Schuster, 1989.

O'Dell Scott. *Island of the Blue Dolphins*. Dell Publishing, 1960.

Osborne, Chester. *The Memory String*. Macmillan, 1984.

Parker, Steve. *Seashore* (Eyewitness Books series). Alfred A. Knopf, 1989.

Pringle, Laurence. *Chains, Webs, and Pyramids: The Flow of Energy in Nature*. Harper Collins, 1975.

Sandok, Cass. R. *The World's Oceans*. Franklin Watts, 1986.

Simon, Seymour. *From Shore to Ocean Floor: How Life Survives in the Sea*. Franklin Watts, 1973.

Simon Seymour. *How to Be an Ocean Scientist in Your Own Home*. J.B. Lippincott, 1988.

Sperry, Armstrong. *Call It Courage*. Macmillan, 1941.

The following videotape titles are produced by PBS. (Check your public library, video rental store, or call 800-344-3337.)
- *Dolphins with Robin Williams*
- *Gray Whales with Christopher Reeve*
- *How Fragile These Frozen Seas*
- *If Dolphins Could Talk*
- *Sea Turtles: Ancient Nomads*
- *The Ancient Mariners*, PBS Odyssey Series
- *Whales!*

The following videotape titles are produced by National Geographic. (Check your public library, video rental store, or call 800-368-2728.)
- *From Here to There*
- *Latitude and Longitude*
- *Let's Explore A Seashore*
- *The Living Ocean*

THEMATIC UNIT—ANCIENT WORLDS

THE ANCIENT WORLDS: GREECE AND ROME

Much of Western Civilization has its origins in the contributions and innovations of the ancient Greek and Roman civilizations. They are the source of much of our art, architecture, philosophy, political thought, mathematics, science, engineering, and theater.

Most states throughout the country mandate an Ancient Civilizations unit, usually in the upper elementary or middle school grades. Greek and Roman myths are also often introduced to students in the younger grades as they study cultures and societies in other parts of the world.

This issue of *Internet Adventures* focuses on two periods of history: the four centuries or so beginning about 800 BC, often called the Classical or Golden Age, when the city-states begin to form, and, secondly, the thousand years from the rise of the Roman Republic (*ca.* 509-27 BC) through the growth of the Roman Empire (*ca.* 27 BC-AD 476).

There are literally hundreds of wonderful sites on the World Wide Web that provide information, illustrations, and photographs of these ancient cultures. Activities in this issue are based on the Social Sciences Frameworks of many states, including CA, TX, FL, and NY. As always, the Newsletter is created so that teachers can integrate social studies, language arts, math, science, art, music, and drama into the overall thematic unit.

In this unit, students will have the opportunity to:

- examine the development of two early civilizations — Greece and Rome;

- consider and compare the contributions of both civilizations—including forms of government, philosophy, science, mathematics, art, architecture, music, theatre, and literature—and the influence of these cultures on our lives today;

- learn about and compare everyday life in ancient Greece and Rome;

- study Greek and Roman values, lore, and ideals;

- create timelines to put historical events in chronological order;

- view maps to understand how and where these societies developed and the diffusion and transmission of ideas, philosophies, and the arts.

- discover the human side of the ancient developers of mathematics and the principles behind the math that students apply each day;

- determine the human qualities of the ancient scientists and the principles behind the natural and social sciences;

- appreciate the origins and development of parts of the English language;

- write descriptive, narrative, and expository compositions incorporating information gleaned from the Internet and other resources.

Begin the unit by displaying for your class the following two sets of items:

(1) various polygons cut from construction paper, an encyclopedia, and pictures of a lighthouse, theater, and boxing;

(2) a calendar, newspaper, and pictures of Roman numerals, a circus, a paved road, and a stop sign. (If you can't find pictures, write the two lists on the blackboard.

Social Studies Connections

Ask students if they know what the common thread is for each of the sets. After generating a list of answers from students, reveal that all of the items in the first set represent contributions of the ancient Greeks. All items in the second set comprise developments by the ancient Romans. Tell students they will use the Internet to help understand the innovations and contributions of both of these civilizations.

The Parthenon, Athens

1. The Ancient World Web is a comprehensive site that has links to wonderful resources for studies of ancient civilizations, including some shown in this issue. (Teachers should note that this site has a Gender and Sexuality link; you may wish to monitor student access. However, keep in mind that this site is one of the best for ancient civilizations and should not be missed.) **http://atlantic.evsc.virginia.edu/julia/AW/meta.html**

2. Asgeir's Library of Antiquity has a large list of sites and links to *The Greek World*, *The Roman World*, *Archaeology*, and *Ancient Science*, among many others. **http://www.uio.no/%7Eaenersen/antiquity.html**

3. Another good site is Diogenes' Links to the Ancient World. **http://www.snider.net/lyceum**   Select the *Ancient Greece* and *Ancient Rome* links.

4. The Greeks developed such things as geometry, the Olympics, drama, public education, libraries, mosaics, and shorthand. Find links to all things Greek at **http://www.snider.net/lyceum/greek.htm** The Romans gave us such things as the circus, concrete, the Julian calendar, newspapers, one-way streets, paved roads, stone bridges, and stop signs. Find links to all things Roman at **http://www.snider.net/lyceum/rome.htm**

5. Older students will find good resources on Greece and Rome, including literature and maps, at the Ancient and Classical Resources site.**http://execpc.com/~dboals/europe.html/** More literature and maps can be found at **http://www.evansville.edu/~wcweb/wc101/grpage.htm**

6. Visit the Kelsey Museum to view the ancient Greek and Roman Gallery.   **http://www.umich.edu/~kelseydb/Outreach/Galleries.html**

7. Another site with excellent resources on ancient civilizations can be found at the University of Michigan. **http://classics.lsa.umich.edu/welcome.html**

8. Have students work in small groups to research the evolution of the city-state, or *polis*. Ask students to think about how Greece's geography affected the development of Greek culture before and after the *polis*. (Small groups of people remained in their local valleys and islands so that many small societies emerged.) Learn about the study of ancient geography. **http://perseus.holycross.edu:80/e-scapes**

9. City-states, such as Athens, had their own governments and traditions and came to think of themselves as separate states or nations built around a single site. Invite students to look at photographic archives of the ruins of the ancient city of Athens. **http://www.indiana. edu/ ~kglowack/Athens/Athens.html**

10. For a brief history of Athens, including information about the status of ruins in Athens today, visit **http://www.vacation.forthnet.gr/athens.html** Learn how 20th century pollutants are affecting the ruins. (See *Science Connections.*)

11. The early Greeks were very interested in geography. They spent much time calculating the heights of mountains, the depths of valleys, etc. Homer even wrote about geography in his epic poem *The Odyssey.* Geographers in ancient Greece made maps based on their own travels and on the stories of other travelers. Geographers also wrote guides to Greek cities. *(See Language Arts Connections.)* View maps of ancient Greece. **http://www.libertynet.org/~terrax/Samples/ greece.html** View maps of ancient Greece and Rome at the Kelsey Museum. **http://www.umich.edu/ ~kelseydb/Outreach/Maps.html**

12. Older students may wish to research city planning in Greece during the Classical Age. Each city-state built a main center, called an *acropolis*, for each town. Streets were laid out in rows that crossed at right angles and houses were arranged in *blocks*. In the center of town was the *agora*, or market place. Other public buildings, such as temples, council halls, and the theater, were grouped around the *agora*. Such larger buildings as the gymnasium and stadium were built on the edge of town. View pictures of the Acropolis, Delphi, Olympia, the Temple of Apollo, and other Greek buildings.**http://libra.caup.umich.edu/ ArchiGopher/GreekArchitecture/ GreekArchitecture.html**

13. Visit The Greek and Roman Cities of Western Turkey site for information. **http://rubens.anu. edu.au/turkeybook/toc1.html**

Scroll down to the *Town Planning* information and select links of interest. Younger students can look at pictures of Athens or other city-states and then recreate them on the classroom floor using blocks.

14. Take a virtual tour of the Acropolis! **http://www.atkinson.yorku.ca/exhibits/ webacropol**

15. Windows on Italy is a site with much textual information on the history of Rome and other Italian cities. **http://www.mi.cnr.it/WOI/explore/explore.html**

16. Learn specifics about Greek and Roman architecture using the Perseus Encyclopedia. **http://www.perseus.tufts.edu/Secondary/ Encyclopedia/encyc.subj.html #Architecture**

17. The CIA Factbook has comprehensive information and statistics on Greece and Italy today. For information on Greece, go to: **http://www.research.att.com/cgi- wald/dbaccess/411?key=95** For information on Italy, go to: **http://www.research.att.com/cgi- wald/dbaccess/411?key=120**

18. How does a city disappear? Encourage students who enjoy mysteries to learn about the present-day search for the lost city of Eliki, once a thriving city-state. Discover what happened to the city and about the attempts of geological oceanographers to find it. Students can even send in their questions to a

scientist who is working on this project.
http://www.ghgcorp.com/geoprobe/eliki.html

19. Learn about another, more famous vanishing city at The Forum at Pompeii site. **http://jefferson.village.virginia.edu/pompeii/forummap.html** Visit the Unguided Tour of Pompeii site. Select the map or the list of sites to see photographs of unearthed ruins taken by a person working on the dig. **http://enterzone.berkeley.edu/ez/e2/articles/frankel/tour1.html** (For more activities on Pompeii, see *Science Connections*).

20. What's the difference between a *democracy* and a *republic*? The ancient Greeks started what we know today as a democratic government, or one ruled directly by the people. The word democratic comes from the Greek *demos*, which means *people* and *kratos,* which means *rule.* Have one group of students research the Assembly. Who spoke at those meetings? What was the job of the Council? Have another group of students research the Republic of Rome. (Republic comes from the Latin words *res publica*, meaning *the affairs of the people).* What was the Senate? Who were the consuls, tribunes, patricians, and plebeians? Have students make a large chart illustrating the major similarities and differences between the two types of governments. Download an activity to help students compare a democracy with a republic. **gopher://bvsd.k12.co.us:70/00/Educational_Resources/Lesson_Plans/Big%20Sky/social_studies/CECsst.181**

Extend the activity by having students create a chart showing the legacy of Greek and Roman political forms in the government of the United States today.

21. Learn about the role of women in Greek mythology and Greek society. **http://www. princeton.edu/~tinalee/women.html**

22. Greek laws were first written down during the Classical Age. The laws related to the family, rights of inheritance, the position of slaves in society, etc. Have students write a list of classroom laws, including issues of listening and speaking, turning in homework late, etc. Form debate teams to argue for or against specific laws. Why are laws written? Invite students to make a list of all the laws they must follow during a single day. Examples include wearing clothes and being driven to school (driver must have a legal driver's license and follow the laws of the road). Visit the Court TV site which discusses laws affecting children. **http://www.courttv.com/kids/law**

23. After the Greeks defeated the Persians, the city-states began to fight with one another. Ask students to research the war between Athens and Sparta. Why was it called the Peloponnesian War and what was the result? Find ancient maps at the Kelsey Museum (See *Social Studies Connections, #11*) to trace the invasion routes.

24. Create a timeline of important events in ancient Greece and Rome to hang across the classroom walls. The events may include important dates in the Archaic Period (8th to 6th century BC), the Classical Period (5th to 4th century BC), and the Hellenistic Period (3rd and 2nd centuries BC). Many students may need an explanation of BC (Before Christ) and AD (Latin: Anno Domini—Year of Our Lord). Non-Christians often use CE (Current Era) and BCE (Before Current Era). Download an activity from Big Sky which helps explain BC numeration and timelines. **gopher://bvsd.k12.co.us:70/00/Educational_Resources/Lesson_Plans/Big%20Sky/social_studies/CECsst.151**

25. Greece Travel Information has links to facts about ancient and modern-day Greece. **http://iris.usc.edu/home/iris/kardaras/tourist.html**

26. The Oracle at Delphi was famous for prophecy. People anxious about the future would visit the oracle to ask a question for a god to answer. Have students research Delphi and then write their own questions and prophecies.

27. The Olympic games started at Olympia, Greece (located in the western part of Peloponnesus) in 776 BC. The games took place every four years until they were abolished by a Roman emperor in 394 AD. The modern Olympic games started again in 1896 and were held in Athens. Have students research all aspects of the ancient games. Were the events similar to the ones played today? Why weren't women allowed to participate or even to be spectators? Why did the men compete in the nude? Why were only those who spoke Greek or were of Greek descent allowed to play? The Historical Stuff site at **http://www.cam.org/~fishon1/olhist.html** offers a great deal of information on the ancient Olympic Games.

28. Another comprehensive site about the Ancient Olympic Games can be found at **http://www. cs.dartmouth.edu/olympic** Students can even submit questions about the ancient Olympic Games to the expert professors at Dartmouth College.

29. The lighting of the Olympic flame still occurs in the valley of Olympia in Greece. Compare the ancient games to the Summer Games to be held in Atlanta this year. **http://www.netroam.com/olympic/index.html** Select the *About the Games* link to get information on each sport. More information can be found on links at the Atlanta Committee for the Olympic Games (ACOG) site. **http://www.atlanta.olympic.org**

30. In ancient Greece, during wartime, a truce was declared for the Games to be played. This tradition was not followed in modern times. Have interested students study the World War periods of 1914-1918 and 1939-1945 when the Olympics were not held. Who called off the games? Have your class host a school Olympics just for fun and/or to raise scholarship or technology funds, by inviting the community to pledge donations.

31. The Roman Games, played at the Colosseum and Circus Maximus, were very different from the Greek Olympic Games. The Roman Games used men, often slaves, as specially trained *gladiators* to fight to the death in an arena. Other games included men fighting with wild animals, chariot races, animal hunts, and even sea battles, conducted by flooding the arena. Encourage interested students to research the gladiators and the Games.

32. Visit the Rome Reborn exhibit. **http://sunsite.unc.edu/expo/vatican.exhibit/ Vatican.exhibit.html**

33. Students can learn about the Roman public baths and see a computer reconstruction of the Hadrianic Baths at Leptis Magna. **http://archpropplan.auckland.ac.nz/People/Bill /hadrians_bath/hadrians_bath.html**

34. Ask a team of students to research public schools in ancient Greece that provided education to all boys ages 7 to 18. Have students create a chart comparing similarities and differences with modern schools.

35. If the great philosopher Socrates was so smart, why did he write no papers or books explaining his philosophies and principles? Have students find out why all of Socrates' teachings or dialogues were recorded by his pupils Plato and Xenophon. Model Socratic questioning techniques (question-and-answer conversations) with your class. Teachers may wish to visit and screen the Ancient Philosophy page. This site has many good sources, but has some links which may not be appropriate for some children. **http://www.liv.ac.uk/~srlclark/classics.html**

36. Read a biography of Julius Caesar, Rome's first Emperor, at Spectrum Magazine. **http://www.autobaun.com/~kbshaw/Biographies/Caesar.html** Learn about all the Roman Emperors and see a map of the Roman Empire at the University of Michigan site. **http://rome.classics.lsa.umich.edu/emperors.html**

Julius Caesar

Socrates

37. Study the warfare and tactics of the Roman military. **http://www.ganet.net/~atulv/roman**

38. Students interested in ancient weapons can visit the Catapult Museum Online. **http://www.nzp.com**

39. Visit the Roman town of Caistor St. Edmund (in England) and take a virtual tour of the ruins. **http://www.sys.uea.ac.uk/Research/ResGroups/JWMP/CaistorRomanTown/crtp1.html**

40. Visit the Ruins of Rione Terra, Pozzouli, for descriptions and illustrations of this ancient Roman settlement near Naples, Italy. **http://www.mimesys.iunet.it/RioneTerra/rioneterraing.html**

Math Connections

1. The contributions of the Greeks in the field of mathematics are extraordinary. Ancient Greeks built upon the basic arithmetic concepts they learned from the Egyptians. They recognized patterns and systems of numbers and applied those systems to just about everything! Encourage students to research some of the great Greek philosopher/mathematicians, including Apollonius, Archimedes, Aristotle, Eratosthenes, Euclid, Ptolemy, Plato, Pythagoras, and Thales, among others. **http://sunsite.unc.edu/expo/vatican.exhibit/exhibit/d-mathematics/ Greek_math.html**

2. More biographies of ancient mathematicians and other historical figures may be found at the Perseus Project at Tufts University. **http://www.perseus.tufts.edu/Secondary/Encyclopedia/encyc.subj.html#Biography**

3. Did Archimedes really discover the principles of water displacement in the bathtub? Learn about his discovery of the level, the pulley, the Archimedean screw (a device for bailing water out of ships), and pi. Learn about Archimedes and other mathematicians at the University of St. Andrews in Scotland, History of Mathematics Archives. **http://www-groups. dcs.st-and.ac.uk:80/~history** Search the database by typing in the name of any mathematician or topic. **Note**: Younger students can experiment with the concept of water displacement by floating and sinking objects. Then download an activity about the pulley especially designed for younger students. **http://sln.fi.edu/tfi/activity/physics/mech-2.html**

4. Archimedes discovered that pi is the ratio of the circumference of a circle to its diameter. Download an activity about the discovery of pi from the Big Sky Telegraph site. **gopher://bvsd.k12.co.us:70/00/Educational_Resources/Lesson_Plans/Big%20Sky/math/CECmath.23**

Another pi activity is available at **http://www.ncsa.uiuc.edu/Edu/RSE/RSEorange/Piactivities.html**

5. Pythagoras has been called one of the founding fathers of science and mathematics. His most famous rule or theorem is what he discovered about right-angled triangles. Learn about his life and work at **http://www-groups. dcs.stand.ac.uk/~history/Mathematicians/Pythagoras.html**

6. What's the difference between a Platonic Solid and an Archimedean Solid? Find out at these two sites, both geared toward older students and adults. **http://www.teleport.com/~tpgettys/platonic.shtml** and **http://www.teleport.com/~tpgettys/archimed.shtml**

7. See three-dimensional models of polyhedra. **http://www.teleport.com/~tpgettys**

8. Interested students can participate in various Geometry projects on the Internet.

   http://forum.swarthmore.edu/geometry/geom.projects.html

9. Visit the Geometry Forum site and select the K-12 link. **http://forum.swarthmore.edu**

10. For more Internet Geometry Projects Online, go to **http://forum.swarthmore.edu/geometry/geom.projects.html**

11. The Internet Geometry Hunt is a fun series of activities for older students. **http://forum.swarthmore.edu/hunt/index.html**

12. Hippocrates was another mathematician/philosopher who is called the father of medicine. Have students read the Hippocratic oath, still taken by doctors today. **http://www.szote.u-szeged.hu/curmed.html#curo5**

13. Eratosthenes invented a table to help find prime numbers, called the Sieve of Eratosthenes. A good explanation of prime numbers can be found at **http://www.c3.lanl. gov/mega-math/gloss/primes/primes.html** Have older students create a Sieve of Eratosthenes chart up to 100 to find prime numbers. (Students can find an example of the chart in Irene Fekete's book *Mathematics*. See *Additional Resources, p.27*.)

14. Discover how Eratosthenes measured the circumference of the Earth. **http://forum. swarthmore.edu/dr.math/problems/ tucker10.7.html**

15. Thales is credited with discovering and proving that vertical angles are equal in measure and that the diameter divides a circle into two halves. Have older students try to prove his discoveries. Younger students who have no experience with formal proofs can still try their hands at using simple logic and measurement. Older students will find math tables, theorems, and proofs for general math, geometry, algebra and other higher level math at **http://www.sisweb.com/math/tables.htm**

16. Older students will enjoy the Geometry Through Art site where they will find hands-on activities and vocabulary organized by grade levels. **http://forum.swarthmore.edu/~sarah/shapiro/ shapiro.handson.html**

17. Another resource for older students is the Gallery of Interactive Geometry at the University of Minnesota. **http://www.geom. umn.edu/apps/gallery.html**

18. Still have questions about ancient mathematicians and their theories? Ask Dr. Math! Submit any K-12 level question(s). **http://forum.swarthmore.edu/dr.math/ dr-math.html**

19. Research how the geometry of the Greeks helped sailors who were busy exploring the world. Download an activity on learning about latitude and longitude. **gopher://bvsd.k12. co.us:70/00/ Educational_Resources/Lesson_Plans/ Big%20Sky/social_studies/CECsst.133**

20. Teachers will find a good central resource for links to ancient math and science at the Cornell Theory Center Math and Science Gateway. **http://www.tc.cornell.edu/ Edu/MathSciGateway/math.html**

21. Find links to Greek math, Ptolemy's geography, and Greek astronomy at **http://sunsite.unc.edu/expo/ vatican.exhibit/Vatican.exhibit. html**

22. The ancient Greeks used coins made of gold or silver or a mixture of both. In the city states, one *drachma* was worth six *obeols*. A loaf of bread cost one *obeol* and the average price of a slave was 150 *drachmae*. Visit a site, created by a numismatist (one who studies coins, tokens, medals, and paper money) to see images of Greek coins. **http://www.arcadis.be/elsen/coinage.htm #greek** To see images of Roman coins, go to **http://www.arcadis.be/elsen/coinage.htm #roman** Compare and contrast the coins. How are they similar? How are they different? Challenge students to create word problems using ancient values. (How many *obeols* would a loaf of bread cost today?)

GREEK COINS

ROMAN COINS

using a Web browser with Java capabilities, the abacus becomes interactive.)
http://www.ee.ryerson.ca:8080/~elf/ abacus. html

25. The Greeks were very interested in symmetry or perfect balance. *(See The Arts Connections)*. Help students to identify lines of symmetry in your classroom. Younger students can look at letters of the alphabet to see which ones can be divided symmetrically. Use the on-line math dictionary to look up *symmetry* and other mathematical terms.
http:/www.mathpro. com/ math/glossary/glossary.html

26. For a discussion of Greek mathematics, music, and proportion, taken directly from the actual essays of Plato, Pythagoras, and others, go to
http://www.scotborders.co.uk/holidaynet/ harmony/harmony.html

23. Palindromes, from the Greek word *palindromos,* meaning "running back again," are any numbers (or words) that read the same from left to right and vice versa. Every number can be used to produce a palindrome. Challenge older students to find out how! (Reverse the order of a number's digits and add the reversed number to the original number. If the sum is not a palindrome, reverse the sum and add again. Keep adding until you reach a palindrome.) See the formula at The Palindrome Quest site where there is information about how computers are being used to check the formula. (So far, numbers less than 10,000 have been tested.)
http://www.fourmilab.ch/documents/ threeyears/threeyears.html

Younger students with limited math skills can find the palindrome of this year (6/9/96) or the year they were born (e.g., 9/8/89). (See *Language Arts Connections* for more palindromes.)

24. The Abacus was first developed by the Romans, then adopted by the Chinese and Japanese. View a picture of an abacus. (As an added treat, if you are

27. Study ancient units of measurement, first developed in Egypt, but also used by the Greeks and Romans. A *cubit* was the length of a man's forearm, a *digit* was the width of a finger (28 digits = 1 cubit). A *palm* was 4 digits and a *hand* was 5 digits. An *inch* was the width of a man's thumb and a *foot* was the length of a man's foot. A *yard* was the distance from a man's nose to the tip of his middle finger and a *stadium* was 606 feet. Invite students to make up silly math problems with these measurements. Ask them why a standard system of measurement was and is important. Read *How Big is a Foot* to younger students for such an explanation. *(See Additional Resources)*. Visit the Common Equivalent Weights and Measures page. **http://chemserv.bc.edu/ weights-n-measures.html**

28. The word tessellation comes from the Latin word *tesserea*, a term that described the small tiles used to create Roman mosaics. In a tessellation, geometric figures cover a surface so that all shapes intersect along their sides or at their vertices and do not leave any spaces or overlap. Have students experiment tessellating squares, equilateral triangles, and other polygons. Download activites relating to tessellations using pattern blocks. Find directions on how to make HyperCard or HyperStudio presentations with tessellations. **http://forum.swarthmore. edu/sum95/suzanne/tess.intro.html** (See *The Arts Connections* for more tesselation activities.)

29. Learn the history of and download activities relating to Roman numerals. **gopher://bvsd.k12.co.us:70/00/Educational_ Resources/Lesson_Plans/Big%20Sky/math/CEC math.41** Have students write their own word problems using Roman numerals.

30. The Romans were phenomenal engineers. They built roads, bridges, walls, sewage systems, and aqueducts with what we would call "primitive" tools. Download an activity about building bridges. **gopher://ericir.syr.edu:70/00/Lesson/Newton_A pple/Lesson_Plan/bridges** Challenge students to build models of bridges, walls, roads, and aqueducts using popsicle sticks, clay, and other readily available materials.

The Colosseum, Rome

31. Practice measurement skills by cooking with authentic ancient Roman recipes. Visit the Antique Roman Dishes site. **http://www.cs. cmu.edu/ ~mjw/recipes/ethnic/historical/ant-rom-coll.html** Along with cooking and sampling the recipes, have interested students research Roman feasts which were often displays of gluttony. **http://www-personal. umich.edu/ ~pfoss/hgender.html** (Students are sure to enjoy reading about how slaves were assigned to help guests regurgitate in order to continue gorging themselves!) On a more serious note, you may wish to have older students research and discuss bulimia and other eating disorders. (The word bulimia comes from the Greek words *bous,* meaning *ox* and *limos* meaning *hunger*).

32. Encourage students to research the fascinating history of mathematical symbols. Challenge them to discover answers to such questions as "Who invented the (°) symbol for degrees and coined the terms *minutes* and *seconds*? What is the origin of the (#) pound symbol? Who used the tally stick for calculations? What does the Latin word *matrix* have to do with pregnant animals and why did the Romans use matrices for solving math problems?"

Science Connections

1. The ancient Greeks made great advances in the study of astronomy. The astrolabe was one of the ancient mathematical instruments they used to measure the altitude of the stars. They used a gnomon, the pointer on a sundial, to observe the night sky. Visit the History of Astronomy site to learn more. **http://aibn55.astro. uni-bonn.de:8000/~pbrosche/astoria.html**

2. The Early Greek Astronomy site is about as comprehensive as it gets! **http://www.perseus. tufts.edu/Greek Science/ Students/Ellen Early Gk Astronomy.html**

3. Another good site for information on Greek Astronomy is **http://www.ncsa.uiuc.edu/SDG/Experimental/ vatican.exhibit/exhibit/d-mathematics/ Greek_astro.html**

4. The Greeks invented the latitude and longitude system of measurement. Download a related activity at the Explores site by selecting the *Student Activities* link. **http://thunder.met. fsu.edu/explores/latlon.html**

5. Signs of the Zodiac, meaning "wheel of life," come from ancient Greece. Have students create a mural showing each sign, along with its constellation.

6. After learning about what the ancients thought of the night sky, have your students go star gazing any time of the day! Paint the constellations on large pieces of butcher paper, using glow-in-the-dark paints. Then hang the constellation murals on the ceiling. Turn off the lights, close the blinds, and enjoy!

7. View the Science of the Summer Games site for very interesting background information on the ancient Olympic Games. **http://www. algorithm.com/summer96/summer96.html**

8. The ancient Roman towns of Pompeii and Herculaneum, near Naples in Italy, were destroyed after the volcano Vesuvius erupted in AD 79. The towns were covered with lava and ash. Have students visit the Volcano World site to learn more and to see pictures of the ruins. Find out what it takes to become a volcanologist and send questions to a volcanologist on call! **http://volcano.und.nodak.edu/vw.html**

9. Teachers may wish to visit the Volcano Mall to purchase photographs of volcanoes from space, posters, and other items. **http://volcano.und. nodak.edu/vwdocs/vwstore/vw_store.html** Older students can download free software (Windows and DOS only) showing a volcanic eruption. **http://volcano.und.nodak.edu/vwdocs/vwstore/ software.html**

Younger students will enjoy creating their own volcanoes using vinegar, baking soda, liquid soap, and food coloring.

10. The Greeks and Romans made water clocks to help limit the speeches of lawyers in Court. Go to A Walk Though Time and select the *Earliest Clocks* link. **http://physics.nist.gov/GenInt/Time/time.html** Read more about water clocks in *This Book is About Time*. (See *Additional Resources).* Then have students make their own.

11. How do we know so much about ancient worlds? What do archaeologists do? Visit the Archaeological Resources site to gather information and view photographs of past and current archaeological digs around the world. Select the *Greece* and *Italy* links. **http://www.indiana.edu/~classics/AIA/internet/ internet.html**

12. The Ancient World Web has a link to *Breaking News,* which gives updates on what's recently been discovered in digs around the world. **http://atlantic.evsc.virginia.edu/julia/ AncientWorld.html**

13. Learning to Read Rome's Ruins is a good site for older students who are interested in the field of archaeology. **http://sunsite.unc.edu/expo/vatican.exhibit/ex hibit/b-archeology/ Archaeology.html**

14. The WWWorld of Archaeology provides more information about archaeological digs underway around the world.**http://www.he.net/~archaeol/ wwwarky/wwwarky.html**

15. Have students study how the environment helps preserve or destroy artifacts. What do long periods of dryness or freezing conditions do? How are artifacts affected by high humidity, acid soil, and air pollution? Today, air pollution and acid rain in Athens is gradually eating away at the Parthenon. Since marble dissolves in acid, it has suffered severe damage. Have students research what is being done. **http://www.vacation.forthnet.gr/athens.html** Select the *Unfair to Athens* link.

16. Go to the Archaeology Magazine to learn more about the field of archaeology. **http://www.he. net./~archaeol/index.html** Then divide students into teams to become archaeologists. First, start with a "trashcan" archaeology game. Either empty a class trashcan or prepare a box of selected trash for students to scrutinize. Have them log data. What inferences can they draw about the people who threw away these items? Extend this project by having students work in groups to create or collect fictional "artifacts" to represent a fictional culture. (Pottery pieces can be made with clay. Once dried, break them into pieces to be buried. Other items might include rope, bone, scraps of documents, painted rocks, etc.) Once created, have each team bury the items in deep boxes of sand and then exchange the box with another team. Remind students to integrate both subtle and blatant clues in their artifacts.
Each student on the team should be assigned a specific job, similar to real archaeological teams: artist, photographer, soil scientist, botanist, zoologist, geologist, anthropologist, paleontologist, ceramist, and epigrapher (expert on decoding ancient languages and symbols). Have each team investigate, dig up the sandbox site, attempt to piece together fragments and clues, and then write up a report with the team's hypotheses about the civilization it has unearthed. Have each team share its findings with the whole class. You may wish to culminate this project by having the class bury a time capsule with stories, illustrations, artwork, and other items that best represent the school year. Then have next year's class unearth and open the capsule.

17. Find another archaeological dig activity at Big Sky Telegraph. **gopher://bvsd.k12.co.us:70/00/Educational_Re sources/Lesson_Plans/Big%20Sky/ social_studies/CECsst.72**

18. Research the many methods of dating artifacts: relative dating, dating by strata, and by typology, radio-carbon dating, and dendrochronology or tree-ring dating.

19. The Greeks designed their theaters and stadiums (or *stadia,* as the Romans would properly say) using

the science of acoustics. Visit the Elementary Music Theory site to learn about acoustics and other properties of sound.
http://www.inch.com/~macmusic/elemtext. html

Language Arts Connections

1. The word *alphabet* comes from the first two letters of the Greek alphabet, *alpha* and *beta*, which they borrowed from Semitic languages. Around 800 BC, the Greeks adopted a set of letters borrowed from the Phoenicians. (This was a system similar to ours; it had twenty letters, each representing a particular sound.) There was one major problem, however. All of the letters were consonants! The Greeks solved this problem by adding vowels to their alphabet. Have a small team of students learn the Greek alphabet and teach it to the class.
http://ripple.bu.edu/Gavin/greek.html and **http://www.njin.net/~flopez/html/ english/a/a.html**
The Exploratorium site sells a chart tracing the evolution of the modern Roman alphabet.
http:///www.exploratorium.edu/publications/C harts.html

2. Compare the Greek alphabet to the alphabets of ancient Italy. **http://www.netaxs.com/~salvucci/ VTLalphabet.html**

3. Believe it or not, your students can read on-line the entire text of Homer's *The Iliad* **gopher://gopher.vt.edu:10010/02/99/1** or *The Odyssey!* **http://darkwing.uoregon.edu/~joelja/ odyssey.html**

4. Older students will want to visit the following sites to read and compare some ancient Greek and Roman myths and legends. **http://www. intergate.net/uhtml/.jhunt/greek_myth/greek_ myth.html** or **http://pubpages.unh. edu/ ~cbsiren/myth.html#greek** Select the *Greek and Roman Myth* links. Have students make lists of familiar words or phrases that come from Greek characters. Teachers of younger students should select a good abridged version of Greek myths or even a book of fables and legends to read aloud to their students. *(See Additional Resources)*

Discuss why people create myths, including efforts to explain natural happenings that they can't understand. Then have students write their own myths by inventing explanations for unexplained events. Publish a class book of myths to share with other classes. Younger children can dictate their stories to the teacher or an older student. Older children may wish to work in teams to write their own constellation myths or legends about other natural phenomena.

5. Older students will also enjoy Sir James Frazer's Summary of Greek Myths site.
http://medusa.perseus.tufts.edu/Texts/ apollod.summ.html

6. The Minneapolis Institute of the Arts has two great sites for students interested in the myths and legends of ancient civilizations.
http://www.mtn.org:80/MIA/mythology and **http://www.mtn.org:80/MIA/mythology/ ancientgreekandroman.html**

7. Visit Bulfinch's Mythology site.
   gopher://gopher.vt.edu:10010/11/53

8. The Greek gods had Roman counterparts. For example, in Greek mythology, Zeus was the ruler of the gods, while Jupiter was the ruler in Roman mythology. The Greeks said Poseidon was the god of the sea, while the Romans gave that title to Neptune. View the Name Cross-Reference site.
   http://www.intergate.net/uhtml/.jhunt/greek_myth/gvrXref.html
   Have students create a large chart showing the names, traits, and storylines of each mythical character.

   Have a small group of students create a family tree, semantic "web" map, or other type of graphic organizer to show the relationships of the mythological gods and goddesses. Students can add to the organizer as they learn about the characters throughout the unit. Display in class for all to refer to and enjoy.

Plato

9. After conducting research and viewing maps of the ancient Greek and Roman empires *(see Social Studies Connections)*, invite student teams to write travel brochures to guide tourists through ancient Athens or Rome.

10. Invite interested students to research some of the major authors of ancient Greece, including Sophocles, Euripides, Homer, Hippocrates, Plato, Aeschylus, Aristotle, and Aristophanes. Information on Plato and Aristotle can be found at **http://www-und.ida.liu.se/~y92bjoch/filosofer/platon.html** Information about other authors, their works, and an analysis of Greek words can be found at Tufts University.
    http://www.perseus.tufts.edu/Texts/chunk_TOC.grk.html

Aristotle

11. Many modern languages, including Spanish, French, and English, have thousands of root words derived from Greek and Latin. Greek words include *democracy, politics, drama, comedy, tragedy, orchestra, and history.* Latin words include *algae, bacteria, cactus, curriculum, and octopus.* Invite

students to make their own dictionary of English words derived from Greek and Latin. Ask students to clip advertisements from magazines and newspapers showing logos or brand names based on mythological characters. For example, Cupid icons for Valentine's Day ads or Ajax Cleanser. Then have them create their own ads for fictional products, using mythological characters as logos or brand names. Visit the New Latin Grammar site. **http://osman.classics.washington.edu/libellus/ aides/allgre/allgre.contents.html**

12. The ancient Greeks wrote poetry in iambic hexameter. Have students read and write poetry in this meter. Then they can submit their work to the Positively Poetry site where students ages 5 to 15 are invited to read and write poetry. **http://iquest.com/~e-media/kv/poetry.html**

13. The word pseudonym comes from the Greek word *pseudonymos*, meaning "bearing a false name." Many authors have used fictitious names, among them Lewis Carroll and Mark Twain. Ask students to research other famous authors who have used fictitious names and find out why they did so.

14. A palindrome, from the Greek word *palindromos,* "running backwards," is a word, group of words, or numbers that reads the same forward and backward. (See *Mathematics Connections.*) Examples include: *bib, civic, refer, peep, 6776.*) Ask students to work in small groups to invent the longest possible palindrome. A rather strange but humorous Web site called The Fishy Palindrome **http://www. big.com/fishy/pal.html** lists many palindromes, some with fish themes. Other palindrome sites on the Internet include a few palindromes created with expletives or other questionable material for children. Teachers ONLY may want to visit these two sites to find appropriate palindromes to share with students. **http://cerc.wvu.edu/~alexey/pal.html** and **http://stekt.oulu.fi/~jopi/humor/palindromes**

15. Have older students read some translated Greek manuscripts. **http://www.stg.brown. edu/projects/mss/overview.html**

16. The Classics Archive includes a searchable collection of Greek and Roman texts and other related links. **http://the-tech.mit.edu/Classics**

17. Did you ever wonder about the meanings of the names of the days of the week? Upon which ancient civilization is our calendar based? After which Roman emperor was the Julian Calendar named? Find out at **http://mendel.mbb.sfu.ca/berg/breden.lab/dot w.html**

18. What better way to learn about the fathers of philosophy than to read what they had to say in their own words? The Perseus Project has an index of text translations from many Greek philosophers/authors. **http://www.perseus. tufts.edu/Texts/chunk_TOC.html**

19. Author Edith Hamilton noted that "One of the qualities of the Greeks that distinguished them from other peoples was their expression of the joy of life." Invite students to respond to this statement in a response journal. Is this true? Why or why not? What evidence do we have?

20. Have students research the legend about the founding of Rome by the brothers Romulus and Remus. Older students can read Plutarch's account. **http://the-tech.mit.edu/Classics/Plutarch/ romulus.sum.html**

21. Look for links in the Ancient World Web **http://atlantic.evsc.virginia.edu/julia/AW/meta. html** to discover how the Romans contributed to the newspaper we read today. Create a classroom version of a Roman newspaper, with students taking on the roles of journalists reporting on events in the Republic.

22. The Greeks invented a coded message in which the letters of an original message were rearranged in a meaningless order. The Romans invented a code in which each letter was replaced by another letter, symbol, or figure. Have students use the Greek and Roman methods of codes to write notes to one another and then attempt to break the codes. As an added challenge, have students write the codes using the Greek alphabet. (Messages can be written

on hand-made "scrolls" from paper towel rolls.) Ask students why they think the Greeks and Romans used these codes and ciphers. Interested students may want to search the Internet to find information on the art of cryptology, using either of these search engines: **http://www.yahoo.com** or **http://www. webcrawler.com**

The Arts (Fine, Dramatic, Music) Connections

1. Learn about Greek and Roman Art history on the Web. **http://www.dsu.edu/departments/liberal/ artwork/ArtH.html** Then make models of Doric, Ionic, and Corinthian columns, and Roman friezes using paint, clay, and/or papier mâché.

2. Greek and Roman architecture dominates the government buildings of Washington DC and many other cities across the USA. Learn about the parts of ancient temples and other buildings, including the porch, antefix, cornice, mutule, metope, triglyph, frieze, architrave, abacus, and echinus. View examples of Greek architecture styles. **http://www.tulane.edu/lester/text/Western.Arch itect/Greece/Greece.html** View examples of Roman architecture styles. **http://www.tulane.edu/lester/text/Western.Arch itect/Rome/Rome.html**

3. Use the Perseus Encyclopedia to study ancient Greek and Roman architectural terms. **http://www.perseus.tufts.edu/Secondary/ Encyclopedia/encyc.subj.html#Architecture** After researching, have students use papier mâché and clay to construct models of Greek and Roman architecture.

4. Architects in Greece and Rome were not only specialists in designing buildings, but also specialists in mathematics. They used math systems to help them build beautifully proportioned, symmetrical buildings. Have students look for examples of symmetry in class. Children of all ages will enjoy making positive and negative design creations. *(See A Handbook of Arts and Crafts, Additional Resources.)* Have students look at the work of Dutch artist Maurits (M.C.) Escher at the Escher Page **http://www.texas.net/escher** to learn more about symmetry and tessellations and visit the Louvre in Paris **http://www. emf.net/louvre/paint/auth/escher** Select the *Symmetry Effects and Mirrors* links.

5. The Archimedia Project at the University of Haifa in Israel shows students how ancient buildings were constructed. **http://www-lib. haifa.ac.il/www/art/archimedia.html**

6. Visit the Art Museum site for links to museums around the world. **http://cedar.evansville. edu/~ss37/museums.html**

7. View examples of Roman art, including bas-relief and mosaics. **http://www.ncsa.uiuc.edu/SDG/Experimental/ anu-art-history/architecture.images.html** Then have students make their own bas-reliefs using terra cotta clay.

8 View Greek vases and learn art terminology. **http://www.perseus.tufts.edu/Secondary/ Encyclopedia/encyc.subj.html#Vase shape** Then have students make their own vases using terra cotta clay. Once the clay has dried, students can paint the vases black and decorate them with red tempera paint to make traditional-looking urns.

9. Mosaics are designs made by arranging many small cubes of marble, stone, or glass, called *tesserae*. Although the art was developed in ancient Greece, the Romans took the art to great heights, creating beautiful mosaic ceilings and floors. View some examples of Roman mosaics. **http://www-personal.umich.edu/ ~pfoss/gal.html** Have students make paper mosaics using small, torn or cut pieces of paper. *(See A Handbook of Arts and Crafts, Additional Resources.)*

Frieze from the Parthenon (British Museum, London)

10. Have students paint a frieze to tell the story of what's been happening in their class to date. Hang the long frieze around the walls of the classroom. Invite other classes to visit and to try to "read" the frieze storyline.

11. Many decorative arts flourished in ancient Rome. The most common material was terra-cotta, which was used to make countless objects. Have students use terra-cotta clay to make pots, statues, and other decorative items.

12. The Greeks originally recorded their writing on thin rolls of papyrus, a kind of coarse paper made from Egyptian reeds. The Romans used the same material and also later wrote on vellum, a type of fine calfskin. Visit the University of Michigan's Papyrology site.
http://www-personal.umich.edu/~jmucci/papyrology

13. Pythagoras said that the cube represented the earth, the pyramid represented fire, the octahedron represented air, the icosahedron represented water, and the dodecahedron represented the universe. Invite students to use construction paper to create each of the solids and/or create a large mural showing the platonic solids and Pythagoras' visions.

14. Invite younger students to create collages by using only geometric shapes.

15. Learn how the ancient Romans made and used glass.
http://www.umich.edu/~kelseydb/Exhibits/WondrousGlass/MainGlass.html

16. Pythagoras was a busy fellow. Besides all of his work in the field of mathematics, he observed number patterns that explained how musical notes worked. Learn about ancient Greek and Roman instruments using the Perseus Encyclopedia.
.http://www.perseus.tufts.edu/Secondary/Encyclopedia/encyc.subj.html#Music

17. Visit the Greek-American Folklore Society for links to song, dance, and folklore resources. **http://www.columbia.edu/~svs1/gafs.html**

18. For information on Greek and Roman drama, dance, and music visit **http:/www.warwick. ac.uk/didaskalia/Didintro.html** Select the *About Ancient Theater* link to view pictures, including some of the Theater of Dionysus in Athens.

19. Have students learn about theater and drama in the Perseus Encyclopedia. **http://www. perseus.tufts.edu/Secondary/Encyclopedia/enc yc.subj.html#Theater and Drama**

20. Invite students to dramatize the original myths they wrote or read *(See Language Arts)* to perform for the class.

21. Mythology in Western Art is a site created at the University of Haifa. Students can view beautiful photographs of ancient Greek and Roman art and coins. **http://www-lib.haifa. ac.il/www/art/mythology_westart.html**

22. There were many different types of craftsmen in ancient Greece and Rome. They included leathercutters, dyers, weavers, modelmakers, cobblers, ropemakers, roadbuilders, coppersmiths, carpenters, and stonemasons. Have students research these jobs and then write fictional Help Wanted ads for apprenticeships.

23. The theater was very popular in ancient Greece. Tragedies and comedies based on stories about the gods and about current events were performed regularly. A group of dancers and singers called a "chorus" commented on the play as it went along, giving it a broader, deeper meaning. The actors wore large masks that showed various emotions very clearly so that even people sitting far away could understand how the characters were feeling. Women were not allowed to perform, so men played both male and female parts. Read the complete plays of Aeschylus, Aristophanes, and Euripides at **http://www.wsu.edu:8080/~dee/InternetResou rces.html** After reading about the theater, have students make masks and costumes (togas, tunics,

chitons, himatrons, and cloaks). Perform abridged versions of famous Greek plays. Make masks from paper bags or from balloons covered with papier mâché. *(See A Handbook of Arts and Crafts, Additional Resources.)*

24. Read what some of the most important playwrights of the ancient world—including Aeschylus, Sophocles, Euripides, Aristophanes—had to say. **http://www.cc.columbia.edu/acis/bartleby/ bartlett/470.html**

25. Have students create a mural and/or a book of the myths and monsters in Greek mythology. *(See Language Arts Connections.)* Encourage younger children to make a monster mobile to hang from the ceiling.

26. Make models of the armor worn by the Greeks and Romans after looking at examples. **http://www.nzp.com/02contents.html**

27. The Greeks and Romans played variations of the games we know as backgammon, chess, and jacks. Invite students to learn how to play these games. Beginners can learn the rules of backgammon at **http://www.io.org/~takeith/bg/main.html** and the rules of chess at **http://www.traveller.com/chess/beginner/ index.html**

Additional Resources

Bellingham, David. *An Introduction to Greek Mythology*. Chartwell Books, 1989.

Bombarde, Odile and Claude Moatti. *Living in Ancient Rome*. Young Discovery Library, 1988.

Burns, Marilyn. *This Book Is About Time*. Little, Brown, and Co. 1978.

Castle, Barry and Naomi Lewis. *Cry Wolf and Other Aesop Fables*. Oxford, 1988.

Caselli, Giovanni. *Life Though the Ages*. Dorling Kindersley, Ltd., 1992.

Corbishley, Mike. *Ancient Rome. Cultural Atlas for Young People*. Facts on File, 1989.

D'Aulaire, Ingri and Edgar D'Aulaire. *D'Aulaires' Book of Greek Myths*. Doubleday, 1962.

Evans, Margaret, illus. *A Child's Book of Myths and Enchantment Tales*. Checkerboard Press (Macmillan), 1989.

Fekete, Irene and Jasmine Denyer. *Mathematics: The World of Science*. Facts on File, 1984.

Ganeri, Anita. *Romans*. Gloucestor Press, 1992.

Gay, Kathlyn. *Science in Ancient Greece*. Franklin Watts, 1988.

Gluok, Shirley. *The Art of Ancient Rome*. Athenum, 1963.

Guirand, Felix, ed. *New Larousse Encyclopedia of Mythology*. The Hamlyn Publishing Group, Ltd. 1972.

Hall, James. *Dictionary of Subjects and Symbols in Art*. Harper & Row, 1979.

Hamilton, Edith. *Mythology: Timeless Tales of Gods and Heroes*. Meridian, 1989.

Kottmeyer, William, ed. *Greek and Roman Myths*. McGraw-Hill, 1962. (A good source for low level readers.)

Leeming, David Adams. *The World of Myth: An Anthology*. Oxford University Press, 1990.

Levi, Peter. *Atlas of the Greek World*. Facts on File, 1984.

Macaulay, David. *City: A Story of Roman Planning and Construction*. Houghton Mifflin, 1974.

Millard, Anne. *How People Lived*. Dorling Kindersley Ltd. 1989.

Mulvihill, Margaret. *Roman Forts*. Gloucester Press, 1990.

Myller, Rolf. *How Big Is a Foot?* Dell, 1991.

Peach, Susan and Anne Millard. *The Greeks.* Usborne, 1990.

Pierre, Miquel. *Life in Ancient Rome*. The Hamlyn Pulishing Group Limited, 1978.

Robinson, Charles Alexander Jr. *Ancient Greece*. Franklin Watts, 1984.

Segal, Arthur. *City Planning In Ancient Times*. Lerner Publications Co., 1977.

Usher, Kerry. *Heroes, Gods and Emperors from Roman Mythology*. Peter Bedrick Books, 1992.

Wankelman, Willard and Philip Wigg. *A Handbook of Arts and Crafts*. Wm. C. Brown Company Publishers, 1983.

THEMATIC UNIT—RAIN FORESTS

Rainforest Introduction

The world's rain forests are teeming with life. They play an essential role in the ecological balance of the planet. They are home to more than half of all known plant and animal species. One-fourth of all medicines we use, including antibiotics, anesthetics, and cancer drugs are derived from rain forest plants and trees. To date, only one percent of tropical rain forest species have been studied for their potential medicinal benefits. Tropical and temperate rain forests help to regulate Earth's weather by absorbing solar energy and aiding the atmosphere's circulation. Trees help absorb pollution and provide oxygen for people and animals to breathe. Rain forest ecosystems are complete life support systems. In addition, these forests are home to indigenous peoples who have lived there for thousands of years.

And yet, half of the world's rain forests have already been burned or clear-cut. In fact, rain forests are being destroyed at a rate of 150 acres per minute. That's 75 million acres per year. Plants and animals aren't the only species that are at risk of extinction. The culture, traditions, and physical survival of the indigenous tribal groups are also at stake.

The World Wide Web (WWW) offers a vast array of resources from which students may learn about the essential treasures of Earth's rain forests and about their systematic destruction by humans. Sites on the WWW connect students with all sides of the environmental, cultural, political, and economic issues surrounding rain forest destruction. Interdisciplinary classroom activities in this issue of Internet Adventures focus not only on the magnificent biodiversity of the rain forests and multiple threats to their survival, but also on ways in which all individuals—even children—can help preserve them.

Internet Adventures *Newsletter* encourages all teachers to blend content areas—rather than teach them in clinical isolation from each other—so that the classroom becomes a better reflection of the real world, full of multidimensional experiences and interdisciplinary approaches to the discovery, transmission, and application of knowledge.

"When we try to pick out anything by itself we find it hitched to everything else in the universe."
— John Muir

The Rain Forests

To allow students to participate in the shaping of the study, start the unit by creating a chart on the chalkboard or poster board. Divide the chart into three columns labeled:

(1) What We Think We Know About Rain Forests;

(2) What We Would Like to Know About Rain Forests;

(3) What We've Learned About Rain Forests.

Invite students to generate a list of items for the first column and record their responses on the chart. Don't be concerned if their "facts" are incorrect; students will have a chance to correct themselves as they do research. The second column allows students to take ownership of their own learning. What kinds of things do they want to know? Where do they think they should go to find out? What resources are available to them on the Internet? The third column should be added to throughout the unit, as students find answers to their questions.

Be sure to revisit the chart at the end of the unit to help bring closure to the study. Which facts in the first column weren't correct? What was the most surprising thing students learned in this unit? Which questions remain unanswered? Where might answers be found?

NOTE: While many organizations involved with rain forests have created a new, one word term—rainforests—it has not yet gained general acceptance. Therefore, we are using the more common two word form in the descriptive text of the newsletter.

What is a Rain Forest?

There are two types of rain forests in the world: tropical and temperate. Tropical rain forests are hot, humid forests that grow in rainy areas near the equator. Some evergreen trees reach heights of 200 feet above the forest floor, branches intertwined to form a dense canopy that shades the forest. Few shrubs can grow here. Thick vines wrap around tree trunks and epiphytes (air plants) grow on high branches. Tropical rain forests receive between 100 and 400 inches of rainfall each year. The largest tropical rain forests are found in South America, Africa. Southeast Asia, Sumatra, and New Guinea.

Smaller tropical rain forests are found in Central America and Australia.

Temperate rain forests grow in wet, high-latitude regions, such as on the northwest coast of North America, in Chile, Tasmania, Australia, and New Zealand. These forests are homes to such deciduous trees as maples, oaks, and redwoods. There are fewer plant and animal species in temperate rain forests but their soils are made very rich by fallen, decomposing leaves. Enough light shines through to the forest floor to enable many shrubs and herbs to grow.

"I never saw a discontented tree. They grip the ground as though they liked it, and though fast rooted they travel about as far as we do. They go wandering forth in all directions with every wind, going and coming like ourselves, traveling with us around the sun two million miles a day, and through space, heaven knows how fast and far!"

— *John Muir*

"The Amazon is a tropical property of humankind. It's not only Brazilian; it belongs to the whole community because there is no such thing as these forests anywhere else in the world."

— Jacques-Yves Cousteau

"Never doubt that a group of thoughtful citizens can change the world; indeed it is the only thing that ever has."

— *Margaret Mead*

Social Studies Connections

1. Have students find out what rain forests are and where in the world they are found. Visit the Rainforest Action Network's (RAN) WWW site for a wealth of information. **http://www.igc.apc.org/ran/** Select the *Kid's Action* link to learn about life in the rain forests. (Teachers will also find a list of books, recordings, and videotapes in the *Kid's Action* link.) Additional rain forest information can be found at the Gaia-Forest Archives site. **http://forests.lic.wisc.edu/forests/gala.html**

2. Have students use a globe or world map to identify and mark the countries where both tropical and temperate rain forests grow. (One-third of the world's remaining rain forests are located in Brazil.) Then visit the interactive Map Viewer at Xerox Palo Alto's Research Center's site to determine the latitude and longitude of rain forest areas. **http://pubweb.parc.xerox.com/map/**

3. Visit a Vanishing Rainforests site created by an Austin, Texas sixth grade class. They've posted information, maps, poems and original illustrations. **http://www.hipark.austin.isd.tenet.edu/rainforests/main.html/** Invite students to view The Rainforest Workshop site for great links to information and pictures. There are also classroom activity ideas here for teachers. **http://mh.osd.wednet.edu/Rainforest_Home_Page.html/** Challenge your students to conceptualize and publish their own WWW site to share their research, writings, and illustrations with other students around the world.

4. View two temperate rain forests in Canada—the Clayoquot and the Walbran—to find out about the flora and fauna living in each and why both forests are being clear-cut. **http://vvv.com/clayoquot/** **http://pinc.com/walbran/**

5. View additional pictures of temperate rain forests at the Ecotrust site. **http://www.well.com/user/ecotrust/**

6. Students might be surprised to know there are even rain forests in Alaska and Hawaii. For information and to view a photograph of a bear and its cubs at Brooks Falls, Katmai Peninsula, Alaska, select this site: **http://www.sierraclub.org/ecoregions/alaska.html/**

   To learn about flora and fauna on the Big Island of Hawaii and about Lava Tree State Monument, which used to be a rain forest, go to the following WWW site: **http://www.book.uci.edu/Books/Moon/hawaii.html** Select the Puna link.

7. The Gaia Forest Archives offer many kinds of background information and up-to-the-minute data on issues affecting the world's rainforests. **http://gaia1.ies.wisc.edu/research/png fores/welcome.html/** Select the *Search Forest Conservation Articles* link. Encourage students to look at the resources available through Gaia's gopher servers. **gopher://gaia1.ies.wisc.edu:70/11/research/wforests/**

8. Learn about the countries where rain forests grow. Students may wish to get started at **http://www.lonelyplanet.com/dest/dest.html/** In addition, students may search the Internet for resources by using one of the Search Engines on **http://home.netscape.com/home/ Internet.search.html/**

9. Approximately 1,000 indigenous tribal groups still live in rain forests worldwide. As the forests are vanishing, so too are these tribal communities. Divide students into small groups to research these fascinating and endangered cultures. (Examples include the Yanomami Indians of Brazil, the Huaorani Indians of Ecuador, the Bambuti Pygmies of West Africa, the Penan tribe in Malaysia, the Efe of Zaire, and Gaya Hill Tribe People of Indonesia). Encourage students to visit the Native Web site to begin research. **http://web.maxwell.syr.edu/nativeweb** Select *Geographic Regions or Subject Categories* link. Have students consider the following questions: How long has each tribe lived in the rain forest? Why is it important for them to remain in the forests? What kinds of things can Western civilization learn from indigenous tribal groups? What impact has the modern world had on these groups?

10. More information on indigenous tribal groups, including articles written in Spanish by tribal leaders, can be found at the Amazonia WWW site. **http://www.charm.net/~perezoso/amazonia.html/**

11. The Center for World Indigenous Studies (CWIS) offers information on **organizations** that help protect the rights of indigenous people worldwide. **http://www.halcyon.com/FWDP/cwisinfo.html/**

12. Encourage interested students to visit the Rights of Indigenous People WWW site to read the *Universal Declaration of Indigenous Rights*. **http://www.ciesin.org/TG/PI/RIGHTS/indig.html**

13. Learn about the status of The Papua New Guinea rain forests by selecting *The Papua New Guinea Rain Forest Campaign* link. **http://www.yahoo.com/Science/Agriculture/ Forestry/** Students may also wish to view the Forest Conservation Education Materials Distributed in Papua New Guinea Villages. **http://gaia1.ies.wisc.edu/research/png fores/**

14. Other people live and work in the rain forests, including rubber tappers, fishermen, anthropologists, archaeologists, botanists, zoologists, and ethnobotanists. Have students work in teams to report on what each job entails. Do a search of these jobs using the YAHOO search engine. **http://www.yahoo.com/** Enter the name of the job or another keyword or phrase into the text field and select Search.

15. International governments, banks, and industries play a role in rain forest deforestation through development projects, logging, mining, and agriculture. International funding agencies, such as

the World Bank and the International Monetary Fund, have been at the center of the controversy for years. Encourage teams of students to debate the issues. Ask one team to take on the role of World Bank representatives. Have them visit the World Bank's site to learn about its views.
http://www.worldbank.org/html/ Students can learn about the World Bank's view of Latin American and Caribbean environmental issues by going to **http://www.worldbank.org/html/lat/english/ default.htm/** and selecting the Environment link. Invite the other team to take on the role of activists involved in protecting the rain forests. Ask them to research RAN's WWW site for simple explanations of the politics and economics behind global deforestation, including a very different perspective on the World Bank.
http://www.ran.org/ran/ran_campaigns/ world_bank/overview.html/

16. Invite students to learn about the industries involved in rain forest destruction, such as logging, agriculture, cattle ranching, and mining. Research alternatives to these industries.

17. After learning about the locations of rain forests, have students work in pairs to create geography mysteries to stump their classmates. For example, "I am a U.S. commonwealth; most of my rain forests have been cleared for agriculture and other development; I am home to El Yunque, the Caribbean National Forest. Who am I?" (Puerto Rico).

18. Learn about languages spoken by indigenous groups living in rain forests by searching the Ethnologue database, a listing of over 6,500 languages spoken around the world. Select the *Search by Country or Area* link.
gopher://sil.org:70/11/gopher_root/ethnologue/

19. Individuals and companies that are concerned about our environment are sometimes called green since

> **"In wilderness is the preservation of the world."**
>
> — Thoreau

the word and color green have become symbols of the ecology movement. Have students read books that tell about how to be green. RAN has a comprehensive book list.
http://ran.org/ran/kids_action /sources_kids. html

20. Visit the Internet Green Marketplace where you can search by company name or product
http://www.envirolink.org/greenmarket/ and The Whole Foods Market site
http://www.wholefoods.com/wf.nonfood.html/ to learn about businesses selling products that do not harm the environment.

21. Many American and foreign companies still contribute to the destruction of the rain forests. Ask students to find out who these companies are and what individuals can do to encourage them to stop commercial logging, slash-and-burn agriculture, and clear-cutting for ranching, farming, and hydroelectric projects.
http://www.igc.apc.org/ran/ran_campaigns/ index.html/

22. People value the world's rain forests for different reasons. Divide students into teams to discuss the economic vs. ecological issues. Invite each team to take on the role of economists, ecologists, tourists, anthropologists, ranchers, biologists, and/or representatives of indigenous tribes. Discover the major principles of ecotourism by visiting two sites:
http://www.greenbuilder.com/mader/ecotravel/e tour.html/ and
http://134.121.164.23/ecoventure.htm/

23. Many rain forest protection groups say that people should "think globally and act locally." Ask students what they think this means. What are some of the things that they can do as individuals and as a class to help protect the forests? For some ideas, visit RAN's Action site
http://www.igc.apc.org/ran/info_center/aa/ index.html/

24. Are there local environmental issues in your community in which students might wish to become involved? Invite a local chapter of an environmental group, such as the Sierra Club, to speak with students. Check the EINet Galaxy WWW site for many

environmental group listings.
**http://galaxy.einet.net/galaxy/Community/
Environment.html/**

25. Chico Mendes was a rubber tapper who lived in Brazil. He spent many years of his life fighting the ranchers who came to clear the rain forest in the state of Acre, near the far west region of Amazonia. He worked hard to show people the rain forest's renewable resources. He helped people organize themselves in non-violent ways, such as forming human chains to block bulldozers. He was also the President of the National Council of Rubber Tappers, a trade union. Mendes is credited with saving approximately three million acres of rain forest before he was assassinated in 1988. Ask interested students to research and report on his life and work. To learn about the work of rubber tappers in Brazil, including Chico Mendes, visit the following site:
**gopher://gaia1.ies.wisc.edu:70/00/research/wfor
ests/brazil/rubber.txt/**
In addition, the Gaia archives offer an article on Chico Mendes and others who have been killed because they worked to protect the rain forests.
**gopher://gaia1.ies.wisc.edu:70/00/research/
wforests/brazil/killgone.txt/**
(See Additional Resources—Films)

26. Have students find out what actions they can take to save the rain forests.
**http://www.igc.apc.org/ran/what_you/
index.html/** Students may wish to host a school event to raise funds to help protect rain forest land. Select the ***Protect An Acre*** link for information.

27. Visit Montañas Verdes—an organization that works to save the rain forests of the Ecuadorian Andes—to view pictures of forest land and to find links to many other rain forest resources.
http://www.xs4all.nl/~monver/

28. Students will enjoy visiting the following sites to learn more about the rain forests in Honduras and Costa Rica: A Walkabout in the Rio Platano Biosphere, La Mosquitia, Honduras.
http://www.cam.org/~derekp/index.html/
Costa Rica.
http://vanbc.wimsey.com/~droland

Math Connections

The words *economics* and *ecology* are derived from the same Greek root—*oikos*—which means *house* or *home*. Ask students what connection they think the two fields have. (Many ecologists have said that deforestation, pollution, and other environmental problems are primarily economic problems that must be understood and fought in economic terms.) Encourage students to keep this in mind as they work on the following activities.

1. Ask students what they think a fast-food hamburger, a pencil, and a teak table have in common? (All contain products that were harvested by destroying rain forest land.) What does a rubber band, caramel corn, and aloe hair conditioner have in common? (Each contains renewable resources that help preserve tropical rain forests and indigenous cultures.) Some companies, such as The Body Shop,
http://www.the-body-shop.com/bsinc.html/ travel to rain forests to hire indigenous groups to manufacture products using renewable local resources. By doing so, they show the world that the rain forests are more profitable when left standing than when being burned or cut down. Items sold in these stores include rubber figurines, buttons made from tagua nuts, instruments made from palm fronds and rain forest plant reeds, natural pesticides, and cosmetics that use rain forest plant oils.

Other companies, such as Ben and Jerry's Ice Cream, purchase Brazil nuts, cashew nuts, and vanilla from rain forests. Visit Ben and Jerry's site to read about the philosophy of their company.
http://www.benjerry.com/aboutbj.html/ Select the ***Statement of Mission*** link. View their product line, including "Rainforest Crunch" ice cream. **http://www.benjerry.com/product/
bulkflavors.html/** For more information, visit the Show Brazilians Value of the Forest site.
http://newciv.org/worldtrans/BOV/BV-302.HTML/

Extend this activity by asking students to invent their own new flavor of ice cream using a renewable rain forest resource! Send the suggestions to Ben and

Jerry via snail mail only: Ben and Jerry Homemade, Inc., P.O. Box 240, Waterbury, VT 05676.

2. View Green Seal Products to see how this company helps protect rain forests. Is it more or less expensive to buy "green?" Why? **http://soltice.crest.org/ environment/GreenSeal/index.html/**

3. Some trees in tropical rain forests grow to heights of 200 feet or 60 meters above the forest floor. Have students create bar graphs comparing the average heights of rain forest trees (at each layer) with the average heights of trees in their own neighborhoods. So, how does one measure a tree using simple geometry? Visit **http://ericir.syr.edu/Newton/Lessons/ redwoods.html/** to download a tree measurement activity created by PBS's Newton's Apple and The National Science Teachers' Association.

4. When discussing rain forests in other countries, students will find that the literature often uses metric measurements. What is a *hectare*? How long is a *kilometer*? How much is a *kiloliter*? Help students learn about Metric Equivalents by visiting the Common Equivalent Weights and Measures page. **http://chemserv.bc.edu/ weights-n-measures.html/** You may want to extend this activity by using colored chalk to mark lengths and areas on the school yard in both Metric and English System units so that students can make comparisons.

5. Have students create a chart or graph comparing the average temperature and average rainfall amount in your city with both tropical and temperate rain forests. Learn about the rain or hydrologic cycle to discover how and why rain forms and falls on the planet. **http://thunder.met.fsu.edu/explores/ h2ocycle.html/** Select the *Return* link for activities.

6. Have students work in teams to create word problems based on rain forest facts. For example, "If 150 acres of forest land are being destroyed every minute, how many acres will be destroyed in a month? 6 months? One year?" Find basic facts at **http://www.igc.apc. org/ran/kids_action/questions.html/**

7. Ask a small group of students to create pie graphs

showing the changes in the average rainfall amounts in the Brazilian rain forest over the last 50 years. What might these changes mean?

8. A Venn diagram is a graphic organizer used to sort or classify objects or information, according to some attribute(s). Have students create a Venn diagram classifying statistical information about rain forest temperature, rainfall, or plant and animal species.

9. Thousands of rain forest plants are edible, and therefore are a sustainable or renewable resource. Have students do research on some of those plants. Cooking is a wonderful ways to introduce or review measurement and estimation skills. If you have cooking facilities, encourage students to find international recipes that use renewable rain forest resources at Stanford University's Yahoo WWW site to cook and share with the class. **http://www.yahoo.com/entertainment/Food/**

10. Determine how long it takes a tree to grow in a tropical rain forest. Create a time line comparing the various lengths of time required for different species of trees to grow. Find out why rain forest trees can't be replanted to replenish clear-cut areas.

11. Ask students to determine by research the percentage of rain forests still intact. Have them create pie graphs to show the results.

12. Economics plays a large role in the deforestation of rain forests. Many developing countries that have borrowed money from wealthier countries are now cutting down their own forests to earn money to repay those debts. Some groups have started debt-for-nature swaps in which such organizations as The Nature Conservancy raise money to pay all or some of the debt at discounted prices. In return, the borrowing governments agree to set aside rain forest land as natural, protected reserves. Read about the originator of the debt-for-nature swap program. **http://www.envirolink.org/orgs/wqed/ lovejoy.html/** Invite students to learn how governments and individuals borrow money and how interest is calculated. Another site of interest is Pro-Natura, an organization that helps preserve the South American rain forests. **http://www.jungleroses.com/ jungleroses/natura.html/**

Science Connections

1. What is the rain forest's "ideal" ecosystem? Have students study all the layers of the rain forest: floor, understory, umbrella, and canopy. How do these layers help the plants and animals that live there? Why do only certain animals and plants live in each layer of the rain forests? How do these layers affect the food chain? What are the predator/prey relationships? A great deal of information can be found at these two sites:
gopher://gaia1.ies.wisc.edu:70/11/research/wforests/ and **http://mh.osd.wednet.edu/Rainforest_Home_Page.html/**

2. Encourage students to research such unique rain forest plants as epiphytes, which are not rooted in soil. Have them discover the advantages of the canopy layer which provides shade, prevents soil erosion, maintains water absorption in soil, and provides a favorable temperature. Have students also research what happens to the flora and fauna when the forests are cut and burned. View Moody Garden, Galveston Island to see parts of a ten-story rain forest exhibit. Select the *Photo Tour* link.
http://www.sccsi.com/Moody/pyramid.html/

3. Students can view rain forest mammals, amphibians, and birds and find out about which species camouflage themselves at the following three sites:

   http://mh.osd.wednet.edu/Homepage/Mammals.html/

   http://mh.osd.wednet.edu/Homepage/Amphibians.html/

   http://mh.osd.wednet.edu/Homepage/Birds.html/

   Teachers will also find lesson plans and activities at these sites.

4. In 1994, a group of scientists and explorers visited the Mayan ruins and rain forests of Belize. Visit the Jason 5 WWW site for a wealth of information and interviews with the scientists.
http://seawifs.gsfc.nasa.gov/seawifs.html Learn more about the Mayan culture by visiting MECC's Maya Quest Home Page at **http://www.mecc.com/ mayaquest.html** Select the *What's Next* link to learn how your class can participate in the new MayaQuest adventure scheduled for March and April, 1996.

5. Ethnobotany is the study of how people use plants. Ethnobotanists work alongside indigenous societies to learn from them which plants can be used for medicine, food, fuel, and fiber. They learn from traditional healers about the medicines they make from plants so that pharmacological researchers can then study the plants' chemistry. Learn about the medicinal uses of Native American plants at the National Agricultural Library. Search by plant name, family, genus, tribe, or use.
http://probe.nalusda.gov:8300/cgi-bin/browse/foodplantdb/
Research medicinal uses of some Hawaiian plants.

http://hawaii-shopping.com/~sammonet/
medicalplants1.html/
Have students compile an illustrated booklet with
information about medicinal plants from the rain
forests.

6. Learn how the Mayas used corn and download a
wonderful ethnobotany activity for your class.
http://ericir.syr.edu/Newton/Lessons/ethnobot.html/

7. Learn about what some ethnobotanists are doing as
they conserve and study the biodiversity of Mt.
Kinabalu, Sabah, Malaysia.
http://nabalu.flas.ufl.edu/kinahome.html/ Select
the link to *Kinabalu Ethnobotany Project.*
View the Brazilian Atlantic Rain Forest Wildlife site to
learn about the EarthCorp teams working in rain
forests around the world.
http://gaia.earthwatch.org:70/WWW/
Xkeuroghlian.html/

8. Over 70 percent of the plants identified by the
National Cancer Institute as useful in cancer
treatments are found only in rain forests. Have
students use Internet search engines to conduct
research to find out more.
http://home.netscape.com/home/
Internet.search.html/

9. View Amazonia from space!
http://www.inpe.br/grid/quick-looks/

10. Human beings are causing planetary changes that
may endanger our very survival. The Future Earth
Exhibit at The Franklin Institute Science Museum site
shows that although our environmental problems are
serious, we can all work to solve them.
http://sln.fi.edu/tfi/exhibits/f-earth.html/

11. How does deforestation affect the Earth's climate?
What exactly is the Greenhouse Effect? Challenge
students to find many answers to their questions as
they visit Greenpeace's WWW site.
http://meer.net/greenpeace/ Select My Green
Brazilian Notebook link to see pictures and hear
sounds of the Amazon.

12. Study how rainforests regulate the weather. Create a
class weather station by having students design and
create simple bottle barometers and weather vanes.
Instructions to make a barometer can be found at
http://ericir.syr.edu/Projects/Newton/12/
tryit. html. Have students make predictions about
the weather in your city each week and then graph
actual readings. Visit CREST' Environmental
Education Center site.

http://solstice.crest.org/environment/eol/
toc.html/ Select the *Forest and Biodiversity*
link and the *Ozone Depletion* link to find out
what deforestation has to do with the Greenhouse
Effect.

13. Learn about photosynthesis, the ozone layer, global
warming, and the effects of carbon dioxide on the air.
Download simple experiments.
http://www.nbn.com/youcan/warm/warm.html/

14. Learn about different sources of energy and what
hydroelectric power has to do with the rain forests
on Yahoo's Energy Page.
http://www.yahoo.com/Science/Energy/

15. Have students work in teams to research the kinds
of weather experienced by people living near the
equator. What explains these patterns? Are seasonal
changes obvious to these people? Why or why not?

Read up-to-the-minute weather maps, view climate images, check the current weather, climate outlooks, precipitation forecasts, and soil moisture forecasts anywhere in the world! **http://grads.iges.org/pix/head.html/** For a more in-depth study, visit the Schools of the Pacific Rainfall Climate Exhibit. **http://aaron.uoknor.edu/spam/aparcc/index.html/**

16. Create a chart showing how people adapt to different climates. Examples can include clothing, shelters, and food sources. What do people wear, what foods do they eat, and where do they live in the rain forests?

17. Many of the foods we eat originate in rain forests. If possible, arrange a field trip to your local grocery and have students list products they think contain renewable rain forest resources. (Examples include avocado, banana, nuts, corn, coffee, cocoa, and vanilla.) Visit Good Green Fun: The Tropical Marketplace. **http://www.tropicalmarketplace.com/** Be sure to check all the links for news about tropical regions, recipes, and activities for children.

18. Rain forests have both renewable (nuts, beans, grains, plant oils) and non-renewable (beef and beef products, hardwood) resources. Ask students to walk through the classroom and then their own homes to find examples of renewable and non-renewable resources. List their findings on tag board or create a database. **http://envirolink.org/**

19. Chocoholics take note! Did you know that chocolate comes from the cacao bean which grows in the rain forest? Find out all about it and download an activity to measure the pH of chocolate. **http://mh.osd.wednet.edu/Homepage/chocolate.html/**

20. Visit the Sierra Club site to find links to areas that tell about current programs to help protect the environment. **http://www.sierraclub.org/ecoregions/**

21. Interested students can research oil development in areas such as the Ecuadorian Amazon. What happens when petroleum wastes seep into rain forest streams and soils? How does this affect the food chain? Have students create diagrams illustrating the effects.

22. Organize a schoolwide tree planting ceremony. Create posters to publicize the event. (See Language Arts). Visit Plant-It 2000 to find out about the benefits of planting trees. **http://www.iits.com/~PLANTIT2000/** For simple directions on the method and care of planting trees at: **http://www.nltl.columbia. edu/staff/DLH/mypage/ForestPlantTrees. html/**

23. Can't organize a field trip to the Amazon? No problem. Have students create miniature tropical rain forests (terrariums) in the classroom. Be sure to use plants that do well in high humidity, such as small ferns, fittonia, creeping fig, dwarf palm, spider plant, and petite philodendrons. Have students bring from home clear glass (or plastic) recycled containers. (Mayonnaise jars, aquariums, and small fish tanks work well.) Place a layer of gravel in the bottom of the container, then charcoal chips and potting soil. Leave ample growing room between plants. Once plants are in place, have students use florist's sheet moss, pebbles, or wood moss to carpet the terrarium. Keep the soil moistened. If desired, add lizards, toads, or salamanders.

Be sure to place the terrariums in an area of the classroom that is well-lit but out of direct sunlight. When covered, the balance of sunlight and moisture will create similar growing conditions to those found in the tropical rain forest. As the plants grow, have students observe how the taller plants overshadow the smaller ones, thereby cutting off their light.

24. Find out about acid rain and what we can do to stop it. Download a simple experiment for students to test for acid rain. **http://www.nbn.com/youcan/acid/acid.html/** To find additional information go to EcoNet's Acid Rain Resources site. **http://www.igc.apc.org: 80/acidrain/**

25. Do your students think it's difficult to motivate their peers and parents to recycle? Have them check out the Artificial Intelligence Lab at the University of Chicago where graduate students are trying to teach a robot to recycle! Learn the history of the program

and get information about Chip, the robot. **http://cs-www.uchicago.edu/~firby/publicity/chronicle-chip.html/**
Operate the laboratory camera and try to get a glimpse of a graduate student teaching Chip. **http://vision.cs.uchicago.edu/cgi-bin/labcam/**

Language Arts

1. Visit the Indigenous People's Literature site. **http://kufacts.cc.ukans.edu/~marc/natlit/native_lit_main.html/**

2. Create posters and pamphlets to tell about the state of the rain forests today. Have students work in teams to organize a schoolwide Rain Forest Awareness Program. This could include tree plantings, fund-raisers, information booths, and exhibits of students' writing and artwork related to the rain forest. A good way to learn about the status of rain forests is by forming pen pal connections with children who live in areas with tropical or temperate rain forests such as American Samoa, Australia, Borneo, Brazil, Guatemala, Hawaii, Madagascar, Mexico, Papua New Guinea, Puerto Rico, and Sumatra. Classes can sign up at The Intercultural E-Mail Classroom Connection's WWW site. **http://www.stolaf.edu/network/iecc/**

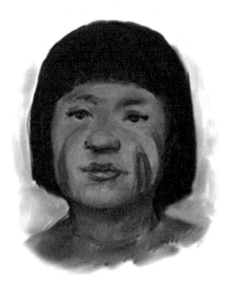

3. Have students write to the some of the firms/organizations involved in rain forest destruction to ask questions, to tell them what they think, or to suggest alternatives. Fax or e-mail the letters. **http://www.igc.apc.org/ran/what_ you/fax_email.html/**

4. Students can fax or e-mail a note to their Representative to find out what Congress is doing to protect the rain forests. **http://www.igc.apc.org/scripts/ran/search.pl?/congress/**

5. Research the origins of rain forest plant names. Examples include *epiphytes*, *kapok*, and *rosy periwinkle*. Study Greek and Latin root words by looking up plant and animal species' names in Webster's Hypertext Dictionary. **http://c.g p.cs.cmu.edu:5103/prog/webster/**

6. Write poems and stories after viewing and learning about the rain forests. Write an article from the point of view of an ethnobotanist, a rancher, a tribal spokesperson, a representative of the World Bank, or an activist from the RAN. Submit stories for publishing to the Children's Voice on The Web site. **http://schoolnet2.carleton.ca/arts/lit/c-voice/welcome.html/**
Select *Examples* link to see what stories and poems other children have written. Your class may also wish to submit news or feature articles about rain forest issues or about their own involvement in ecological issues to the International Student Newswire **http://www. vsa.cape.com/~powens/kidnews.html**

7. In the field, John Muir kept a detailed journal in which he recorded his observations and sketches of plants, wildlife, and his feelings about nature. He kept 84 journals from 1867 to 1913. Encourage students to read excerpts from some of Muir's books at the U.C. Davis site. **http://ice.ucdavis.edu/John_Muir/Harolds_favorite_John_Muir_quotations.html/**
Select the *John Muir Exhibit* picture link to get more information about the life and works of Muir. Then have students start their own journals. Take your class outside to appreciate the beauty of nature. Encourage them to write and sketch.

8. Read creation legends and traditional wisdom of indigenous tribes. Get started at **http://www.ozemail.com.au:80/~reed/global/ mythstor.html/** Read a retelling of a traditional Indonesian folktale by students at Fahan School. **http://www.tas.gov.au/fahan/Compute/Flores/ pgone.html/**

9. Encourage students to read for information and for pleasure! See the recommended book list at RAN's site. **http://www.igc.apc.org/ran/kids_action/sources _kids.html/** and the Additional Resources list.

10. Create word searches and crossword puzzles using newly learned vocabulary such as *renewable, sustainable, global warming, ecosytem, temperate,* and *tropical.* Create an illustrated rain forest dictionary. **http://www.igc.apc.org/ran/kids_action/ glossary.html/**

11. Compile a classroom newsletter for students to take home to parents, informing them of the issues surrounding rain forests. Help parents to understand how their shopping, recycling, and energy-use habits all have an effect on the rain forests. Send copies to the editors of your local newspapers to let them know what your class is doing. Visit 40 Tips To Go Green, a site by Jalan Hijav, a Singapore-based environmental group. **http://www.ncb.gov.sg/jkj/env/greentips.html/**

12. Ecotravel is one way that environmental groups are helping local governments and politicians to understand how forests are more valuable uncut than if logged or burned to make room for cattle grazing. Have students write a travel brochure about visiting a particular rain forest in order to help people understand how to make a profit from tourism instead of from logging and agriculture dollars. View the National Parks, Refuges, and Reserves of Costa Rica site. **http://www.sig.net/~amt/parks.html/**

13. Write and illustrate a question/answer trivia book about the rain forests for younger children. Then share it with a kindergarten or first grade class. Invite the classes in to show them some of the best sites on the Internet. Visit the Wildlife of the Amazon Rain Forest—Descriptions and Photo Explorations. **http://www.hipark.austin.isd.tenet.edu/ rainforests/wildlife/wildlife.html/**

14. Teachers may wish to join a mailing list dedicated to discussions about all aspects of rain forests. To subscribe, contact **listserv@gdarwin.cox.miami.edu/**

The Arts (Fine, Dramatic, Music) Connections

1. Natural dyes come from berries, leaves, roots, fruits, flowers, and nuts. Have students crush and soak some plants to see what colors they can make. Find recipes for simple natural dyes in *Making Things* by AnnWeisman. (See Additional Resources). Learn about how ancient Polynesians used plants in Hawaii.
http://www.aloha.net/nation/canoe/wauke.html/

2. Make papier mâché masks such as those some indigenous tribes use for dances and dramatic productions. Visit the Javanese Mask Collection to see masks from Indonesia.
http://www.bvis.uic.edu/museum/exhibits/javamask/javamask.html/

3. View beautiful pictures of the Carib Indians who live in the tropical rain forest of Surinam as you download sounds of the forest animals and tribal drums. **http://www.euronet.nl/users/mbleeker/suri_eng.html/**

4. Recycle newspapers to make new paper to help reduce the demand for both tropical and temperate rain forest timber. (See Additional Resources for books with instructions on making recycled paper.) Use this paper to publish your class newsletter. (See Language Arts). Visit the American Museum of papermaking **http://www.ipst.edu/amp/** Select the *Virtual Tour* link to learn how paper is made and recycled. Encourage students to make collages using recycled materials.

5. View beautiful paintings of the Peruvian Amazon rain forest and indigenous tribal groups at The Electric Gallery site.
http://www.egallery.com/amazon.html/

6. Have students create dioramas and/or murals showing each layer of the rain forest and the plants and animals living in the rich ecosystem.

7. Visit Tree Mountain—A Living Time Capsule. This site was created by an artist from Finland who has started a unique project as a way to contribute to saving the environment.
http://nttad.com/asci/ad.html/

8. Create a class rain forest theme quilt by having each student illustrate a scene, using natural dyes, on a 12" x 12" piece of unbleached fabric. Students may want to show plant and animal species that are already extinct because of aggressive deforestation. Then have students assemble the quilt by hand, stitching each piece and each row together. Add batting and backing. Tie or stitch the quilt to finish.

9. Build a rain forest to scale in the classroom using chicken wire and papier mâché . Use large butcher paper to decorate the walls (from floor to ceiling) to represent the rain forest from forest floor to canopy. Illustrate animals, insects, birds,plants, and indigenous people.

10. Create mobiles of the rain forest animals and birds that live in the canopy. Hang the mobiles from the ceiling. (See Additional Resources)

11. Research musical instruments and songs from the rain forest. View the RAN Audiovisual Resources link for teachers **http://www.igc.apc.org/ran/kids_action/index.html/** and Deep Forest, songs with voices of Pygmies of Central African rain forests.
http://www.sony.com/music/ArtistInfo/DeepForest.html/

12. Culminate the unit by creating skits that tell about the status of the world's rain forests. Perform for parents and other classes.

13. Batik is an art of dyeing fabric that originated in Malaysia. Have students batik their own fabric or t-shirts. (See Additional Resources for a book on batiking.) Visit the Crafts of Malaysia site.
http://www.ncb.gov.sg/EDM/Craftspage.html/

14. Many indigenous groups weave baskets from such rain forest resources as cane, rattan, and fibers. Invite students to weave simple wall hangings or baskets. (See Additional Resources)

15. The Cuna Indians of Central America live off the coast of Panama on the San Blas Island. They make beautiful reverse-appliqued cloth panels used for decoration and clothing. Learn about this art at the Wingspread: Textiles As Art site. **http://www.wingspread.com/fa/fa035.html/** Also view the Enthnographic Art site. **http://www.wingspread.com/30k/k25.html/** Have students create their own paper or fabric molas. (See Additional Resources)

16. Many indigenous groups wear headpieces, ear attachments, ankle bracelets, or paint their faces and bodies as religious symbols or for ceremonial dress. Some rituals are seasonal. View photos of some indigenous tribes of the Amazon at the Brazilian Mall site. **http://www. brazilianmall. com/brazil/index.html/** Select the *Art Gallery* link. Ask students to illustrate or make clay models of some of these adornments.

Other Informative Sites for Teachers

1. Environmental Education Server
   http://www.yahoo.com/Society_and_Culture/ Environment_and_Nature/Indices/

2. Halting Deforestation Global Curriculum Unit Proposal
   http://www.nltl.columbia.edu/staff/DLH/ mypage/Forest/GlobalCurric.html/

Additional Resources

1. Caulfield, Catherine. *In The Rainforest.* Alfred A. Knopf, 1985.

2. Cherry, Lynne. *The Great Kapok Tree.* Guliver Books/HBJ, 1990.

3. Elkington, John Hailes, et al. *Going Green: A Kid's Handbook to Saving the Planet.* Viking Penguin, 1990.

4. George, Jean Craighead. *One Day in the Tropical Rain Forest.* Thomas Y. Crowell, 1990.

5. Goodman, Billy. *A Kid's Guide to How to Save The Planet.* Byron Preiss Visual Publications, Inc/Avon Books, 1990.

6. Gutnik, Martin J. *Experiments That Explore Acid Rain.* The Millbrook Press, 1992.

7. Gutnik, Martin J. *Experiments That Explore The Greenhouse Effect.* The Millbrook Press, 1991.

8. Hare, Tony. *Vanishing Habitats.* Gloucester/Watts, 1991.

9. Hollender, Jeffrey. *How to Make the World A Better Place: A Guide to Doing Good.* Quill, 1990.

10. Jacobs, Marius. *The Tropical Rainforest: A First Encounter.* Springer-Verlag, 1988.

11. Jaggendorf and R.S. Boggs. *The King of the Mountains: A Treasury of Latin American Folk Stories.* Vanguard Press, 1960.

12. Johnson, Revecca L. *The Greenhouse Effect: Life on a Warmer Planet.* Lerner Publications Co., 1990.

13. McVey, Vicki. *The Sierra Club Book of Weatherwisdom.* Sierra Club Books/ Little, Brown and Co., 1991.

14. Perry, Donald. *Life Above the Jungle Floor.* Simon and Schuster, 1986.

15. Pringle, Laurence. *Global Warming: Assessing the Greenhouse Threat.* Arcade Publishing, 1990.

16. Weisman, Ann. *Making Things: The Hand Book of Creative Discovery.* Little, Brown and Co., 1973. (Instructions for making recycled paper, weaving, batik, and molas.)

17. Weisman, Ann. *Making Things Book Two: A Hand Book of Creative Discovery.* Little, Brown, and Co., 1975. (Instructions for making mobiles, natural dyes, weaving, and recyling paper.)

Films/Videos

1. *Amazonia: A Celebration of Life.* Produced by Andrew Young, 1983. Available through the State University at Stony Brook, NY (516) 632-6484.

2. *Chico Mendes: A Voice from the Amazon.* Directed by Miranda Smith, 1989. Available from The Cinema Guild, 1697 Broadway, Suite 802, New York, NY 10019. (212) 246-5522.

3. *Contact: The Yanomami Indians of Brazil.* Produced by Geoffrey O'Conner, 1985. Available through Realis Pictures, 32 Union Square East, Suite 816, New York, NY 10003. (212) 505-1911.

4. *Emerald Forest.* 1985 Available for rent at local video stores.

5. *Rainforest,* 1983. Produced by National Geographic Videos. Available for rent at local video stores.

PERFORMANCE—BASED ASSESSMENT IN THE CLASSROOM: A PLANNING FRAMEWORK

JAY McTIGHE
MARYLAND ASSESSMENT CONSORTIUM

STEVEN FERRARA
MARYLAND STATE DEPARTMENT OF EDUCATION

Ongoing assessment of student learning is an essential aspect of effective teaching. Teachers can use a variety of assessment methods to diagnose students' strengths and needs, plan and adjust instruction, and provide feedback to students and parents regarding progress and achievement. We believe the primary purpose of classroom assessment is to inform teaching and improve learning, not to sort and select students or to justify a grade.

Although the choice of particular assessment methods should vary according to the purpose of the assessment, the content of the curriculum, and the age levels of students, we discuss a set of common principles underlying effective classroom assessment. We also consider the strengths and limitations of a variety of performance-based classroom assessment approaches and methods and present a series of vignettes to illustrate these methods in action.

Finally, we offer a set of guiding questions and a framework for planning performance—based classroom assessments to improve teaching and learning.

Principles of Effective Classroom Assessment

A wide variety of methods for assessing student learning is available to teachers (Airasian 1991, Cross and Angelo 1988, Ferrara and McTighe 1992). Regardless of the particular methods employed, effective classroom assessment is guided by three fundamental principles: (1) assessment should promote learning, (2) assessment should use multiple sources of information, and (3) assessment should provide fair, valid, and reliable information.

The first principle is based on the premise that the primary purpose of classroom assessment is to inform teaching and improve learning (Mitchell and Neill 1992). This premise suggests that classroom assessment be viewed as an ongoing process instead of a single event at the conclusion of instruction. Rather than waiting until the end of a unit or course to assess students, effective teachers employ formative assessments at the beginning of instruction to determine students' prior knowledge. They assess regularly throughout the unit or course to obtain information to help them adjust their teaching based on the learning needs of students. They recognize that assessment results can inform them about the effectiveness of their teaching as well as the level of student learning.

When using performance-based assessments, teachers can make their evaluative criteria explicit in advance to serve as a focus for both instruction and evaluation. Effective teachers help their students understand that criteria describe the desired elements of quality (Ferrara, Goldberg, and McTighe 1995). They provide regular feedback to students based on the identified criteria, and they allow students to revise their work based on this feedback. They also actively involve students in improving their own performance by asking them to use the criteria to evaluate themselves and their peers.

Assessment for learning recognizes the mutually supportive relationship between instruction and assessment. Like a mobius strip, where one side appears to seamlessly blend into the other, classroom assessment should reflect and promote good instruction. For example, teachers following a process approach to teaching writing would allow their students to develop drafts, receive feedback, and make revisions as part of the assessment. Likewise, if we teach science through a hands—on, experimental approach, our assessment should include hands-on investigations.

A second principle of sound classroom assessment calls for a synthesis of information from several sources. A single assessment, such as a written test, is like a snapshot in that it provides a picture of student learning. Although a snapshot is informative, it provides incomplete information because it portrays an individual at one moment in time in one particular context. To use a one-time snapshot of student performance as the sole basis for drawing conclusions about how well a student has achieved desired learning outcomes is inappropriate. The classroom context offers a distinct advantage over large-scale assessments administered once or twice a year because it allows teachers to take frequent samplings of student learning using an array of methods. To continue the photographic analogy, classroom assessment enables us to construct a "photo album" containing a variety of pictures taken at different times with different lenses, backgrounds, and compositions. The photo album reveals a richer and more complete picture of each student than any single snapshot can provide. Applying the principle of multiple sources is especially important when the assessment information is used as a basis for important summative decisions, such as assigning report card grades or determining promotion.

A third principle of classroom assessment concerns validity, reliability, and fairness. Validity has to do with whether an assessment measures what it was intended to measure. For example, if a media specialist seeks to assess students' ability to conduct research using primary and secondary sources, she should observe their use of these sources directly as they work on their research projects. For this learning outcome, a paper—and-pencil test of students' knowledge of library references is an indirect and less valid assessment because it does not reveal the ability to actually use the references purposefully.

Reliability refers to the dependability and consistency of assessment results. If the same assessment yields markedly different results with the same students (without intervening variables such as extra instruction or practice time), one should question its reliability. Performance assessments present an additional challenge because they call for judgment-based evaluation of students' products and performances. A truly reliable evaluation results in equivalent ratings by the same rater on different occasions. For instance, an observation checklist can be used reliably as long as teachers are careful to ensure that their ratings will not differ substantially from occasion to occasion (e.g., Monday morning versus Friday afternoon). When teachers are involved in school- or district-level evaluations based on a set of criteria used throughout the school or district, inter-rater reliability must also be considered. In this case, scores on a writing assessment are considered reliable if different raters assign similar scores to the same essays.

Fairness in classroom assessment refers to giving all students an equal chance to show what they know and can do. Fairness is compromised when teachers assess something that hasn't been taught or use assessment methods that are incongruent with instruction (e.g., asking for recall of facts when the emphasis has been on reasoning and problem solving). The fairness of teacher judgments is also challenged by the "halo" and "pitchfork" effect, where expectations based on students' past attitudes, behaviors, or performances influence the evaluation of their current performance.

Subtle and unintended racial, ethnic, religious, gender, or other biases also present roadblocks to the fair assessment of students. Such biases may negatively influence students' attitudes toward, and per— formances on, Classroom assessments. For example, the junior high mathematics teacher who routinely uses sports statistics as a main source for problem-solving tasks could irritate students who are not sports fans. Likewise, insensitivity to diverse religious beliefs (e.g., choosing reading passages involving only Christian holidays), gender and racial images (e.g., depicting all doctors as white males), or socioeconomic status (e.g., assuming that all kids have access to a telephone or home computer) may result in unfair evaluation of individuals or groups. Teachers must be on guard so that biases do not influence their evaluations of a student's performance.

Key Questions in Planning Classroom Assessments

Just as teachers can choose from numerous instructional techniques and strategies, so too can they select from a variety of methods for assessing learning. Figure 1 outlines some important questions that should influence the selection of assessment methods. The first question concerns learning outcomes, or the intended results of our teaching: What *do we want students to understand and be able to do?* Learning outcomes typically fall into three categories: (1) declarative knowledge—what we want students to understand (facts, concepts, principles, generalizations, (2) procedural knowledge—what we want students to be able to do (skills, processes, strategies), and (3) attitudes, values, or habits of mind—how we would like students to be disposed to act (e.g., appreciate the arts, treat people with respect, avoid impulsive behavior). The choice of specific assessment methods should be determined in large part by the nature of the learning outcomes being assessed (Marzano, Pickering, and McTighe 1993). For example, if we want students to demonstrate the capacity to write an effective persuasive essay, then our assessment should involve gathering samples of persuasive writing and evaluating them against specified criteria. In this case, a multiple—choice test would be ill-suited to measure the intended outcome. Likewise, if we want students to develop the ability to work cooperatively on a research project, then we should assess group processes and products as well as individual performance.

KEY QUESTIONS FOR CLASSROOM ASSESSMENT PLANNING

Learning Outcomes *What do we wantstudents to understand and be able to do?*	**Purpose(s) for Assesment** Why *are we assessing and how will the assessment information be used?*	**Audience(s) for Assesment** *For whom are the assessment results intended?*
■ —————— —————— —————— ■ —————— —————— —————— ■ —————— —————— —————— ■ —————— —————— ——————	⊓ to diagnose student strength and needs ⊓ to provide feedback on student learning ⊓ to provide a basis for instructional placement ⊓ to inform and guide instruction ⊓ to communicate learning expectations ⊓ to motivate to; to focus student attention and effort ⊓ to provide practice applying knowledge and skills ⊓ to provide a basis for student evaluation (e.g., grading) ⊓ to obtain data for site-based management ⊓ to gauge program effectiveness	⊓ teacher/instructor ⊓ students ⊓ parents ⊓ grade level/department team ⊓ other faculty ⊓ school administrators ⊓ curriculum supervisors ⊓ business community ⊓ higher education ⊓ general public ⊓ other:_____

Source: McTighe and Ferrara 1994.

FIGURE 1

In addition to considering outcomes, we need to raise questions related to the purposes and audiences for classroom assessments: Why *are we assessing? How will the assessment information be used? For whom are the assessment results intended?* The purposes and audiences for assessments

influence not only the methods selected, but the ways in which the results of the assessments are communicated. For example, if we wish to provide the parents of a primary-grade student with an interim report of progress in language arts, we might arrange a conference to give the parents a developmental profile of the child's reading skills and to review samples of the child's writing.

Performance-Based Approaches to Assessing Student Learning

Given identified outcomes, purposes, and audiences, how might we assess student learning in our classrooms? The Framework of Assessment Approaches and Methods in Figure 2 offers a systematic guide to the purposeful selection of assessment methods. Each of the five columns in the framework identifies an assessment approach and contains examples of specific assessment methods corresponding to that approach. Given the focus of this chapter on performance-based assessment, we'll skip the first column (selected-response formats) and concentrate on the approaches in the second through fifth columns of the framework. We'll describe each general approach, examine the strengths and limitations of each, and provide vignettes of teachers using particular assessment methods in their classrooms.

Performance—based assessment refers to assessment activities that directly assess students' under—standing and proficiency. These assessments allow students to construct a response, create a product, or perform a demonstration to show what they under-stand and can do. Because they call for students to apply knowledge and skills, rather than simply to recall and recognize, performance-based

FRAMEWORK OF ASSESSMENT APPROACHES AND METHODS

How might we assess student learning in the classroom?

PERFORMANCE BASED ASSESSMENTS

Selected Response Items	Constructed Responses	Products	Performances	Process-Focused
⊓ multiple choice ⊓ true-false ⊓ matching	⊓ fill in the blank • word(s) • phrases(s) ⊓ short answer • sentence(s) • paragraphs ⊓ label a diagram ⊓ "show your work" ⊓ visual representation • web • concept map • flow chart • graph/table • matrix • illustration	⊓ essay ⊓ research paper ⊓ log/journal ⊓ lab report ⊓ story/play ⊓ poem ⊓ portfolio ⊓ art exhibit ⊓ science project ⊓ model ⊓ videotape/ audiotape ⊓ spreadsheet	⊓ oral presentation ⊓ dance/ movement ⊓ science lab demonstration ⊓ athletic competition ⊓ dramatic reading ⊓ debate ⊓ musical recital	⊓ oral questioning ⊓ observation ("kid watching") ⊓ interview ⊓ conference ⊓ process description ⊓ "think aloud" ⊓ learning log

Source: McTighe and Ferrara 1994.

FIGURE 2

assessments are more likely to reveal student understanding than traditional assessments. They are well suited to assessing the application of content—specific knowledge, the integration of knowledge across subject areas, and lifelong learning competencies such as effective decision making, communication, and Co-operation (Shepard 1989).

Constructed Response Assessments

Unlike selected-response items that call for a selection from given alternatives, constructed—response assessment tasks ask students to generate brief responses to open—ended questions, problems, or prompts. Short written answers and visual representations (e.g., concept map, flow chart, graph) are examples of widely used constructed-response assessment methods. Although constructed-response tasks may seek a correct or acceptable response (e.g., fill- in-the-blank), they are more likely to yield a range of responses. Thus, the evaluation of student responses requires judgment, guided by criteria. This approach may be used for assessing declarative knowledge and procedural proficiency. In addition, constructed responses can provide insight into understanding and reasoning when students are asked to show their work and explain or defend their answers in writing.

Constructed responses offer several advantages as classroom assessments. Because the response to each item is short, this assessment requires less time to administer than other types of performance-based assessments. A variety of constructed—response tasks can easily be used to assess multiple outcomes. Evaluation of student responses is fairly straightforward, guided by criteria or model responses.

Constructed responses are limited in their ability to adequately assess attitudes, values, or habits of mind. In addition, as with any open—ended assessment, judgment—based evaluation takes time and introduces potential problems of scoring reliability and fairness. For summative assessments, teachers should take care not to repeat constructed-response tasks so as to avoid having students give memorized responses to known questions and tasks.

Classroom Examples

1. A middle school science teacher involves her students in an investigation of the absorbency rates of different brands of paper towels. Following the investigation, they record the results of their data collection on a chart and state their conclusions in writing. Students are evaluated on (a) the effectiveness of their charts in communicating results and (b) the accuracy of their written conclusions.

2. A 5th grade mathematics teacher asks her students to show their work as they attempt to solve multi—step word problems. In addition to examining their solutions, she looks at their work for evidence of the appropriate use of algorithms and problem-solving strategies. She provides feedback through brief written comments.

Product Assessments

Student products provide tangible indicators of the application of knowledge and skills. Many educators believe that product assessment is especially "authentic" because the process closely resembles what students will encounter when they enter the work force. Teachers may evaluate written products (e.g., essays, research papers, laboratory reports), visual products (e.g., two-and three-dimensional models, displays, videotapes), aural products (e.g., an audiotape of an oral presentation), and other types of products to determine degrees of proficiency or levels of quality.

One application of product assessment occurs when representative samples of student work are systematically collected over time in portfolios. Portfolios allow teachers, students, parents, and others to observe a student's development and growth in learning. Over the years, portfolio assessment has been widely used in the visual arts, architecture, and certain technical areas, and now educators are witnessing a growing use of portfolios to document learning in other subject areas, especially the language arts.

The use of products and portfolios is appealing because of their instructional relevance. When students are given opportunities to produce authentic products, they often become more engaged in, and committed to, their learning. Unlike standardized assessments, which strive for uniformity, product assessments often present students with opportunities to express their individuality. Product assessments highlight what students can do, while revealing what they need to learn or improve. The criteria used to evaluate products, when made public, make the elements of quality known to students and serve as a guide for peer- and self-evaluation. Previously developed products can serve an instructional purpose when they are presented as models of excellence for students (Wiggins 1992).

Despite their benefits, product assessments have their drawbacks. Criteria for judging the products must be identified and agreed upon, and product evaluation can be a time-consuming process. When evaluating student products, teachers must be careful that their judgments aren't unduly influenced by relatively extraneous variables, such as neatness or spelling. Practicality must also be considered. The time required to develop high—quality products may compete with other instructional priorities. Product assessments require resources, including funds for materials and space for display and storage.

Classroom Examples

1. Students develop a computer program for an advanced high school computer class. Their teacher evaluates students' programming knowledge and skills by examining the program's written code for accuracy and efficiency. In addition, students must run the program to demonstrate that it performs the specified functions. Students must "debug" unsuccessful programs until they satisfy the requirements.

2. A 2nd grade teacher collects biweekly examples of representative student work in a language arts portfolio. During mid-year conferences, the teacher reviews the collected student samples with parents. The portfolio provides parents with tangible illustrations of their child's literacy development. The teacher uses the actual products, along with a developmental scale of reading and writing for the primary grades, to discuss the student's skill strengths and point out areas needing special attention.

3. Fifth grade art students create landscape paintings using tempera paints. Using a skills check list, their art teacher assesses their paintings to determine their proficiency in using the medium. He also assesses their understanding of the use of compositional elements for creating an illusion of depth. Individual teacher-student conferences give students additional feedback on their work.

4. A middle school science teacher reviews her students' laboratory reports to determine how effectively students have applied the experimental procedures and collected accurate data. Her written comments in the margins point out errors and offer specific suggestions for improvement. The reports are returned, discussed, and then filed in the students' science folders for future reference.

Performance Assessments

Using performance assessments, teachers are able to observe directly the application of desired skills and knowledge. Performance assessments can be among the most authentic types of student assessments because they can replicate actual performances required in the world outside of school. Performances have been widely used to assess learning in certain disciplines, such as vocal and instrumental music, physical education, speech, and theater, where performance is the natural focus of instruction. Teachers in other subjects, however, can also routinely include performances such as oral presentations, demonstrations, and debates as part of a broad array of assessment methods.

The evaluation of performances becomes instructionally valuable when students apply the scoring tools for peer and self-evaluation. This kind of involvement helps students internalize the elements of quality embedded in the criteria. Many teachers have observed that students are motivated to put forth greater effort when they perform before "real" audiences of other students, staff, parents, or expert judges. In addition to the influence on students, schools often benefit from positive public relations when students perform for the community.

Despite their positive features, performance assessments can be time-consuming and labor-inten sive for students and teachers. Time must be allocated for rehearsal as well as for the actual performances. The evaluation of performances is particularly susceptible to evaluator biases, making fair, valid, and reliable assessment a challenge.

Classroom Examples

1. Students in the school orchestra participate in a dress rehearsal two weeks before the public performance. The music teacher works with the students to evaluate their performance during the rehearsal and identify areas of weakness. During the ensuing practices, the orchestra members concentrate on making improvements in these areas prior to the actual performance before a live audience.

2. A high school social studies teacher sets up an in-class debate as a culminating activity for a contemporary issues unit. Students work as part of a team to debate the issue of gun control. The teacher will rate students' performances in the debates on several dimensions, including their understanding of the Bill of Rights, the persuasiveness of their arguments, their use of supporting factual information, their effectiveness in countering rebuttals, and their obser vance of the rules of debating.

3. An elementary phys ed teacher uses a skills checklist during the unit on introductory gymnas tics to assess students' proficiency. Each student receives a copy of the checklist and works with a partner to try to perform the identified skills. The completed checklists constitute one component of the culminating grade for the unit.

Process-Focused Assessments

Process-focused assessments provide information on students' learning strategies and thinking-processes. Rather than focusing on tangible responses, products, and performances, this approach seeks to gain insights into the underlying cognitive processes used by students. A variety of process-focused assessments are routinely used as a natural part of teaching. For example, teachers may elicit students' thinking processes using oral questions (e.g., "How are these two things alike and different?") or by asking students to think out loud as they solve a problem or make a decision. Teachers may also ask students to document their thinking over time by keeping a learning log. Finally, teachers can learn about students' thinking processes by observing students as they function in the classroom. This "kid watching" method is especially well suited to assessing the development of attitudes or habits of mind, such as persistence.

Process-focused assessments are formative in that they provide diagnostic information to teachers and feedback to students. They also help students develop metacognition by heightening their awareness of cognitive processes and worthwhile strategies. Process-focused assessment methods are typically used over time, rather than on single occasions. Thus, they are rarely used in standardized, high-stakes evaluations of students.

Classroom Examples

1. A high school literature teacher regularly poses oral questions to assess students' interpretation of a text. Their responses sometimes reveal misunderstandings that need clarification by the teacher.

2. A kindergarten teacher interviews her students at the beginning of the school year. This informal assessment provides useful information about cognitive and linguistic development, social skills, and areas of personal interest.

3. A middle school social studies teacher carefully observes students to assess their cooperative skills as they work on a social studies project in learning groups. He also selects students to serve as process observers, giving them a checklist of observable indicators of cooperative skills. The teacher and student observers periodically provide feedback to the class on the effectiveness of their interactions in cooperative groups.

4. A high school mathematics teacher asks students to describe their reasoning processes by thinking out loud during the solution of open-ended problems. By listening to students as they articulate their thoughts, the teacher can identify fallacious reasoning, evaluate students' understanding of Strategies, and then provide needed assistance.

Evaluating Student Work and Communicating Assessment Results

In addition to making choices about classroom assessment methods, teachers should consider options for evaluating student work and for communicating assessment results. Figure 3 outlines some important questions to consider in deciding which options to use.

EVALUATION AND COMMUNICATION METHODS

Evaluation Methods *How will we evaluate student knowledge and proficiency?*	**Evaluation Roles** *Who will be involved in evaluating student responces, products, or performances?*	**Communication/Feedback Methods** *How will we communicate assessment results?*
Selected Response Items: ⊐ answer key ⊐ scoring template ⊐ machine scoring **Performance-Based Assessments:** ⊐ generic rubric ⊐ task-specific guide ⊐ rating scale • bipolar • hierarchical ⊐ checklist ⊐ written/oral comments	**Judgement-Based Evaluation by:** ⊐ teacher(s)/instructor(s) ⊐ peers ⊐ expert judges (external raters) ⊐ student (self evaluation) ⊐ parents/community members ⊐ other _____	⊐ numerical score • percentage scores • point totals ⊐ letter grade ⊐ developmental/proficiency scale • generic rubric • task specific guide • rating scale ⊐ narrative report (written) ⊐ checklist ⊐ written comments ⊐ verbal report/conference

Source: McTighe and Ferrara 1994.

FIGURE 3

Evaluation Methods

How will we evaluate student knowledge and proficiency? The selection of evaluation methods should be determined largely by the assessment approach and the nature of the student responses to the assessment item or task. Performance-based assessments result in a wider range of responses, products, or performances that reflect different strategies, varying degrees of quality, and different levels of proficiency. We rely on judgment-based methods to evaluate responses to these open-ended assessments. Five primary types of evaluation methods are used in conjunction with performance-based assessments: scoring rubrics, task-specific scoring guides, rating scales, checklists, and written and oral comments.

Rubrics

Because performance-based assessments generally do not yield a single correct answer or solution method but allow for a wide range of responses, evaluations of student products or performances are based upon judgments. The evaluative judgments are guided by criteria that define the desired elements of quality. One widely used scoring tool is a *rubric,* a generic scoring tool used to evaluate the quality of products and performances in a given outcome area. Rubrics consist of a fixed measurement scale (e.g., 4 points) and a list of criteria describing the characteristics for each point on the scale. Rubrics are frequently accompanied by examples of student products or performances to illustrate each of the points on the scale. These examples are called *anchors.*

Scoring rubrics can be *holistic* (intended to provide an overall impression of the elements of quality and levels of performance in a student's work), *analytic* (designed to indicate the level of performance of a student's work on two or more separate elements of quality), or *primary trait* (global in nature, like holistic rubrics, but focused on a specific feature, such as language usage).

Task-Specific Scoring Guides

In contrast to generic rubrics, task-specific scoring guides are designed for use with a specific assessment activity (e.g., an open-ended question about a particular reading assignment or concept from a class discussion). Although they also contain a fixed scale and descriptive criteria, task-specific scoring guides cannot be used to evaluate responses to different performance tasks (Goldberg 1993).

Both rubrics and task-specific guides are most effectively used for evaluation or instruction when they are accompanied by examples of responses for each point on the scale These examples, or anchors, provide tangible illustrations of the possible scores. Perhaps the greatest advantage of rubrics and task-specific guides lies in their capacity to clearly communicate elements of quality to students and evaluators. The clarity provided by criteria and anchors assists raters in reliably evaluating student responses, products, or performances. The criteria also provide targets toward which teachers can teach and students can aim. When students internalize the criteria contained in rubrics or guides, they are better equipped to evaluate and revise their own work.

These evaluation methods require time to collect or develop rubrics and task-specific guides, to identify representative anchors, to develop proficiency in applying them reliably, and to use them for evaluating student products and performances. Some schools and districts have recognized the significant professional development benefits of providing opportunities for teachers to work together on scoring student products and performances and identifying anchors.

Rating Scales and Checklists

Rating scales and checklists are also helpful in evaluating responses to open-ended questions and tasks. Although these scoring tools are easy to use, they generally do not provide the detailed, explicit criteria found in rubrics and guides.

Written and Oral Comments

Through written and oral comments, teachers can clearly and directly communicate with their students about elements of quality, expected standards of performance, areas of strength, and needed improvements. Although these methods are timeconsuming, they allow teachers to provide specific evaluative feedback to students. The effectiveness of comments may diminish, however, if teachers provide only negative feedback (identifying errors or problems), make nonspecific positive comments that do not acknowledge particular aspects of student effort and work, or regularly make comments that do not address all the important elements of quality.

Roles in Classroom Assessment
Who will be involved in evaluating student responses, products, or performances? As always, this guiding question should be answered with assessment outcomes, purposes, audiences, and methods in mind. The question also reminds us of the opportunity to involve others in the evaluation process. When students are engaged in applying criteria for self- and peer-evaluation, they begin to internalize elements of quality and performance standards in ways that can lead to improvements in the quality of their work and learning. Teachers may also involve other staff members, parents, or community experts in the evaluation of student products (e.g., science fair projects) and performances (e.g., public speaking exhibitions).

Communication Methods
How will we communicate assessment results? A variety of methods can be used to communicate assessment results, including numerical scores, letter grades, developmental or proficiency scales, checklists, verbal and written comments or reports, and conferences. The choice of communication methods should be determined by the assessment purposes and methods, the evaluation methods, the feasibility considerations (e.g., time required), and, especially, the audience for the assessment.

A Message to Students
Assessment is an essential component of the teaching-learning process. Without effective classroom assessment, it is impossible for us to know whether our students are hitting the target—that is, learning what is important for them to learn. The significance of classroom assessment, however, extends beyond the role of measuring learning. What we assess, how we assess and evaluate, and how we communicate results sends a clear message to students about what is worth learning, how it should be learned, what elements of quality are most important, and how well we expect students to perform. By considering the key questions and principles presented here, teachers will be better equipped to develop and use classroom assessments that provide fair, valid, and reliable information that will inform teaching and promote learning.

REFERENCES

Airasian, P.W. (1991). *Classroom AssessmenL* New York: McGraw-Hill.

Cross, K.P., and TA. Angelo. (1988). *Classroom Assessment Techniques: A Handbook for Faculty.* (Technical Report No. 88-A-004.()). Ann Arbor: University of Michigan, National Center for Research to Improve Postsecondarv Teaching and Learning.

Ferrara, S., G. Goldberg, and J. McTighe. ~995). "Ways in Which Teachers Communicate Performance Targets,Elements of Quality, and Standards of Performance." Paper presented at the annual meeting of the American Educational Research Association, San Francisco. Ferrara, S., andj. McTighe. (1992). "Assessment: AThoughtful Process." In *IfMinds Matter:A Foreword to the Future,* Vol.2, edited by A. Costa, J. Bellanca, and R. Fogarty. Palatine, Ill.: Skylight Publishing.

Goldberg, G. ~993). *Scoring MSPAP: A Teacher's Guide.* Baltimore: Maryland State Department of Education.

Marzano, R., D. Pickering, andj.McTighe. *(1993).Assessing Student Outcomes: Performance Assessment Using the Dimensions ofLearning Model.* Alexandria, Va.: ASCD.

McTighe, J., and S. Ferrara. (1994). *Assessing Learning in the Classroom.* Washington, D.C.: National Education Association.

Mitchell, R., and M. Neill. (1992). *Criteria For Evaluation of Student Assessment Systems.* Washington, D.C.: National Forum on Assessment.

Shepard, L. (April 1989). "Why We Need Better Assessments." *Educational Leadership 46,* 7: 4–9.

Wiggins, G.P. (February 1992). "Standards, Not Standardization: Evoking Quality Student Work." *Educational Leadership* 4, 5: 18–25.

Expedition Experience

CHAPTER CONTENTS

Staff Development

Substance Abuse

Surfing Adventures

Shareware and Software

Useful, Cool Internet Services

EDUCATIONAL WEB SITES

In this chapter, you will find many valuable Internet resources to explore. Resources include:

- ✏ Collections of K12 Educational Resources—GOLMINE resource sites.

- ✏ Online global collaborative projects.

- ✏ Resources for content domains.

- ✏ Resources for students to use in their class work and assignments.

- ✏ Resources for research.

- ✏ Resources for the college-bound students.

- ✏ Web sites that are interesting to visit that serve as examples of how the Internet can be used to present information and to communicate with Net visitors.

- ✏ Web sites for finding shareware and software.

EDUCATIONAL RESOURCES

Collections of K12 Educational Resources

BUSY TEACHERS' WEB SITE
http://www.ceismc.gatech.edu/BusyT
This Web site was put together by Carolyn Cole while on spring break from Georgia Institute of Technology. Realizing that teachers were busy people that needed quick access to quality source materials, she put together this excellent educational resource site.

EDUCATION HOTLIST
http://sln.fi.edu/tfi/hotlists/education.html
A list of educational resources.

EDUCATION WORLD
http://www.education-world.com/
This excellent Web site is updated daily with many wonderful educational resources.

FIGURE 7.1
Home Page—Education World

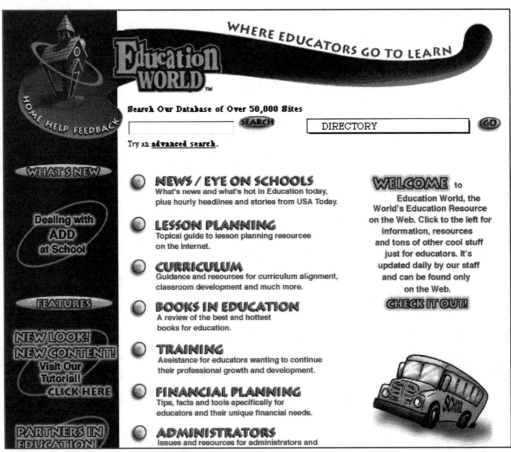

EDUCATIONAL HOT LINKS
http://www.ucalgary.ca/~jross/Links.html
This site has over 400 links to resources for elementary school children and their teachers.

SCHOOLS ON THE INTERNET
http://rrnet.com/~gleason/k12.html
Links to schools across the country that are on the Internet.

YAHOO'S K12 COLLECTION
http://www.yahoo.com/Education/K_12/

Yahooligans

http://www.yahooligans.com

A collection of Web resources for students.

FIGURE 7.2
Home Page—Yahooligans

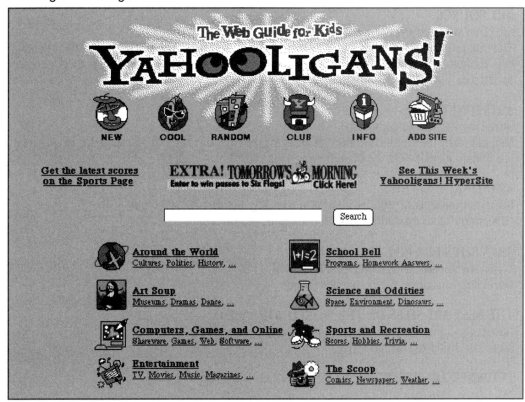

Art Resources

ARCHEOLOGY
http://www.cr.nps.gov/archeo.html
The National Park Service Archeology and Ethnography program is a leading authority on archeological and cultural resources in the United States. This site has a link to the National Archeological Database—a computerized communications network for the archeological and historic preservation community.

ARCHITECTURE IN EDUCATION
http://whyy.org/aic/page2.html
A must-see for educators looking for ways to blend the arts into their curricula. This site provides classroom activities, curriculum ideas, and much more.

ART CRIMES—THE WRITING ON THE WALL
http://www.gatech.edu:/desoto/graf/Index.Art_Crimes.html
Graffiti art from all over the world. Visit this fascinating Web site and answer this question, "Is graffiti crime?"

ART HISTORY RESOURCES ON THE WEB
http://witcombe.bcpw.sbc.edu/ARTHLinks.html
An associate professor of art history maintains this page with loads of great links for prehistoric, ancient, and medieval art.

ART HOTLIST
http://sln.fi.edu/tfi/hotlists/art.html
A collection of links to art galleries, museums, and artists.

ART SOURCE
http://www.uky.edu/Artsource/artsourcehome.html
This site provides a collection on art and architecture resources on the Net including original materials submitted by librarians, artists, and art historians. For electronic exhibitions select the link to Exhibitions.

ARTSEDNET
http://www.artsednet.getty.edu
Maintained by the Getty Education Institute for the Arts, this site offers links to lesson plans and curriculum ideas. Select the Classroom Resources link.

ARTSLINK
http://pathfinder.com/@@jfC00AUAw4GkloKX/twep/artslink/morfogen/
Links to museum exhibitions around the United States.

ARTS SITES FOR K-12 EDUCATORS
http://www.ceismc.gatech.edu/BusyT/art.html
Good links that appear to be updated often.

THE BEST ART SITES ON THE WORLD WIDE WEB
http://www.bev.net/education/schools/admin/art-hot-spots.html
More good sites to check out.

INTERNET ART RESOURCES
http://artresources.com
A complete guide to the visual arts with links to galleries, museums (over 1100 listed worldwide), art schools, artists, and much more.

OODLES OF DOODLES CHILDREN'S ART
http://nebula.on.ca/oodles/howto.htm
Peruse the online gallery of children's art and encourage students to submit their own!

Environmental

EE-LINK
http://www.nceet.snre.umich.edu
Maintained by the National Consortium for Environmental Education and Training, this site has excellent information and links to other sites that help explore our environment. Educators will find an excellent list of classroom resources, conferences and workshops, and professional development opportunities.

THE ELECTRONIC DRUMMER
http://www.teleport.com/~rot/
This site is a Web newsletter created by the Thoreau Institute. Articles include such topics as forestry, urban planning, and public land-use.

ENVIROLINK
http://www.envirolink.org
A virtual community that unites hundreds of environmental organizations and volunteers around the world and is dedicated to providing the most comprehensive, up-to-date environmental resources.

ENVIRONMENTAL SITES ON THE INTERNET
http://www.lib.kth.se/~lg/eindex.htm
Sponsored by the Royal Institute of Technology in Sweden, this site is a goldmine of information. In June 1996 it was selected as the Best Comprehensive Environmental Directory by CESSE (Center for Economic and Social Studies for the Environment), Brussels, Belgium.

ENVIRONMENTAL VOTING RECORDS OF CONGRESSMEN (BY REGION)
http://www.lcv.org/index2.html
The League of Conservation Voters keeps track of how each congressperson is voting on all environmental issues.

ENVIRONMENTAL WEB DIRECTORY
http://www.webdirectory.com
The directory is a GOLDMINE of online environmental resources.

EXPLORES! TEACHER'S RESOURCE GUIDE
http://thunder.met.fsu.edu/explores/resources.html
Loads of links to online projects and curriculum guides related to environmental education science.

GAIA FOREST ARCHIVES
http://forests.org/gaia.html
Wonderful articles on such issues as deforestation, forest conservation, the survival of indigenous tribes, and other ecological issues.

LINKS TO ECOLOGY
http://ecology.umsl.edu/links.html
The University of Missouri and the Association for Tropical Biology have compiled a great list of links that include such resources as academic ecology, government research groups, and museums and institutes that focus on ecology.

INDIGENOUS PEOPLES RESOURCES
http://www.halcyon.com/FWDP/othernet.html
The Internet has many other sources of information regarding indigenous peoples. This is an
AWESOME list of resources.

RAINFOREST ACTION NETWORK
http://www.ran.org
RAN is a wonderful site, full of up-to-the-minute information about the remaining tropical and temperate rainforests around the world. Children, teens, and adults will find age-appropriate materials
here. Be sure to check out their Tribal Links to find a comprehensive list of other relevant sites.

RAINFOREST ALLIANCE
http://www.rainforest-alliance.org
Another rainforest preservation group that has a well-designed web site. Children and adults will
enjoy the What's Your Eco-Rhythm and Jungle Journey game. Be sure to register (no charge) to get
your own Rainforest Spirit Name and identity!

WWF-GREENWEB DIRECTORY
http://www.panda.org/index/netindex.htm
The World Wildlife Fund shows us how well-organized and informative the Internet can be! It's a
one-stop, must-see site for anyone interested in the environment. Subject areas include: general
ecology, forests, species, water, climate, and wildlife.

Geography

CIA WORLD FACT BOOK
http://www.odci.gov/cia/publications/95fact/index.html
Published by the Central Intelligence Agency (CIA), The World Fact Book has a subject index for
researching facts about countries.

GEOGRAPHIC NAME SERVER
http://www.mit.edu:8001/geo
Type in a name of a place you want to look up and this search tool will get you information.

GEOGRAPHY RESOURCES
http://www.ipl.org/ref/RR/GEN/geography-rr.html
The Internet Public Library has a wonderful collection of geography links.

GEONET
http://www.hmco.com/hmco/school/geo/index.html
An entertaining game based on the National Geography Standards.

THE GREAT GLOBE GALLERY
http://hum.amu.edu.pl/~zbzw/glob/glob1.htm
This AWESOME site has links to every type of map or globe imaginable.

HOW FAR IS IT?
http://www.indo.com/distance/
A marvelous geography site to determine the distance between any two cities. Students can access
statistics about the states and can view maps showing their relative locations in the world.

INDIGENOUS PEOPLES RESOURCES

http://www.halcyon.com/FWDP/othernet.html
The Internet has many other sources of information regarding indigenous peoples. This is an AWE-SOME list of resources.

NATIONAL GEOGRAPHIC

http://www.nationalgeographic.com
Use the boarding pass to National Geographer's adventure travel online.

THE PERRY-CASTAÑEDA LIBRARY MAP COLLECTION

http://www.lib.utexas.edu/Libs/PCL/Map_collection/Map_collection.html
Electronic maps of the world.

ONLINE MAP CREATION

http://www.aquarius.geomar.de/omc/omc_intro.html
Make your own maps!

WORLD WIDE WEB VIRTUAL LIBRARY—GEOGRAPHY

http://www.icomos.org/WWW_VL_Geography.html
A collection of geography resources.

XEROX PARC MAP VIEWER

http://pubweb.parc.xerox.com/map
A wonderful resource for teaching geography.

Global Online Projects

ADVENTURE ONLINE

http://www.adventureonline.com/
This site has current, upcoming, and archived projects. Check often for new projects. Projects in 1997 include:

- Eco-Adventures
- IGE: International Greenland Adventures
- Magellan Global Adventure

ELECTRONIC SCHOOLHOUSE: AMERICA ONLINE

If you are an America Online subscriber, visit the Electronic Schoolhouse (keyword: ESH). There you will find many collaborative projects hosted by schools around the country. You can also announce your own project(s) there, and even find keypals (electronic pen pals) for your students

GLOBAL SCHOOLNET FOUNDATION

http://www.gsn.org
Links to hundreds of current projects, listed by the month in which they begin. If you and your students decide to host your own project, you can list it on the Global SchoolNet Foundation site as well.

IEARN

http://www.iearn.org/iearn/projects.html
The International Education and Resource Network hosts global projects that focus on how students can make a difference in the world.

THE JASON PROJECT VIII—JOURNEY FROM THE CENTER OF THE EARTH
http://seawifs.gsfc.nasa.gov/scripts/JASON.html
This expedition, led by Robert Ballard and his team of scientists, highlights different types of "movement"—of volcanoes and glaciers, of birds and other wildlife, and of people. Iceland, Yellowstone National Park, and the environment near your own community will be featured.

JOURNEY NORTH—A GLOBAL STUDY OF WILDLIFE MIGRATION
http://www.ties.k12.mn.us/~jnorth
Hosted by Annenberg/CPB Math and Science Project, this project has two levels of participation: Level 1 is free and Level 2 requires a small fee.

MAYAQUEST '97
http://www.mecc.com/mayaquest.html
Join bicyclist Dan Buettner and his team as they explore ancient civilizations of Central America. There is a fee to participate, although many of the resources are still provided free over the Internet.

NASA K-12 INTERNET INITIATIVE: ONLINE INTERACTIVE PROJECTS
http://quest.arc.nasa.gov/interactive/index.html
This site lists upcoming projects as well as archives of past projects. Examples of several exciting projects scheduled in the 1996-1997 school year include:
1) Live From Mars
2) Live From Antarctica2
3) Women of NASA
4) Shuttle Mir/Online Research Experience

OREGON TRAIL
http://www.mecc.com/ies/oto/oto.html
Join an Internet wagon train and follow its learning journey. There is a fee to participate, although many of the resources are available free over the Internet.

WHERE ON THE GLOBE IS ROGER?
http://www.gsn.org/gsn/proj/rog/index.html
Follow Roger Williams and his truck, Bubba, as they drive around the world.

Government

FEDERAL GOVERNMENT AGENCIES
http://www.lib.lsu.edu/gov/fedgov.html
A collection of over 200 government sites.

GOVERNMENT AGENCY LINKS
http://www.fjc.gov/govlinks.html
Links to the federal courts and other government agencies.

GOVERNMENT DOCUMENT LINKS
http://thorplus.lib.purdue.edu/reference/gov.html
Purdue University has an impressive collection of online U.S. Government documents.

LIBRARY OF CONGRESS
http://www.loc.gov

Access The Library of Congress databases, historical collections, exhibitions, publications, links to other electronic libraries, information on copyright, and much more.

PRESIDENT
http://sunsite.unc.edu/lia/president
A Web site with a collection of presidential resources and an exhibit on the First Ladies of the United States.

SOCKS THE CAT WHITE HOUSE TOUR
http://www.whitehouse.gov/WH/kids/html/home.html
Feline docent, Socks the Cat, takes you on a tour of his famous house.

TEXAS A&M'S WHITE HOUSE ARCHIVES
http://www.tamu.edu/whitehouse
A collection of information about the White House and those that have resided there, dating back to 1992.

THE WHITE HOUSE
http://www1.whitehouse.gov/WH/Welcome.html
Visit this site and explore the virtual library for a collection of Presidential documents, speeches, and photos.

History of Internet and Computers

THE ABACUS
http://www.ee.ryerson.ca:8080/~elf/abacus.html

CALCULATING MACHINES
http://www.webcom.com/calc/mult_maps.html

COMPUTER HISTORY WEB SITE
http://granite.sentex.net/~ccmuseum/hist_sites.html

HISTORY OF COMPUTERS AND THE INTERNET
http://www.yahoo.com/Computers_and_Internet/History/

HOBBES INTERNET WORLD
http://info.isoc.org/guest/zakon/Internet/

HOBBES INTERNET TIMELINE
http://info.isoc.org/guest/zakon/Internet/History/HIT.html

LIBRARY OF CONGRESS—HISTORY OF THE INTERNET
http://www.loc.gov/global/internet/history.html

PUBLIC BROADCASTING SYSTEM— HISTORY OF THE INTERNET
http://www.pbs.org/internet/history/

TRIUMPH OF THE NERDS — PBS
http://www.pbs.org/nerds/

VIRTUAL MUSEUM OF COMPUTING
http://www.comlab.ox.ac.uk/archive/other/museums/computing.html

Language Arts

AUTHOR'S PEN
http://www.books.com/scripts/authors.exe
A large collection of links with comprehensive resources to over 625 authors. Author areas contain one or more home pages plus interviews, biographies and complete bibliographies.

CHILDREN'S LITERATURE WEB GUIDE
http://www.ucalgary.ca/~dkbrown/index.html
One of the best children's and young adult's literature sites ever created on the Web! A must see for students, teachers, parents, and anyone who appreciates good literature.

THE COMPLETE WORKS OF WILLIAM SHAKESPEARE
http://the-tech.mit.edu/Shakespeare/works.html
This site not only has an electronic version for each work of Shakespeare, but also links to related resources and discussion forums.

DRAGONFLY
http://miavx1.muohio.edu/~Dragonfly
Language arts activities and an online magazine.

THE GUTENBERG PROJECT
ftp://mrcnext.cso.uiuc.edu
http://www.w3.org/pub/DataSources/bySubject/Literature/Gutenberg/Overview.html
http://www.cs.waikato.ac.nz/~nzdl/gutenberg/text/query.html
A collection of great works of English-language literature. Gutenberg's goal is to make available 10,000 texts online by the year 2001.

INTERCULTURAL E-MAIL CLASSROOM CONNECTIONS
http://www.stolaf.edu/network/iecc
Students can sign up for keypals anywhere in the world. Great for multicultural studies.

KIDNEWS
http://www.vsa.cape.com/~powens/Kidnews3.html
Monitored discussion groups for students to discuss current news and to publish news articles, creative stories, etc.

THE LANGUAGE ARTS PAVILION
http://pen.k12.va.us/Anthology/Pav/LangArts/LangArts.html
Students can correspond with well-known book characters, visit literary giants, publish poetry, and write about their own towns. This site, maintained by Virginia's Public Education Network, also has great resources, projects, and lesson ideas for teachers.

THOREAU CYBERSAUNTER
http://umsa.umd.edu/thoreau
This growing site is the home of a wealth of knowledge about the life and works of Henry David Thoreau. Coming in the near future, an interactive tour of Concord and Walden.

ULTIMATE BOOK LIST AND WRITER'S PAGE
http://www.acpl.lib.in.us/information_resources/ultimate_book_list.html
A collection of book-related sites on the Internet. The ULTIMATE!

WORLD WIDE WEB VIRTUAL LIBRARY OF LITERATURE RESOURCES
http://sunsite.unc.edu/ibic/guide.html
Another collection of book-related resources on the Internet.

Maps

BIG BOOK
http://www.bigbook.com
Big Book has an interactive map service—enter the street name, city, and state and Big Book will generate a map for you. Big Book has street-level locations of 11 million U.S. businesses. Zoom in or pan out on maps for more detailed information.

MAGELLAN MAPS
http://pathfinder.com/@@RUvpagcAJhE*G*3i/Travel/maps
Magellan Maps is a Time Warner Pathfinder site with links to maps worldwide.

FIGURE 7.3
Home Page—Magellan maps

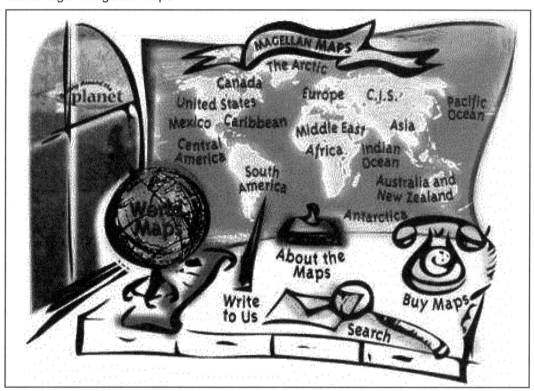

MAPQUEST

http://www.mapquest.com
This site features Interactive Atlas with a street guide for access to maps anywhere in the world. Trip Quest is a driving travel aid that provides city-to-city driving directions in the continental United States, Canada, and Mexico!

MICROSOFT AUTOMAP ROAD ATLAS
http://www.microsoft.com/automap/default.htm
Try this interactive route planner with detailed driving instructions between any two of 6,700 places in the United States.

NATIONAL PARKS MAPS
http://www.lib.utexas.edu/Libs/PCL/Map_collection/National_parks/National_parks.html
This site has links to maps of United States national parks and monuments.

Mathematics

ASK DR. MATH
http://forum.swarthmore.edu/dr.math/dr-math.html
Submit any math-related questions to have them answered by Swarthmore College math students. Also, search extensive archives of past questions/answers.

CALCULATORS ONLINE
http://www-sci.lib.uci.edu/HSG/RefCalculators.html
More than 100 types of calculators used in all walks of life.

EINET MATH GUIDE
http://galaxy.einet.net/galaxy/Science/Mathematics.html
A collection of mathematics resources from the search directory EINet Galaxy. Teachers will find wonderful links here.

EISENHOWER NATIONAL CLEARINGHOUSE: MATH AND SCIENCE
http://www.enc.org/
Wonderful links to activities and resources for K-12 educators.

MATH PAGES
http://www.seanet.com/~ksbrown
This site contains over 300 articles on a variety of mathematical topics, including number theory, combinatorics, geometry, algebra, calculus, differential equations, probability, statistics, physics, and the history of mathematics.

MATH RESOURCES
http://forum.swarthmore.edu/math.topics.html
Selected math resources by subject. Math subjects are divided into K-12, College, and Advanced.

MATH AND SCIENCE GATEWAY
http://www.tc.cornell.edu/Edu/MathSciGateway
This collection of math and science resources—for students grades 9-12—is maintained by Cornell University. Resources include astronomy, biology, chemistry, engineering, medicine, physics, meteorology, mathematics, earth, ocean, and environmental resources.

MATHEMATICS INFORMATION SERVERS

http://www.math.psu.edu/OtherMath.html
An impressive collection of worldwide math resources.

MEGA-MATH
http://www.c3.lanl.gov/mega-math/
Los Alamos National Laboratory has created a wonderful Web site to turn kids (and adults) on to math. Find mind benders, games, and challenges for kids of all ages here.

TREASURE TROVE OF MATHEMATICS
http://www.astro.virginia.edu/~eww6n/math/math0.html
Although this collection has been compiled by an individual who provides a disclaimer at the top of his home page, the alphabetical listings are impressive.

THE VIRTUAL MATHEMATICS CENTER
http://www-sci.lib.uci.edu/~martindale/GradMath.html
Martindale's award-winning graduate and undergraduate mathematical center has an impressive collection of math resources. DEFINITELY MUST EXPLORE site.

Music

ARTIST UNDERGROUND
http://www.aumusic.com
The award-winning site is the place to discover artists and their music.

CLASSICAL NET
http://www.classical.net
The site provides an extensive collection of classical music resources—over 2000 in all—as well as over 1800 links to other interesting Web sites.

DIGITAL TRADITIONS FOLK SONG DATABASE
http://www.deltablues.com/dbsearch.html
A wonderful site for anyone interested in the roots of and/or lyrics of international folk songs.

INTERNET MUSIC RESOURCES
http://www.music.indiana.edu/music_resources
A collection of Internet music resources from the Indiana University.

YAHOO MUSIC RESOURCES
http://www.yahoo.com/Entertainment/Music
An extensive collection of music resources.

News Publications

CNET.COM
http://www.cnet.com/Content/Reviews/Bestofweb/cat.html
CNET.COM offers a well-done, high quality, and timely news site. This outstanding site offers daily up to the minute technology and computer news for which there is no print counterpart. This site offers more than news. You will find reviews of software and hardware, links to interesting stories found in other online publications, news sections on major topics, collections of programs and games to download, and much more. They also produce several TV shows that air on the Sci Fi channel on Sunday: Web, Edge, and CNET. A must visit site to stay up to date on the latest technolo-

gy news.

HOT WIRED

http://www.hotwired.com

Visit this innovative digital storefront that contains services, advertising, opportunities for advertising, special guest appearances, chat rooms, and much more. This site is an excellent example of the Internet's capabilities for the interactive delivery of information.

NEWSPAGE

http://www.newspage.com

NewsPage is one of the Web's leading sources of daily business news, with thousands of categorized news stories updated daily.

NEW YORK TIMES

http://nytimesfax.com/index.html

This site delivers highlights from the daily newspaper as well as articles on technology. You will need to download a copy of Adobe Acrobat reader (free) before you can read the Times online.

NATIONAL PUBLIC RADIO

http://www.realaudio.com/contentp/npr.html

Stop by NPR online to see how audio is being used on the Internet. Visit the NPR archive to find your favorite programs.

NEWSLINK

http://www.newslink.org/

This excellent site provides links to over 2,000 news sites.

NEWSPAGE

http://www.newspage.com

With 500 information sources and 25,000 pages refreshed daily, NewsPage is the most comprehensive news site on the Web. To use NewsPage, simply select an industry and drill your way through categories and topics to today's news, hot off the virtual presses.

THE OTIS INDEX

http://www.interlog.com/~gordo/otis_pubpubs.html

This site helps you search the Internet to find software, on-line books, commercial sites, newsgroups, and electronic publications.

PBS ONLINE

http://www.pbs.org

The latest news from Public Broadcasting Station as well as links to popular PBS series and other news-related resources.

POINTCAST NETWORK

http://www.pointcast.com/products/index.html

Voted one of the best Internet applications, the PointCast Network (PCN) broadcasts news, financial news, stock quotes, weather, sports, and more to your desktop 24 hours a day. The PointCast Network is the first news network to use the Internet to broadcast news and information to a viewer's computer screen. The service is free, financed by advertising on the PointCast page. With "pointcasting" you can personalize the network to get just the news that interests you.

FIGURE 7.4
PointCast Network application

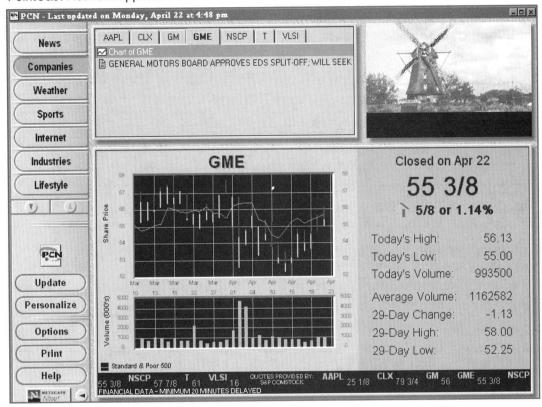

SAN JOSE "MERCURY NEWS"
http://www.sjmercury.com/main.htm
The Mercury Center Web is the first complete daily newspaper on the World Wide Web. This service offers continually updated news coverage, the complete text of each day's final edition of the San Jose Mercury News, including classified ads, and a variety of special features.

TIME WARNER
http://www.pathfinder.com
Pathfinder from Time Warner is an excellent Web site for discovering how an information-providing company pushes the capabilities of the new Internet medium.

THE WALL STREET JOURNAL
http://www.wsj.com
This online version of The Wall Street Journal has hyperlinks to money and investing updates, a variety of Journal offerings including headlines from today's paper, and The Wall Street Journal Classroom Edition—the Journal's award winning educational program for secondary school students and teachers.

WALL STREET NEWS
http://wall-street-news.com/forecasts
Stop by WALL STREET - U.S.A. and drop in on the Internet Broadcasting Super-Station. Meet the News Director, Dr. Paul B. Farrell, who has a unique approach to financial news—the forecasting business. The news comes directly from financial newsletters published by Wall Street's leading forecasters. WSTN goes beyond just reporting the news, they forecast tomorrow's news today.

WALL STREET RESEARCH NET
http://www.wsrn.com
Wall Street Research Net consists of over 110,000 links to help professional and private investors perform fundamental research on actively traded companies and mutual funds, and locate important economic data that moves markets. A MUST VISIT site for those who want to find information on companies.

Science

ASTRONOMY LINKS FROM NASA
http://quest.arc.nasa.gov/lfs/other_sites.html
An AWESOME collection of astronomy links from NASA.

CHEMISTRY RESOURCES
http://www.rpi.edu/dept/chem/cheminfo/chemres.html
A collection of resources related to chemistry and associated fields.

DISCOVERY CHANNEL ONLINE
http://www.discovery.com
This site changes weekly. Loads of interesting articles, activities, and links related to the themes of the television show.

EARTH PAGES
http://starsky.hitc.com/earth/earth.html
Earth Pages, sponsored by NASA, is a search and index tool to help navigate the Internet for data, information, and resources related to earth science.

EINET GALAXY
http://galaxy.einet.net/galaxy/Science.html
A collection of science and math resources.

EXPLORATORIUM
http://www.exploratorium.edu
Enjoy hands-on activities at this Science and Art Museum in San Francisco.

GEOLOGICAL TIME MACHINE
http://www.ucmp.berkeley.edu/help/timeform.html
Hop into this virtual time machine and experience time travel from the very early Precambrian to Quaternary present day.

THE HEART—AN ONLINE EXPLORATION
http://sln.fi.edu/biosci/heart.html
Explore the heart. Discover the complexities of its development and structure. Follow the blood through the blood vessels. Wander through the weblike body systems. Learn how to have a healthy heart and how to monitor your heart's health. Look back at the history of heart science.

HOTLIST: ONLINE EXHIBITS
http://sln.fi.edu/tfi/jump.html
Interactive exhibits for students including tele-robotic arms (move things remotely from your own computer), and live cameras on the Internet.

INFOSEEK SCIENCE
http://guide.infoseek.com/Science
Infoseek's collection of science resources.

INQUIRY ALMANACK
http://sln.fi.edu/qanda/qanda.html
A monthly, online magazine hosted by the Franklin Institute Science Museum. Great activities and brain-teasers for all ages.

THE MAD SCIENTIST NETWORK
http://128.252.223.239/~ysp/MSN/
Ask questions of scientists and peruse the archives of questions and answers.

MAINE SOLAR HOUSE
http://solstice.crest.org/renewables/wlord
This award-winning site is a MUST VISIT stop even if you have no interest in solar power.

NASA
http://www.nasa.gov
Learn more about what lies beyond planet Earth by visiting the NASA site. Stop by the Gallery where you will find video, audio clips and still images to download. In the Aeronautics section you will find aeronautics research and links to related Webs. In Space Science there is information on NASA's planetary exploration, astronomy and research into the origins of life. Mission to Planet Earth is dedicated to understanding the many ways the Earth is constantly changing and how human beings influence those changes. Human Space Flight provides links to the space shuttle research.

SCIENCE HOBBYIST
http://www.eskimo.com/~billb
This COOL site is an example of how individuals can contribute valuable information for the global universe. There are many unusual places to explore. A DEFINITELY MUST VISIT site.

SCIENCE TABLES AND DATABASES
http://www.sci.lib.uci.edu/~martindale/Ref3.html
Another Martindale site with an AWESOME collection of science tables and database resources.

THE SPACE STATION
http://www.aros.net/~create/space/space.htm
An exceptional resource for space-related links.

THE TREE OF LIFE
http://phylogeny.arizona.edu/tree/phylogeny.html
The Tree of Life is a collection of World Wide Web pages that present information about the world's organisms. This site is designed to illustrate the diversity and unity of living organisms. Each page presents information about a particular group. This is an example of the beetles page.

UNIVERSITY OF NEVADA, SEISMOLOGICAL LAB
http://www.seismo.unr.edu
Older students and adults will enjoy accessing information about earthquakes and can even view a live Web camera pointed at earthquake helicorder drums in the laboratory.

VIRTUAL ASTROPHYSICS AND SPACE CENTER
http://www-sci.lib.uci.edu/~martindale/GradSpace.html
Martindale's award-winning graduate and undergraduate space center has an impressive collection of resources. DEFINITELY MUST EXPLORE site.

VIRTUAL BIOSCIENCE CENTER
http://www-sci.lib.uci.edu/~martindale/GradBioscience.html
A Martindale site with an exhaustive collection of bioscience resources including genetics, proteins, biology, botany, ecology, marine biologygenetics, and other resources such as Periodic Tables, dictionaries, and publications.

VIRTUAL CHEMISTRY CENTER
http://www-sci.lib.uci.edu/~martindale/GradChemistry.html
Martindale's graduate and undergraduate center for chemistry resources.

WHALENET
http://whale.wheelock.edu
Links to all things whale.

WINDOWS TO THE UNIVERSE
http://www.windows.umich.edu
An AWESOME Astronomy collection from the University of Michigan is heavily designed with beautiful graphics. Although it seems to be designed for K-12, it is definitely worth a visit.

YAHOO SCIENCE RESOURCES
http://www.yahoo.com/Science
An extensive collection of science resources.

Social Studies

THE AMERICAN CIVIL WAR HOME PAGE
http://funnelweb.utcc.utk.edu/~hoemann/warweb.html
An AWESOME collection of Civil War resources.

THE ANCIENT WORLDS META INDEX
http://atlantic.evsc.virginia.edu/julia/AW/meta.html
A GOLDMINE of resources on the ancient world.

ARCHIVING EARLY AMERICA
http://earlyamerica.com
Original documents from 18th century America. Literally brings history alive!

BYZANTINE & MEDIEVAL STUDIES
http://www.fordham.edu/halsall/med/medweb.html
Anything you every wanted to know about Byzantine and Medieval history can probably be found in this amazing collection.

FROM REVOLUTION TO RECONSTRUCTION
http://www.let.rug.nl
This award-winning site has original source resources on American history from the colonial period until modern times.

GATEWAY TO WORLD HISTORY
http://neal.ctstateu.edu/history/world_history/world_history.html
This site has provides a collection of history archives and historical resources on the Internet.

THE INTERNET ENCYCLOPEDIA OF ANCIENT LANDS
http://www.oise.utoronto.ca/~dchamberlain/ancientlands.html
Greece, Egypt, China, Aztecs, Mayas, and more. You name it, it's here.

K-5 CYBERTRAIL: MULTICULTURAL CURRICULUM RESOURCES
http://ernie.wmht.org/trail/explor02.htm
Great links for multicultural studies.

KATHY SCHROCK'S GUIDE FOR EDUCATORS: HISTORY AND SOCIAL STUDIES
http://www.capecod.net/Wixon/history.htm
An excellent compilation of some of the best social studies sites on the Web. The site is updated regularly.

MIGRATION TO AMERICA: ELLIS ISLAND
http://www.turner.com/tesi/html/migration.html
Turner Broadcasting hosts this excellent resource for multicultural studies. Both students and teachers will find information about and photographs of the immigrant experience.

SOCIAL STUDIES RESOURCES
http://www.teleport.com/~vincer/social.html
Great place for students to find links for specific research projects.

US HISTORICAL DOCUMENTS ONLINE
http://w3.one.net/~mweiler/ushda/ushda.htm
Another site for viewing original historical documents and reading their content.

Weather

CNN WEATHER UPDATES
http://www.usatoday.com/weather/wfront.htm
Find current weather and 5-day forecasts for the U.S. and locations worldwide.

INTELLICAST
http://www.intellicast.com
Microsoft's NBC Web site has links to U.S. and worldwide weather, as well as ski conditions and general news.

THE WEATHER CHANNEL
http://www.weather.com
The Weather Channel is a 24-hour television network devoted entirely to weather. Each day The Weather Channel broadcasts local forecasts for more than 4,000 National Weather Service zones across the country.

WEATHERNET
http://cirrus.sprl.umich.edu/wxnet
WeatherNet, sponsored by The Weather Underground at the University of Michigan, connects you to the world of weather. This site provides access to thousands of forecasts, images, and the Net's

largest collection of weather links. WeatherNet is perhaps the most comprehensive and up-to-date source of weather data on the Web.

IMPROVING STUDENT GRADES

Using the Internet as a Communication Tool

Methods of communication have changed dramatically over the past two decades. Before the 1970s, communication was either in person, by telephone, or by U.S. mail. In the 1980s, new communication tools began to emerge with the introduction of fax machines, personal computers, computer networks, electronic mail, express mail, cellular phones, and telecommunication technologies. In the 1990s the Internet emerges as the fastest growing communication medium of all times. Some have called the World Wide Web the fourth media, positioned to take a place with print, radio, and television as a mass market means of communication. Listed in this section are Web-based communication resources.

ANALYSIS FOR INTERNET COMMUNICATION
http://shum.huji.ac.il/jcmc/vol1/issue4/december.html
This very interesting site provides a thought-provoking discussion and analysis on using the Internet for communication.

DIGITAL PLANET
http://www.digiplanet.com/index.html
For anyone who wants to communicate a message, the most important issue is engaging and retaining one's audience. Whether conveying a corporate message or providing entertaining consumer content, Digital Planet explores the interactive medium's power to communicate a message that is entertaining, enlightening, and informative. Visit this site to learn how the Internet is being used to communicate with customers.

THE BUSINESS OF THE INTERNET
http://www.rtd.com/people/rawn/business.html
An introduction to the Internet for commercial organizations with a focus on what the Internet can do for businesses: product analysis, market analysis, expert advice and help, recruitment of new employees, rapid information access, wide-scale information dissemination, rapid communication, cost-effective document transfer, peer communication, and new business opportunities.

GLOBAL VILLAGE COMMUNICATION
http://www.info.globalvillag.com/index.html#NewsStand
Global Village develops and markets communication products and services for personal computer users. Visit the different areas in The Village to learn more about communicating from your computer, including faxing, accessing online services and the Internet, and connecting to remote networks.

THE INTERNET, A REVOLUTION IN COMMUNICATION
http://www.nih.gov:80/dcrt/expo/talks/overview/index.html
This site has information on the Internet as a communication medium and links to information on the Internet revolution as reported in the media.

SANDBOX
http://www.sandbox.net
Sandbox is entertainment with a clue—a free online network that explores how to use the Internet for entertainment.

Composition and Grammar

ELEMENTS OF STYLE
http://www.columbia.edu/acis/bartleby/strunk
The Elements of Style by William Strunk is a book intended for use in English courses in which the practice of composition is combined with the study of literature.

GRAMMAR AND STYLE NOTES
http://www.english.upenn.edu/~jlynch/grammar.html
This award winning Web site has articles on grammatical rules and explanations, and comments on style.

Libraries

Libraries from around the world can be accessed for research. Some libraries require a Telnet connection and require the use of commands to find and retrieve information. Some libraries provide Help menus to assist you; others do not. Many libraries now have World Wide Web access thus eliminating the need for commands to find information. Listed below are library resources on the Web.

ELECTRIC LIBRARY
http://www.elibrary.com
The Electric Library is a virtual library where you can conduct research online. Submit a question and a comprehensive search is launched of over 150 full-text newspapers, 800 full-text magazines, two international newswires, two thousand classic books, hundreds of maps, thousands of photographs, as well as major works of literature and art.

LIBCAT
http://www.metronet.lib.mn.us/lc/lc1.html
An AWESOME guide to library resources on the Internet.

LIBRARY OF CONGRESS
http://www.loc.gov
Access the Library of Congress databases, historical collections, exhibitions, publications, links to other electronic libraries, information on copyright and much more.

LIBWEB
http://sunsite.Berkeley.EDU/Libweb
A collection of online libraries worldwide.

SMITHSONIAN INSTITUTION
http://www.si.edu/newstart.htm
A valuable online research service, the Smithsonian Institution provides over one million resources. Click on the link to Resources and Tours to begin your journey.

WEBCHATS
http://library.usask.ca/hywebcat
Library catalogs on the Web.

Reference Desk

The Internet is the newest and perhaps largest reference library. This rich source of information resource is available to Net users. Listed below are a few reference resources that you will find useful.

ASK AN EXPERT
http://njnie.dl.stevens-tech.edu/curriculum/aska.html
This Web site provides opportunities for you to interact with experts on topics such as computers, economics, literature, and science by sending questions via email.

BARTLETT'S FAMILIAR QUOTATIONS
http://www.ccc.columbia.edu/acis/bartleby/bartlett/index.html
Looking for a quote for your class presentation or paper? Connect to this Web site and search by keyword or choose from a list of people.

BRITANNICA ONLINE
http://www.eb.com
For a minimal fee you can subscribe to the Britannica Online and Merriam-Webster's Collegiate Dictionary. Some of the encyclopedia text is linked to Internet sites.

CIA WORLD FACT BOOK
http://www.odci.gov/cia/publications/95fact/index.html
Published by the Central Intelligence Agency (CIA), The World Fact Book has a subject index for researching facts about countries.

COPYRIGHT HOME PAGE
http://www.benedict.com
This award-winning Web site has everything you will ever want to know about copyright.

DICTIONARIES & THESAURI
http://www.arts.cuhk.hk/Ref.html#dt
A GOLDMINE collection of cyberdictionaries, thesauri, and other subject oriented references.

ENCYBERPEDIA
http://www.encyberpedia.com/ency.htm
The HOTTEST encyclopedia from cyberspace designed to help you find good stuff in the jungle of over 2 million Web Sites.

MLA STYLE SHEET FOR DOCUMENTING ONLINE RESOURCES
http://www.cas.usf.edu/english/walker/mla.html
Information on how to document online research.

MY VIRTUAL REFERENCE DESK
http://www.refdesk.com/main.html
Links to many excellent reference resources including a link to subject directory of resources—My Encyclopedia link.

NOBLE CITIZENS OF PLANET EARTH
http://www.tiac.net/users/parallax
This dictionary contains biographical information on over 18,000 people who have shaped our world from ancient times to the present day. Information contained in the dictionary includes birth and death years, professions, positions held, literary and artistic works and other achievements.

ONELOOK DICTIONARIES
http://www.onelook.com
Type in a word and this search tool will look for multiple definitions from a variety of online dictionaries: computer/Internet dictionaries, science, medical, technological, medical, business, sports, religion, acronym, and general.

ONLINE REFERENCE WORKS
http://www.cs.cmu.edu/Web/references.html
This site has a collection of online reference works such as English, foreign and computing dictionaries, acronym guides, thesauri, quotation resources, encyclopedias, and more.

REFERENCE CENTER
http://www.ipl.org/ref
This virtual library helps to make finding valuable information online easy. Click on a reference shelf and be linked to resources.

REFERENCE DESK
http://www-sci.lib.uci.edu/~martindale/Ref.html
This GOLDMINE site has won multiple awards for its SUPERB resource collection. A go to the top of the bookmark list site.

REFERENCE INDEXES
http://www.lib.lsu.edu/weblio.html
Links to online references such as dictionaries, library catalogs, newsstand, and subject collections.

REFERENCE SHELF
http://gort.ucsd.edu/ek/refshelf/refshelf.html
The University of California, San Diego, sponsors this collection of online reference resources.

RESEARCHPAPER.COM
http://www.researchpaper.com/directory.html
This award-winning online research tool that brings an archive of thousands of magazines, newspapers, books, and photographs.

THE VIRTUAL REFERENCE DESK
http://thorplus.lib.purdue.edu/reference/index.html
Purdue Universities links to an AWESOME list of valuable online resources.

WIRED SOURCE
http://www.wiredsource.com/wiredsource
A collection of search engines to use for your research.

Speeches and Speech Writing

HOW TO WRITE YOUR SPEECH
http://www.coffingco.com/doc/tjwrite.html
Tips for writing a speech for a particular audience.

PUBLIC SPEAKING ANXIETY
http://www.mwc.edu/~bchirico/psanxinf.html
Symptoms of public speaking anxiety (PSA) and how to overcome PSA.

SPEECH WRITING
http://speeches.com/index.shtml
This award-winning site has excellent resources for writing speeches. You're just a click away from everything you need to help you in your speech preparation. There's a speech archive: links to thousands of other speeches on the Web, free help with your speech writing, and the one and only Automatic Wedding Speech Writer.

SPIN DOCTOR'S CLINIC
http://speeches.com/writer.html
Help with your speech draft from the Spin Doctor.

RESEARCHPAPER.COM
http://www.researchpaper.com/directory.html
This award-winning online research tool that brings an archive of thousands of magazines, newspapers, books, and photographs.

VISUAL PRESENTATION ASSISTANT
http://www.ukans.edu/cwis/units/coms2/vpa/vpa.htm
An online tutorial for improving public speaking skills.

WORDS OF MOUTH
http://www.cohums.ohio-state.edu/english/facstf/kol/diverse.htm
The Words of Mouth Home Page has been created to meet two distinct needs of editors and others interested in learning more about communication skills.

Writing Resources

BARTLETT'S FAMILIAR QUOTATIONS
http://www.ccc.columbia.edu/acis/bartleby/bartlett/index.html
Looking for a quote for your class presentation or paper, connect to this Web site and search by keyword or choose from a list of people.

EDITORIAL EYE
http://www.eei-alex.com/eye
The Eye is a resource for writers, editors, designers, project managers, communications specialists, and everyone else who cares about excellence in publishing practices. Any aspect of effective written communication is likely to appear as a topic in the Eye.

RHETNET—A CYBERJOURNAL FOR RHETORIC AND WRITING

http://www.missouri.edu/~rhetnet

RhetNet is a concerted effort to see what publishing on the Net might be in its "natural" form without merely adapting Net publishing to print-based convention. However, print heritage should not be left behind entirely. This site explores the creative possibilites that Net publishing offers. Here you will find links to many electronic publications—essays, Net journals, and other written resources.

SUPERQUOTES

http://www.columbia.edu/acis/bartleby/bartlett

Bartlett's familiar quotations, passages, phrases, proverbs traced to their sources.

UNIVERSITY WRITING RESOURCES

http://www.interlog.com/~ohi/inkspot/university.html

Links to many writing resources.

WRITER'S BLOCK

http://www.magi.com/~niva/writblok/index.html

Writer's Block is a quarterly newsletter that deals with technical writing and the business of documentation. It contains material of interest to communications specialists, including writers, editors, graphic designers, and desktop publishing operators.

WRITING LAB

http://owl.english.purdue.edu

At Purdue, students come to the Writing Lab to talk with tutors about planning and writing their papers. On-line, the Writing Lab offers
other services as well, including some of our materials on writing and useful links to other sources of information.

WRITING PAGE

http://www.stetson.edu/~hansen/writguid.html

This page is designed to provide as much information and resources as possible for writers. While this site has all types of resources and links, its main focus is helping college students improve their writing skills. This page is a companion page to the Write Your Way to a High GPA page.

WRITER'S RESOURCE CENTER

http://www.azstarnet.com/~poewar/writer/writer.html

John Hewitt is the writer and curator of the Writer's Resource Center. Here you will find links to writing tips such as 14 Tips for Sending Effective Press Releases; How to Become an Expert Writer in Any Industry; Technical Writing: Books and Reference Sources; The Art of Networking, and much more.

WRITING RESOURCES

http://www.public.iastate.edu/~psisler/resources.html

Writing resources from the University of Iowa for writing instructors, professional communicators, technical writers, and rhetoric and composition scholars.

WRITING RESOURCES ON THE NET

http://owl.trc.purdue.edu/resources.html

Purdue University has compiled many excellent writing resources on the Internet. If you're looking for good indexes and directories, also check out their extensive collection of Writing Labs on the Internet.

EXTRA CREDIT

Books and Literary Resources

IBIC GUIDE TO BOOK-RELATED RESOURCES ON THE INTERNET
http://sunsite.unc.edu/ibic/guide.html
IBIC (Internet Book Information Center) has an extensive collection of book-related resources that can be found on the Internet: authors, publishers, booksellers, online books and magazines, poetry, short stories, rare books, and more.

THE COMPLETE WORKS OF WILLIAM SHAKESPEARE
http://the-tech.mit.edu/Shakespeare/works.html
An online collection of Shakespeare's work from MIT including resources for discussion, Shakespearean quotations, and links to other related online resources.

LABRINTH
http://www.georgetown.edu/labyrinth/labyrinth-home.html
The Labyrinth is a global information network providing free, organized access to electronic resources in medieval studies through a World Wide Web server at Georgetown University. The Labyrinth's easy-to-use menus and hypertext links provide automatic connections to databases, services, and electronic texts on other servers around the world.

LITERARY RESOURCES ON THE NET
http://www.english.upenn.edu/~jlynch/Lit
This award-winning site is a collection of links to sites on the Internet dealing especially with English and American literature, excluding single electronic texts.

MODERN ENGLISH COLLECTION
http://etext.lib.virginia.edu/modeng.browse.html
An extensive collection from the University of Virginia.

ONLINE BOOKS PAGE
http://www.cs.cmu.edu/books.html
Look here for an index of thousands of online books, and for common repositories of online books and other documents.

SCIENCE FICTION RESOURCE GUIDE
http://sflovers.rutgers.edu/Web/SFRG
A MUST VISIT site for sci fi enthuiasts.

VOICE OF THE SHUTTLE
http://humanitas.ucsb.edu
An AWESOME collection of Humanities resources. An important research site.

PREPARING FOR COLLEGE

Applying for College

CB NET (COLLEGE BOUND NET)
http://www.product.com/cbnet
A student interactive guide to college life from Ramholtz Publishing. Their College Bound Magazine provides information about the college application process.

COLLEGEAPPS.COM
http://www.collegeapps.com
Sharon Barth and Sue Berescik claim to be able to help motivate students to get started in the college application process. The site advertises their book and consulting services for taking the fears out of applying to college, showing how to self-assess and find ones unique qualities and experiences, and giving a sure-fire method of writing essays that LEAP OFF THE PAGE!

COLLEGE LINK
http://www.collegelink.com
Apply to college using your computer. CollegeLink's award winning software simplifies the application process by making it easy to apply to multiple colleges at once. Visit their site to learn more about their customized applications to match the regular forms of hundreds of colleges.

U.S. NEWS COLLEGE AND CAREER CENTER
http://www.usnews.com/usnews/edu
U.S. News provides services to assist high school seniors as they finalize their list of colleges and prepare the applications that will determine what path the next four years of their lives will take.

Usenet newsgroup for college admissions at soc.college.admisions.

Finding a College

Resources for helping find colleges, universities, community colleges, and technical schools.

AMERICAN UNIVERSITIES
http://www.clas.ufl.edu/CLAS/american-universities.html
This site is a collection of home pages for American Universities granting bachelor or advanced degrees.

COLLEGE AND UNIVERSITY HOME PAGES
http://www.mit.edu:8001/people/cdemello/univ.html
Links to more than 3000 colleges and universities.

COLLEGE GUIDE SEARCH FORM
http://www.jayi.com/jayi/ACG/search.html
Use this search form to find the perfect college for you. Use the pull-down menus and keyword to

choose the variables of your preference. Or, if you'd prefer, you may simply view regional and alphabetical lists of colleges.

COLLEGE LINK

http://www.collegelink.com
Apply to college using your computer. CollegeLink's award-winning software simplifies the application process by making it easy to apply to multiple colleges at once. Visit their site to learn more about their customized applications to match the regular forms of hundreds of colleges.

COLLEGE LOCATOR

http://www.ecola.com/college
A tool to help you locate a college or university by city and state.

COLLEGENET

http://www.collegenet.com/cnmain.html
CollegeNET is an AWESOME guide to colleges and universities.
CollegeNET lets you browse institutions by various criteria including geography, tuition, and enrollment. Other resources include a search tool to assist you with finding a college, information on financial aid, and scholarhsips, featured schools, online application forms, graduate programs, and academic resources.

COLLEGE VIEW

http://www.collegeview.com
A free online database of 3,500 colleges and universities, with virtual tours, financial aid information, career planning tools, and electronic applications! Visit the Coffee Shop to find others with similar interests and chat interactively.

COMMUNITY COLLEGES

The following Web sites have links to Community Colleges and technical schools.
http://www.utexas.edu/world/comcol/alpha
http://www.sp.utoledo.edu/twoyrcol.html
http://www.yahoo.com/Education/Higher_Education/Community_Colleges

KAPLAN

http://www.kaplan.com/library/precoll/listing.html
The Kaplan site has links to over 420 online colleges as well as a featured college of the week where you can get their detailed information about what they feel to be some of the best colleges.

PLANET EARTH HOME PAGE

http://www.nosc.mil/planet_earth/uni.html
Planet Earth has an excellent collection of college resources including: university phone directories; an alphabetical listing of academies, colleges, universities; other college and university sources; faculty and student body home pages; department of education; scholarships; career center; job opportunities; and links to other educational resources.

SELECTING A SCHOOL—A GUIDED TOUR

http://www.tgslc.org/adventur/selectng.htm
On this virtual tour you'll find out what characteristics to look for when choosing a college or training program and how to find the best school for you. This well-done site has many links to information from career planning to financing your education to finding a job.

U.S. NEWS COLLEGE AND CAREER CENTER
http://www.usnews.com/usnews/edu/college/cosearch.htm
This excellent site has an interactive tool to help you find a college using your own personal selection criteria. They also have an an online college rating taken from their publication—America's Best Colleges—that shakes up the college world.

Planning for a College Education

The Net sites in this section are for high school and college students: resources to help make the transititon smooth from high school to college; information on the fastest growing careers; student success; internships; and, career programs.

CAREER PLANNING GUIDED TOUR
http://www.tgslc.org/adventur/planning.htm
On this tour, you can find out how to choose a career and how to reach your career goal. You can also pick up useful tips on job hunting, resume writing, and job interviewing techniques.

COLLEGE BOARD ONLINE
http://www.collegeboard.org
This impressive site brings the authoritative educational and information resources of the College Board to your dekstop. Here students and parents will find the Web's most comprehensive menu of information to aid in the transition from school to college. Services include online SAT test dates, online SAT registration, a test question of the day, a college search tool, a financial aid calculator, and much more.

COLLEGEEDGE
http://www.CollegeEdge.com
This award-winning site offers a powerful college search tool, useful links, advice and guidance from an expert college panel. Explore careers and majors. In the CollegeEdge Forums talk to other students about careers and majors. Career Advice provides information on the fastest growing careers as well as advice and information on choosing the right career for you.

EASI
http://easi.ed.gov
EASI (Easy Access for Students and Institutions) is made available from the U.S. Education Department as a resource for families of college-bound students. This site provides links to information on financial aid resources by state, standardized tests for postsecondary schoool admission, student's rights, and loan repayment responsibilities.

KAPLAN EDUCATIONAL CENTER
http://www.kaplan.com
Kaplan helps prepare students for tests and success. Their online resources include links to many fun sites to test yourself—I.Q. tests, personality games, career inventories—an online SAT course, SAT vocabulary flash cards, a college simulator to help determine if you are a scholar or a party animal. You will also find college sites of the week, links to over 460 online colleges, and information for student success.

THE PRINCETON REVIEW
http://www.review.com/index.shtml
The Princeton Review offers students a wealth of free and unique resources. Through special student programs and an informative and comprehensive Web site, students can gather information

about tests, admissions, internships, and career programs. The focus is on helping students.

U.S. NEWS COLLEGE AND CAREER CENTER
http://www.usnews.com/usnews/edu
U.S. News provides services to assist high school seniors as they finalize their list of colleges and prepare the applications that will determine what path the next four years of their lives will take. Get Into College takes you step-by-step through the process, from choosing schools, to filling out the applications, to planning the campus visit. They also have an exclusive college rankings published in their America's Best Colleges and now online.

YAHOO COLLEGE ENTRANCE COLLECTION
http://www.yahoo.com/education/college_entrance
A collection of online resources to help prepare for college.

Tests—Standardized

COLLEGE BOARD ONLINE
http://www.collegeboard.org
The College Board site provides online SAT test dates, online SAT registration, a test question of the day, a college search tool, a financial aid calculator, and much more.

KAPLAN
http://www.kaplan.com/library/precoll/listing.html
Testing services include the opportunity to take a sample SAT or GRE online at no cost. Visit their site to learn more about their test preparation services.

PRINCETON REVIEW
http://www.review.com/undergr/college_homepage.shtml
Visit this site to learn about standardized tests and how to prepare for them. Included is information on SAT, SATII, The ACT, and The PSAT.

TESTPREP.COM
http://www.testprep.com
This Web site offers free online test preparation solutions with thousands of screens of math and verbal lessons and over 700 practice problems.

SYNDICATE
http://syndicate.com
Learning vocabulary can be fun for everyone! Compete for prizes in monthly word puzzle contests. Enjoy grade specific puzzles, comic strips, word games and many other ways to sharpen your skills in preparation for the SAT(R), SSAT, GRE or LSAT tests.

STAFF DEVELOPMENT

ALTERNATIVE ASSESSMENT/PERFORMANCE ASSESSMENT
http://ericae2.educ.cua.edu/intass.htm
A GOLDMINE site with many excellent resources on alternative and performance assessment.

ASSESSMENT—NORTH CENTRAL RESIONAL EDUCATIONAL LAB
http://www.ncrel.org/sdrs/areas/as0cont.htm
Assessment resources from Pathways to School Improvement.

EDUCATION HOTLIST
http://sln.fi.edu/tfi/hotlists/education.html
A list of educational resources including professional development.

EDUCATION WORLD
http://www.education-world.com
This excellent Web site is updated daily with many wonderful educational resources.

EDUCATIONAL PSYCHOLOGY INTERACTIVE
http://www.valdosta.edu/~whuitt/psy702/internet.html
A comprehensive list of Internet resources in the area of educational psychology.

EDWEB HOME ROOM
http://edweb.cnidr.org:90/resource.cntnts.html
Exploring technology and school reform.

PROFESSIONAL DEVELOPMENT RESOURCES
http://www.indiana.edu/~eric_rec/prodev/menu.html
Links to professional development resources.

PROFESSIONAL DEVELOPMENT RESOURCES—
North Central Regional Educational Lab
http://www.ncrel.org/sdrs/areas/pd0cont.htm

WEB66
http://mustang.coled.umn.edu/Howused.html
An AWESOME educational resource with links to the best online educational resources, schools on the Internet, and much more.

WORLDWIDE CLASSROOM
http://www.worldwide.edu/
WorldWide Classroom is a compilation of intercultural and educational programs around the world which welcome international visitors. They include: university study, adult enrichment, foreign language immersion, teen camps, volunteerism, internships, cultural, craft and heritage programs.

SUBSTANCE ABUSE

ADDICTION RESEARCH FOUNDATION
http://www.arf.org
The Addiction Research Foundation develops and makes available knowledge and programs that can be used to reduce the problems caused by the abuse of alcohol and other drugs in Ontario. This site has information on community-based planning and development services, health promotion activities, treatment programs, research, and more.

ALCOHOL & DRUG INFORMATION (FROM NCADI)

http://www.health.org/

NCADI sponsors PREVLINE—Prevention Online. This site has links to information on what to do if someone you love has a problem—resources and referrals, publications, latest press releases, research, surveys, statistics, drug and alcohol databases, online discussion forums, and links to related Internet resources.

CANADIAN CENTRE ON SUBSTANCE ABUSE

http://www.ccsa.ca

Canadian Centre on Substance Abuse is a non-profit organization working to minimize the harm associated with the use of alcohol, tobacco, and other drugs. This site has links to information on substance abuse, statistics, publications, and activities. You can also search their database for information on substance abuse.

CENTER FOR EDUCATION AND DRUG ABUSE RESEARCH (CEDAR)

http://www.pitt.edu/~mmv/cedar.html

CEDAR's mission is to elucidate the factors contributing to the variation in the liability to drug abuse and determine the developmental pathways culminating in drug abuse outcome, normal outcome, and psychiatric/behavioral disorder outcome. Their Internet site supports this mission in providing information on drug and alcohol abuse projects and links to drug-related sites.

CENTER FOR SUBSTANCE ABUSE RESEARCH (CESAR)
http://www.bsos.umd.edu/cesar/cesar.html

CESAR is a research center within the College of Behavioral and Social Sciences, University of Maryland College Park. A primary mission of CESAR is to collect, analyze, and disseminate information on the nature and extent of substance abuse and related problems. Second, CESAR conducts policy-relevant research on specific initiatives to prevent, treat, and control substance abuse, and evaluates prevention and treatment programs. Visit this site and learn more about their services and online support information.

DRUG ENFORCEMENT ADMINISTRATION

http://www.usdoj.gov/dea/deahome.html

Visit this site to learn more about what DEA is doing to combat the war against drugs.

DRUG INFORMATION

http://www.paranoia.com:80/drugs

This Web site has a place to submit and read drug users stories; cold, hard information on substances such as alcohol, marijuana, MDMA, nontropics, opiates, psychedelics, and stimulants; information on the war on drugs; and better living through drug links.

DRUGS AND CRIME

http://www.ncjrs.org/drgshome.htm

Links to information on community efforts and prevention, corrections, courts, drug testing, drug treatment, drug use indicators, enforcement, policy and law, research, and evaluation.

DRUGS IN THE MEDIA

http://www.he.net/~storm/drugs/media.html

Links to articles and special reposts about drugs including the MacNeil/Lehrer News Hour, an article by William F. Buckley, and New York Times and Los Angeles Times stories.

NATIONAL INSTITUTE ON DRUG ABUSE (NIDA)
http://www.nida.nih.gov

The mission of the National Institute on Drug Abuse (NIDA) is to lead the nation in bringing the power of science to bear on drug abuse and addiction. To accomplish this mission, NIDA conducts research across a broad range of disciplines and provides rapid and effective dissemination and use of the results of that research to significantly improve drug abuse and addiction prevention, treatment, and policy. This site has links to NIDA's research and programs.

RAND DRUG POLICY RESEARCH CENTER (DPRC)
http://www.rand.org/centers/dprc

DPRC was established in 1989 to conduct the empirical research, policy analysis, and outreach needed to help community leaders and public officials develop more effective strategies for dealing with drug problems. The center is strongly committed to ensuring that its findings reach those who can make a difference. Visit their Web site to learn more about their work.

SUBSTANCE ABUSE AND MENTAL HEALTH SERVICES ADMINISTRATION (SAMHSA)
http://www.samhsa.gov

SAMHSA's mission is to assure that quality substance abuse and mental health services are available to the people who need them and to ensure that prevention and treatment knowledge is used more effectively in the general health care system. This site provides information on SAMHSA's programs and services, statistical information on drug abuse, funding opportunities, events and conferences, and other related Internet resources.

UNITED NATIONS INTERNATIONAL DRUG CONTROL PROGRAMME
http://www.undcp.org

The United Nations International Drug Control Programme is the United Nations agency responsible for coordinating activities relating to the international control of narcotic drugs and psychotropic substances. Visit this site to learn more about its programs and services as well as links to national drug information.

WEB OF ADDICTIONS
http://www.well.com:80/user/woa

The Web of Addictions is dedicated to providing accurate information about alcohol and other drug addictions. The Web of Addictions was developed due to concerns about the extent of misinforma-

SURFING ADVENTURES

tion about abused drugs on the Internet.

This section features some of the coolest Web sites that present valuable information in visually well-designed interactive environments.

AIRLINES ON THE WEB
http://w2.itn.net/airlines

The Airlines on the Web page is maintained by a graduate student at the University of California—Berkeley Haas School of Business studying the rapid changes in the airline industry for a dissertation. At this site you will find links to most of the passenger carriers worldwide, frequent flyer programs, airline stock quotes, medical airline transports, cargo airlines, manufacturers and suppliers, aviation organizations, airline 800-numbers, related Internet sites, and Airlines on the Web statistics.

ALCATRAZ

http://www.nps.gov/alcatraz

Out in the middle of the San Francisco Bay, the island of Alcatraz is a world unto itself. Isolation, one of the constants of island life for any inhabitant—soldier, prisoner, bird or plant—is a recurrent theme in the unfolding history of Alcatraz. Follow this pelican for a complete tour of the island. Learn about the military and penitentiary history, Native American Occupation, Natural History, or visit the bookstore.

AUDIONET

http://www.audionet.com

The broadcast network on the Internet.

CYBORGANIC GARDENS

http://www.cyborganic.com

Kick off your shoes and wander around the Cyborganic Gardens. A creative, interesting, and fun site.

CYBERTOWN

http://www.cybertown.com/cybertown/index.html

The purpose of Cybertown is to create a virtual community where people can have fun, be entertained, learn things and explore the best of the Earth Internet. Cybertown is set in the latter half of the 21st century and is not far from this galaxy. It is populated mostly by people originally from Earth. Many of them left Earth after the Great War in the hopes that a new start would lead to more peaceful times. Visit Cybertown to continue the journey.

DIGITAL PASSPORT

http://www.rubicon.com/passport.html

This hot Web sit is worth a visit. Valuable and useful information is provided for those interested in international travel: an excellent world exchange rate tool, time zone information, international holidays, embassies, air travel information, and information on international deliveries.

EARTHSHIP

http://www.slip.net/~ckent/earthship

If you're looking for UFO's, aliens, and other such things, this is not the place. Earthships are a new approach to sustainable living. Imagine building a house out of discarded tires and aluminum cans. Imagine using environmentally friendly materials and techniques to create a truly self-sufficient home. Imagine interfacing and harnessing nature to create a dwelling that lives with the land, not on top of it.

ECOMALL

http://www.ecomall.com

A place to help save the earth.

EDWARD ABBEY WEB

http://www.utsidan.se/abbey/abbey.html

Meet Edward Paul Abbey, twentieth-century polemicist and desert anarchist, a character of elaborate contradictions and eccentricities whose words either infuriated or delighted his readers. In a career spanning four decades, he wrote passionately in defense of the Southwest and its inhabitants, often mocking the mindless bureaucratic forces hell-bent on destroying it. "Resist much, obey little," from Walt Whitman, was this warrior's motto.

—from Epitaph for a Desert Anarchist

FIGURE 7.5
Edward Abbey Home Page

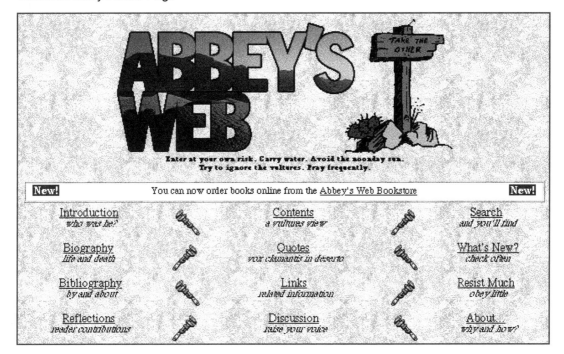

ELECTRONIC ZOO
http://netvet.wustl.edu/e-zoo.htm
Back in the spring of 1993, a veterinarian started a (then) very manageable project of organizing and categorizing veterinary medical information available on the Internet. The project grew and today has become one of the best Web sites with "everything animal."

ESPNET SPORTSZONE
http://ESPNET.SportsZone.com
The latest sports news can be found at ESPNET.

FODOR'S TRAVEL
http://www.fodors.com
http://www.ypn.com/travel
Use Fodor's Trip Planner to prepare for your next vacation. Build a customized miniguide to scores of destinations around the world. The Trip Planner leads you through a series of checklists where you tell Fodor's your destination and exactly what you want in the way of hotels, restaurants, travel info, and more. When you're finished, it uses your choices to build a personalized guide that you can print out for easy reading or to take with you on your trip. The Know Before You Go section links to information on travel advisories, world weather, currency converter, government health advisories, and more.

MEDIADOME
http://www.mediadome.com/About/index.html
CNET and Intel collaborate to bring the best cutting-edge multimedia Web entertainment to your desktop. A new interactive program debuts every two weeks providing the utimate Web experience where you become a participant rather than just an observer.

SONY

http://www.sony.com

The Sony site is an excellent example of how interactivity can be used on the Internet. It contains links to music, film, and electronics. Information can be found on musicians, their tour schedules, sound clips, record cover art, music videos, and special promotions, as well as information on Sony products.

TELEGARDEN

http://www.usc.edu/dept/garden

For the experienced gardener, the TeleGarden offers a search for the soul of gardening. Sowing a single, unseen and untouched seed thousands of miles away might seem mechanical, but it engenders a Zen-like appreciation for the fundamental act of growing. Though drained of sensory cues, planting that distant seed still stirs anticipation, protectiveness, and nurturing. The unmistakable vibration of the garden pulses and pulls, even through a modem. — Warren Schultz

Visit the TeleGarden and interact with a remote garden filled with living plants. At no cost, become a member—plant, water, and monitor the progress of seedlings via the movements of a robotic arm.

SHAREWARE AND SOFTWARE

JUMBO

http://www.jumbo.com

The Biggest, Most Mind-Boggling, Most Eye-Popping, Most Death-Defying Conglomeration of Freeware and Shareware Programs on the Web! 24,582 PROGRAMs at this time.

FREEWARE CENTRAL

http://www.ptf.com/free

Freeware Central is an exploratory news and information resource for the free software community. Topic areas include: archives of free software, calendar of upcoming events related to free software, legal issues related to free software, news about free software, organizations involved with free software, and services related to free software,

MIT'S HYPERARCHIVE

http://hyperarchive.lcs.mit.edu/HyperArchive/HyperArchive.html

Search MIT's archive for software or browse by categories.

SHAREWARE.COM

http://www.shareware.com

An extensive collection of shareware with an online search engine for finding what you are looking for.

TUCOWS (THE ULTIMATE COLLECTION OF WINSOCK SOFTWARE)

http://www.tucows.com

This site has an excellent selection of Internet software for Windows 95. TUCOWS provides Windows 3.x and '95 winsock programs to facilitate PC access to the Internet.

USEFUL, COOL INTERNET SERVICES

AT&T TOLL FREE
http://www.tollfree.att.net/dir800
This Web site is one example of how a company has used the Internet to provide a useful service. The site helps you find 800-numbers of companies.

CAR RENTAL 800 NUMBERS
http://www.travlang.com/carrental.800.html
Toll free numbers for car rental agencies.

FEDEX
http://www.fedex.com/cgi-bin/track_it
Wondering where your FedEx package is, when it got delivered, or who signed for it? Visit FedEx's Package Tracking interactive and fascinating Web site.

HOTEL TOLL FREE NUMBERS
http://www.go-explore.com/CONTENT/USA/hotel800.htm
Click on the first letter of the hotel's name, or scroll through the list to find the toll-free number of a hotel in the U.S. or Canada.

INTERNATIONAL DIALING CODES
http://www.cris.com/~Kropla/dialcode.htm
This site has a listing of Country Codes and IDD (International Direct Dialing) prefixes.

UNITED PARCEL SERVICE
http://www.ups.com
Learn more about how businesses provide useful services by visiting the United Parcel Service's interactive site. This site also helps you track your packages, calculate approximate costs for sending a package, and a form to help estimate how long it will take for your package to reach its destination.

ZIP+4 CODE LOOKUP
http://www.usps.gov/ncsc/lookups/lookup_zip+4.html
Have you ever been frustrated trying to find a zip code. This Web site by the United States Postal System provides a useful Internet resource. Enter an address and, if found in their database, this lookup will standardize the address, return the ZIP+4 Code, and provide the county name.

Foreign Language Center

ACTIVE

Microsoft's response to Java was the ActiveX development platform. This technology makes it possible for Web programmers to create and for Web surfers to view moving and animated objects, live audio, scrolling banners, and interactivity. The ActiveX technology—available in Microsoft Internet Explorer—makes it possible to view many plug-in applications without first downloading and installing the required plug-in. ActiveX makes it possible for desktop applications to be linked to the World Wide Web. For example programs such as Word can be viewed directly from Explorer.

ADMINISTRATIVE ADDRESS

The e-mail address used for sending requests to listservs for either text documents or requests to subscribe to a mailing list.

ANONYMOUS FTP

The method used in file transfer protocol that allows Internet users to log into an FTP server as an unregistered users. Before browsers were used for FTP, users connecting to an FTP server would have to log in by entering a login name and password. The login name was anonymous; the password, your e-mail address.

APPLETS

Mini-applications that a software program such as Netscape downloads and executes.

ASCII (TEXT) FILES

One of the file transfer modes (binary is another mode) used when transferring files on the Internet. ASCII treats the file as a set of characters that can be read by the computer receiving the ASCII text. ASCII does not recognize text formatting such as boldface, underline, tab stops, or fonts.

AVATAR

In online chat environments users create nicknames that they are known by online. In 3D chat worlds an avatar is the graphical representation that a user creates for himself. Avatars can look like a person, animal, or object.

BINARY FILE

Another transfer mode available for transferring Internet files. In the binary mode, files are transferred which are identical in appearance to the original document.

BINHEX (BINARY HEXADECIMAL)

A method for converting non-text files (non-ASCII) into ASCII. Used in e-mail programs that can handle only ASCII.

BIT

A single-digit number, either a 1 or a zero, that represents the smallest unit of computerized data.

BOOKMARKS

A feature providing the user with the opportunity to mark favorite pages for fast and easy access. Netscape's bookmarks can be organized hierarchically and customized by the user through the Bookmark List dialog box.

BOOLEAN OPERATORS

Phrases or words such as "and," "or," and "not" that limit a search using Internet search engines.

BROWSER

A client program that interprets and displays HTML documents.

CLIENT
A software program assisting in contacting a server somewhere on the Net for information. Examples of client software programs are Gopher, Netscape, Veronica, and Archie. An Archie client runs on a system configured to contact a specific Archie database to query for information.

COMPRESSION
A process by which a file or a folder is made smaller. The three primary purposes of compression are to save disk space, to save space when doing a backup, and to speed the transmission of a file when transferring via a modem or network.

COOKIE
Cookie technology allows the storage of personal preferences for use with Internet information and communication tools. A text file is created of your preferences, saved in your browser's folder, and stored in RAM while your browser is running. For example a popular Web audio site, Timecast, allows users to select their personal audio preferences to be played with RealAudio. These personal in your browser folder in a called cookie file. When you connect to the site that uses personal preferences, the server at that site looks for the cookie file on your computer to find your specifications. The problem with cookie technology is that Web sites you connect to can look at your cookie file also to see personal information. Programs, such as Cookie Muncher, have been created to delete cookie files when you log off.

DELAYED-RESPONSE MEDIA
Internet communication tools that require time for an end-user to respond (i.e., electronic mail, list-servs, and newsgroups)

DIGERATI
A community of diverse professionals—computer scientists, film makers, designers, engineers, architects, artists, writers, musicans—who are becoming increasingly wealthy through their creative and innovative use and exploration of digital technology. Louis Rossetto and Jane Metcalfe (Wired magazine) were the first to give name to these digital elite whom they believed were becoming the most powerful people on earth.

DOMAIN NAME
The unique name that identifies an Internet site. Names have two or more parts separated by a dot such as xplora.com.

FINGER
An Internet software tool for locating people on the Internet. The most common use is to see if an individual has an account at a particular Internet site.

FIRE WALL
A combination of hardware and software that separates a local area network into two parts for security purposes.

FLAME
Flaming is a used in Internet communiction (e-mail and newsgroups) to personally attach another person. A flame war occurs when the a flamer is flamed back.

FRAMES
A new feature of Netscape Navigator 2.0 makes it possible to create multiple windows on a Netscape page. This is an example of a Web page divided into several windows called frames. To navigate within frames and to save bookmarks, you will use your mouse. To move forward and back within

frames, position your cursor within the frame and hold down the mouse button (Macintosh users); Windows users hold down the right mouse button. A pop-up menu appears. Choose Back in Frame or Forward in Frame. To bookmark a frame, place your cursor over the link to the frame and hold down the mouse button. A different pop-up menu appears. Select Add Bookmark for this Link. To print a frame, click the desired frame and select Print Frame from the File menu.

FTP (FILE TRANSFER PROTOCOL)
Protocol for transferring files between computers on the Internet.

GIF (GRAPHIC INTERFACE FORMAT)
A format developed by CompuServe, Inc. for storing complex graphics. This format is one of two used for storing graphics in HTML documents.

HELPER APPLICATIONS
Programs used by Netscape to read files retrieved from the Internet. Different server protocols are used by Netscape to transfer files: HTTP, NNTP, SMTP, and FTP. Each protocol supports different file formats for text, images, video, and sound. When these files are received by Netscape, the external helper applications read, interpret, and display the file.

HELPER APPLICATIONS
Stand-alone programs that work with browsers to extend their graphic file abilities. These same helpers also operate on their own outside the browser environment. On example of a helper would be a compression program such as PKZIP or Stuffit Expander.

HISTORY LIST
Netscape keeps track of your Internet journeys. Sites that you visit are listed in the History List found under the Go pull-down menu. Click on an Internet site on your list, and you will be linked to that destination.

HOME PAGE
The starting point for World Wide Web exploration. The Home Page contains highlighted words and icons that link to text, graphics, video, and sound files. Home Pages can be developed by anyone: Internet providers, universities, businesses, and individuals. Netscape allows you to select which Home Page is displayed when you launch the program.

HTML (HYPERTEXT MARKUP LANGUAGE)
A programming language used to create a Web page. This includes the text of the document, its structure, and links to other documents. HTML also includes the programming for accessing and displaying media such as images, video, and sound.

HTTP (HYPERTEXT TRANSFER PROTOCOL)
One protocol used by the World Wide Web to transfer information. Web documents begin with http://

HYPERLINKS
Links to other Web information such as a link to another page, an image, or a video or sound file.

HYPERMEDIA
The combined use of multimedia (text, images, video, and sound) in a Web presentation page.

HYPERTEXT
A document containing links to another document. The linked document is displayed by clicking on a highlighted word or icon in the hypertext.

INTRANET
An intranet is usually owned by a company or corporation for communication within the organizattion. It is referred as a restricted-access network.

IP ADDRESS
Every computer on the Internet has a unique IP address. This number consists of four parts separated by dots such as 198.68.32.1

ISDN
Normal telephone lines are low-bandwidth analog lines. ISDN lines are digital lines that can handle large amounts of information very quickly— up to four times as fast as the standard 28.8Kbps modem. An ISDN line is a single phone wire that makes it possible to download Web pages, send and receive faxes and talk on the phone—all at the same time. An ISDN line is divided into 3 channels: two B channels and one D channel, thus making it possible to surf the Internet with one B channel and have the other 2 channels available for phone calls or faxes.

ISP
Internet Service Provider

JAVASCRIPT
A new programming language developed by Sun Microsystems that makes it possible to incorporate mini-applications called applets onto a Web page.

JPEG (JOINT PHOTOGRAPHIC EXPERTS GROUP)
A file format for graphics (photographs, complex images, and video stills) that uses compression.

LISTSERV MAILING LIST
A listserv is the automated system that distributes electronic mail. Listservs perform two functions: distributing text documents stored on them to those that request them; and, managing interactive mailing lists.

LIVE OBJECTS
Java brings life and interaction to Web pages by making it possible to create live objects. Move your mouse over an image of a house and see the lights go on. Move your mouse to a picture of a woman and hear her welcome you to her Home Page.

MIME (MULTIMEDIA INTERNET MAIL EXTENSION)
Most multimedia files on the Internet are MIME. The MIME type refers to the type of file: text, HTML, images, video, or sound. When a browser such as Netscape retrieves a file from a server, the server provides the MIME type to establish whether the file format can be read by the software's built-in capabilities or, if not, whether a suitable helper application is available to read the file.

MOZILLA
Users of Netscape may run into a little cartoon dragon that pops up on Netscape screens. This characters is called Mozilla—the Netscape mascot. The name originated in the early days of Netscape. The creators of first Web browser—NCSA Mosiac—formed a company and created what we now know as Netscape. The developers code named the first beta version of Netscape "mozilla" for Mosaic mated with Godzilla—a mutant or monstrous version.

MULTIMEDIA
The term used when referring to the use of more than one medium—such as text supplemented with annimation, video, or sound.

NEWSGROUPS
Large distributed bulletin board systems that consist of several thousand specialized discussion groups. Messages are posted to a bulletin board by e-mail for others to read.

NEWS READER
A software program required to read Usenet newsgroups. Netscape has a news reader built in. Explore requires the downloading and installing of the news reader Internet Mail and News.

NNTP (NEWS SERVER)
A server protocol used by Netscape for transferring Usenet news. Before you can read Usenet news, you must enter the name of your news server to interact with Usenet newsgroups. The news server name is entered in the Mail and News dialog box (Options pull-down menu; Preferences; Mail and News).

PAGE
A file or document in Netscape that contains hypertext links to multimedia resources.

PKZIP
A popular compression program for Windows computers.

PLATFORM
Netscape Navigator 2.0 is referred to as a platform rather than a browser. A platform program makes it possible for developers to build applications onto it.

PLUG-IN
Software programs designed to play multimedia files from your browser window or page, running as a system resource as long as they are needed.

POP-UP MENU
Menus that activate software features and navigational aids.

PPP (POINT-TO-POINT PROTOCOL)
A method by which a computer may use a high-speed modem and a standard telephone line to have full Internet access. A PPP or SLIP connection is required to use graphical interfaces with the Internet such as Netscape Navigator and Explorer. Using a PPP or SLIP connection enables you to point and click your way around the Internet.

QUICK LINKS
Microsoft Internet Explorer provides an option for creating toolbar buttons of your favorite sites. This feature is call quick links.

REAL-TIME MEDIA
Internet communication tools where interaction occurs in real-time (i.e., chats, MOOs, MUDs, Internet telephone, and Internet videoconferencing).

.SEA (SELF-EXTRACTING ARCHIVES)
A file name extension indicating a compression method used by Macintosh computers. Files whose names end in .sea are compressed archives that can be decompressed by double-clicking on the program icon.

SEARCH DIRECTORY
Descriptive subject indexes of Web sites.

SEARCH ENGINE
Software programs designed for seeking information on the Internet. Some of these programs search by keyword within a document, title, index, or directory.

SERVER
A computer running software that allows another computer (a client) to communicate with it for information exchange.

SHELL ACCOUNT
The most basic type of Internet connection. A shell account allows you to dial into the Internet at your provider's site. Your Internet software is run on the computer at that site. On a shell account your Internet interface is text-based. There are no pull-down menus, icons, or graphics. Some Internet providers offer a menu system of Internet options; others merely provide a Unix system prompt, usually a percent sign or a dollar sign. You must know the commands to enter at the prompt to access the Internet.

SLIP (SERIAL LINE INTERNET PROTOCOL)
A method by which a computer with a high speed modem may connect directly to the Internet through a standard telephone line. A SLIP account is needed to use Netscape. SLIP is currently being replaced with PPP (Point-to-Point Protocol).

SMTP (SIMPLE MAIL TRANSPORT PROTOCOL)
A protocol used by the Internet for electronic mail. Before using Netscape e-mail, the host name of the Internet provider's mail server must be designated. The mail server name is entered in the Mail and News dialog box (Options pull-down menu; Preferences; Mail and News).

SOURCE FILE
When saved as "source," the document is preserved with its embedded HTML instructions that format the Internet page.

STATUS BAS
A horizontal bar found at the bottom of some browser windows that indicate the status of the document or file that is being transferred to the computer from an Internet site.

STREAMING AUDIO AND VIDEO
audio or video files that flow continuously over the Internet to your computer immediately playing the video or sound file as it arrives at the desktop. RealAudio is an example of one of the more popular streaming audio programs.

SUBMISSION ADDRESS
The e-mail address used to send a message to subscribers of a listserv mailing list.

TCP/IP (Transmission Control Protocol/Internet Protocol)
The protocol upon which the Internet is based and which supports transmission of data.

TELNET

One of the oldest Internet tools that allows users to log onto another computer and run resident programs.

TOOLBAR

Navigational buttons used in graphical interface applications.

URL (UNIFORM RESOURCE LOCATOR)

URLs are a standard for locating Internet documents. They use an addressing system for other Internet protocols such as access to Gopher menus, FTP file retrieval, and Usenet newsgroups. The format for a URL is protocol://server-name:/path.

URL OBJECT

Any resource accessible on the World Wide Web: text documents, sound files, movies, and images.

USENET

Developed in the 1970s for communication among computers at various universities. In the early 1980s, Usenet was being used for electronic discussions on a wide variety of topics and soon became a tool for communication. Today, Usenet groups are analogous to a café where people from everywhere in the world gather to discuss and share ideas on topics of common interest.

VIEWER

Programs needed to display graphics, sound, and video. For example, pictures stored as a GIF image have the file name extension ".gif" and need a gif helper application to display the image. Netscape has the required viewers (external helper applications) built into the software. A list of programs required to view files can be found in the Helper Application menu of Netscape. Open the Options pull-down menu, select Preferences, then Helper Applications.

VRML (VIRTUAL REALITY MODELING LANGUAGE)

A programming language that makes 3-dimensional virtual reality experiences possible on Web pages.

APPENDIX

Finding Web Sites That Have Moved

The Internet is a dynamic and rapidly changing environment. Information may be in one place today and either gone or in a new location tomorrow. New sites appear daily; others disappear. Some sites provide forwarding address information; others will not. As you travel in cyberspace and find that a resource you are looking for can no longer be found at a given Internet address, there are several steps you can take to find if the site has a new address.

- Check for a new Internet address or link, often provided on the site of the old address.

- Shorten the URL.
  The format for a URL is: **protocol//server-name/path**
  Try deleting the last section of the URL (path), so that the URL ends with the domain name or server name (com, edu, net, org). For example, you may be look ing for NASA's links to astronomy sites. Take the original URL provided for the site, in this case **http://quest.arc.nasa.gov/lfs/other_sites.html**, and delete the last part of the address **lfs/other_sites.html** leaving **http://quest.arc.nasa.gov**. You will most likely get to NASA's Home Page and can navigate to the specific topic or category you are looking for.

- Type in a company name for the URL.
  Companies usually use either their name, some part of their name, or an abbreviation as their domain name that becomes their URL. Netscape 2.02 and 3.0 accept abbreviated Net addresses, without the **http://www.** prefix. If you type a single word as your URL, Netscape adds the prefix **http://www.** and the suffix **.com**. For example, to connect to Netscape's Home Page, type **Netscape**. Microsoft Internet Explorer requires the **http://www. prefix**.

- Identify a domain name or server name.
  If you are trying to find an educational institution (edu), non-profit organization (org), networking organization (net), government (gov), or military agency (mil), identify a portion of their name that they may have chosen for their domain name. For example, Rainforest Action Network (RAN), is an non-profit organization (org) that has changed the location of its Web site several times. Typing in an old address **http://gaia1.ies.wisc.edu/research/png fores/welcome** gives this message: **HTTP/1.0 404 Object Not Found**

  To find the Rainforest Action Network, look at their name and try to identify what they may have chosen for their domain name. Since Rainforest Action Network is long, perhaps they chose their acronym, RAN. Try entering a URL using **RAN** and **org**. In this instance type **http://www.ran.org**. This URL connects to the Rainforest Action Networks' Home Page.

- Do a keyword search using search engines.

Example 1: Finding a new URL for the Rainforest Action Network

When researching the new URL for the Rainforest Action Network, a search engine such as Infoseek Ultra, Alta Vista, or Excite can be used. For this example, we will use Infoseek Ultra. Type in the keywords *rainforest action network* and enclose the keywords with quotation

marks as suggested by this search tool. Otherwise all instances of the words *rainforest, action*, and *network* will be found and returned in the search results.

Entering "rainforest action network" in Infoseek Ultra produced the link to RAN's Home Page.

Infoseek Ultra seems to provide the highest relevant returns for keyword searches at this time.

When the same search was done using Infoseek Ultra, and the word *rainforest* was made into two words *rain forest*, the search did not immediately provide the Home Page for RAN. It is important to use the same keywords as the organization or company uses. In this case, *Rainforest Action Network*, not *Rain Forest Action Network*. Although the Web site will eventually be found, it may take longer to review an extensive list of returns.

Example 2: Finding a new URL for Bucknell Engineering Beast project
When the URL **http://www.eg.bucknel.edu/~beast96** for Bucknell Engineering's Beast 96 project was entered, Netscape returned this message.

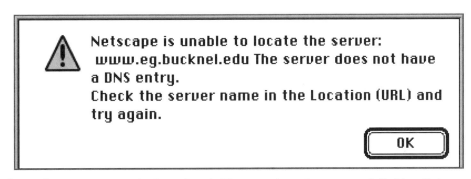

Since no forwarding URL was given, the Infoseek Ultra search engine was used. To identify key-words for the search, refer to the Web site information in your book (in this case, *Internet Investigations in Electronics,* page77).

Beast96 is a project with Bucknell Engineering Animatronics Systems Technology. The key-words selected for the search were *Bucknell Engineering*. Since two words are being entered in the search, use Infoseek's suggestions to place keywords in quotation marks, limiting the search to only returns that contain both words *Bucknell* and *Engineering*.

Infoseek Ultra used for keyword search

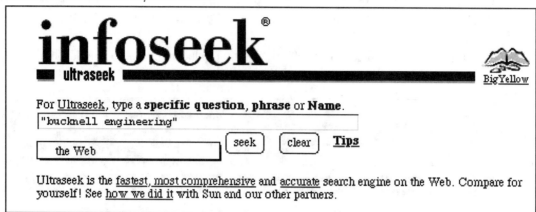

The search produced the following results.

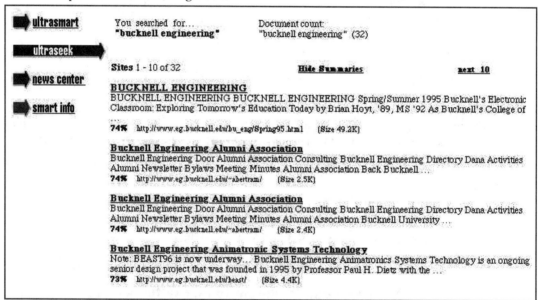

Review the search engine returns for the Web site you are searching for. In this case, the fourth return indicated that the Beast project could be found at the given site **http://www.eg.bucknell.edu/beast**.

Finding information on the Internet, is often a Treasure Hunt. Become an Explorer and your Journey will become an Adventure.

Index

Page references to sites on the Internet appear in bold. In most cases, types of locations other than web sites have been noted in parentheses.